Bettina Al-Sadik-Lowinski
Alpha Males and Alpha Females

Bettina Al-Sadik-Lowinski

Alpha Males and Alpha Females

—

Male executives from around the world on how to
increase gender diversity in senior management

DE GRUYTER

German edition: Alpha-Mann und Alpha-Frau – Internationale Topmanager über Strategien zu mehr Gender Diversität und gemischten Führungsspitzen (978-3-11-105064-5)
Translated by Dr Andrew Godfrey-Collins, UK

ISBN 978-3-11-116942-2
e-ISBN (PDF) 978-3-11-117265-1
e-ISBN (EPUB) 978-3-11-117391-7

Library of Congress Control Number: 2023933675

Bibliographic information published by the Deutsche Nationalbibliothek
The Deutsche Nationalbibliothek lists this publication in the Deutsche Nationalbibliografie; detailed bibliographic data are available on the Internet at http://dnb.dnb.de.

© 2023 Walter de Gruyter GmbH, Berlin/Boston
Cover image: Fabia Matveev c/o kombinatrotweiss.de
Printing and binding: CPI books GmbH, Leck

www.degruyter.com

Contents

1 The global companies need to harmonise men's and women's strengths

The stereotype of the alpha male is well known: the successful, high-earning, competitive man who dominates and dazzles in business or politics thanks to his assertive, charismatic personality. Such men are often figures of awe and mystique. Alpha females, by contrast, are less common. They're so rare, in fact, that the very term provokes some perplexity. Alpha women tend to be viewed more critically and associated with more ambivalent qualities. Either they're selfish careerists who've clawed their way to the top at the expense of their children and family (if they have children at all – many are childless), or they're victims of male discrimination. It's only in more recent times that they've also begun to be admired for their independence and courage.

This book will seek to set aside the traditional stereotypes and consider gender roles from a new perspective, with a focus on men and women who've been highly successful in the business world. Both sexes need certain qualities to reach the top. Until recently, company boardrooms were the exclusive preserve of alpha men; it's only in the past few years that women have begun to make inroads too, and in many parts of the world they're still a rarity in senior management. But companies that want to succeed need to productively combine men's and women's strengths. So how can diverse leadership teams be made the norm at international companies?

To find answers to this question, in-depth interviews were conducted with male CEOs and senior executives from eleven countries, most of whom are fathers of daughters. These men have a wealth of relevant experience to offer. In the interviews, they shared their perspectives on how more women can rise to the top of the corporate ladder and then successfully master the challenges of senior management. The men are firmly on the side of their female colleagues, are keen to support qualified women and agree that women and their abilities should be better represented on company boards. The interviews reveal their thoughts on diverse leadership as well as the conflicts they sometimes experience with women in management. The interviewees also discussed what, in their view, women should do if they want to achieve their career ambitions. The men believe one cause of the current imbalance is that many highly capable women are reluctant to pursue their ambitions. Another is that women are held back by existing power structures. Men fear losing face and being shown up by strong women. They crave recognition, rather than aggression, from their female colleagues. The interviews also touched on sensitive topics such as #MeToo and the effects of 'erotic capital', as well as the much-discussed 'old boys' networks' and the question of whether men and women have distinct leadership qualities. Several interviewees identified women's positive, calming influence in male-dominated meetings as one of their strengths. Just like the women trying to make it into management, the men are still on a learning curve when it comes to changed gender roles. They've also observed a dissonance among their male colleagues, who on the one hand are supportive of women's advancement, but on the other aren't taking the action needed for real change.

https://doi.org/10.1515/9783111172651-001

Throughout this book, the male senior executives have been quoted in their own words (translated into English and edited for clarity where applicable). Excerpts from interviews with women in top management have also been included to provide a complementary, alternative perspective.

Alpha Males and Alpha Females is intended to promote greater equality at senior level in global companies, with more diverse leadership teams made up of both talented men and talented women. It offers a fresh perspective on gender roles that moves away from the old paradigm of male domination and female victimhood. It gives women who are interested in pursuing a management career an insight into men's views, as well as guidance on their personal career development. It suggests ways that company executives can strengthen diversity and build more successful mixed-gender leadership teams. And last but not least, it gives men with an interest in the topic an opportunity to learn from the experiences of their international colleagues and apply those lessons in their own spheres of influence.

Why listen to male executives' thoughts on this topic?

The vast majority of existing publications and studies on gender equality in management mainly involve women. So there's a pressing need to also consider the perspectives of men who've had high-flying international careers. During the current transitional period from male dominance to diverse leadership teams, there's value in hearing men's views on this important topic, as doing so will open up fresh perspectives and pave the way for more effective collaboration between the genders in senior management. Companies that want to be successful and viable in future will need to harmonise typically male and typically female strengths, so this kind of collaboration is vital (both between men and women, and between other groups). A lot of work is still needed to build bridges and improve mutual understanding of men's and women's different leadership styles and ways of resolving conflict. The men who currently hold positions of power need to recognise the benefits of mixed boards and to stop worrying so much that women threaten their sense of identity and purpose. And women, in their well-intentioned struggle for greater gender equality in management, should remember this goal can only be achieved if everyone works with, rather than against, each other. Empathy is already one of women's strengths, which they can use to better understand men's points of view and so position themselves more effectively.

> Chinese CEO in Hong Kong: I don't want to overstate it. As if ignoring the gender issue would be a fatal failure for a leader. I think that would be exaggerated. But if a male leader doesn't understand women's contribution to their business, they've definitely missed the boat. If that's the case, their chance of failing is definitely higher than those who understand the importance of diversity.

Our international business world is closely intermeshed. Yet the opportunities for women in senior management continue to vary from place to place around the globe, depending on sociocultural context. Many of the interviewees have worked in multiple countries and can bring a global perspective to this topic. What strategies do these experienced managers believe could help to encourage more diverse leadership teams at international companies? What factors shape the relations and interactions between male and female executives? These and other questions will be explored in this book.

Together for success: the alpha men's perspective

A few main strands can be discerned in the literature on men and women in senior management.

One widely studied idea is that harmonising the leadership strengths of highly qualified men and women allows companies to improve their performance and make themselves fit for the future. It also creates an environment that people like working in, as they feel equally represented. A survey of 21,980 listed companies in ninety-one countries conducted by the Peterson Institute for International Economics found that the proportion of women in leadership positions is positively correlated with a company's profitability (Noland et al., 2016). Studies by McKinsey (2012) and Catalyst (2004) suggest that having more women on boards results in higher profits, higher return on sales and better overall performance. Numerous other international studies have come to the same conclusion. These findings point to a positive way forward to a business world where both genders are represented – and companies reap the benefits.

An alternative, deficit-focused strand of research asks whether women lack the skills, qualities or motivation needed to rise up through the ranks at companies. Deficit-focused studies hypothesise that women are unable to meet the demands of management, lack leadership ability or don't actually want top management careers. They typically measure women against the standard of leadership qualities and career advancement norms, defined by reference to men. In her 2011 book *Das dämliche Geschlecht* (literally, 'The Stupid Sex'; the pejorative term *dämlich* is derived from *Dame*, or 'woman'), Barbara Bierach took her fellow women to task and asked why they are so willing to settle. She concluded that German women don't really want to rise to senior level and that it's their own fault if they let men walk all over them when it comes to their careers, their salaries or a fair distribution of household chores.

There are still relatively few studies that undertake international comparisons of female role models who have successfully progressed to leadership positions at companies. *Women in Top Management* (Al-Sadik-Lowinski, 2020), the predecessor to this book, is premised on the idea that women from around the world learn more effectively from other women than they can from management and leadership principles devised solely for men. It analyses the career paths and patterns of over 110 female senior managers from five industrialised nations.

A contrasting perspective focuses on how women's careers are obstructed by men upholding the status quo. On this view, male executives are systematically preventing capable women from advancing in their careers. Studies in this strand of research look to apportion blame and victimhood, exploring issues such as discrimination and prejudice against women in senior management. Sometimes, this prejudice can come from women themselves, who reject female top managers due to traditional stereotypes and obstruct their advancement. Successful leaders are supposed to possess male characteristics, and it's against this standard that female leaders are measured. In response to this problem, Wittenberg-Cox (2010) formulated the dictum that 'women do not need to be fixed, men do not want to be blamed'. Meanwhile, the new stereotype of 'old white men', synonymous with the exclusion of women from male-dominated circles of power, has become a widespread media trope.

In the academic debate on gender issues, very little attention has been paid to the thoughts and experiences of male top managers, even though in most companies and countries it is still men who hold the majority of leadership positions. The new study conducted for this book shifts perspective and focuses on men's viewpoints, with the goal of promoting gender diversity in management. The book is about the experiences and perspectives of high-flying men with regard to women in management and diverse leadership teams. What do successful male CEOs and senior executives think about successful women and the way that men and women treat each other in the boardroom? What are their perceptions of successful and less successful women? What conflicts have they experienced with female colleagues in senior leadership roles? And what specific steps do they think companies can take to effectively address some of these problems? The interviewees' responses set out approaches and strategies that they believe will help more women to make it into top management roles. The analysis of the men's viewpoints is complemented by comparing the perspectives of women who have already made it onto company boards.

This book is intended to foster discussion of diverse leadership teams, in which men and women harmonise their strengths and work together to bolster their company's performance, and to suggest ways that the number of women in senior positions can be increased. This goal has still not been achieved in many countries of the world. Among leading global economies, Germany and Japan are still stuck in the bottom third of the world rankings for the proportion of women in senior management roles. But at least in Germany, there is a trend towards increased participation of women.

The Global Women Career Lab: rigorous research and consultancy services to promote diversity in companies round the world

This book is based on an empirical study, in which confidential, in-depth qualitative interviews were conducted with twenty-eight male senior executives from eleven countries. What is distinctive about the way the research findings are presented in the book is that the alpha men themselves are allowed to speak in their own words. These authentic quotations provide highly personal insights into their experiences and thoughts on the topics of diversity, mixed-gender leadership teams and ways of supporting women. The study participants were aware from the outset that the primary goal of this research is to support women's careers and promote effective collaboration between men and women in the boardroom. Another goal is to share facts and insights that will help other men think through this important topic as well. All the study participants are in leadership roles at international companies (in most cases, as CEOs) and were selected using a predefined theoretical sampling method. The broad selection of countries was intended to represent a cross section of leading economies, including the USA, the UK, Australia, China and Russia. The interviewees come from eleven countries in total, and are also familiar with many other countries thanks to their international careers and postings abroad. The majority are aged between forty-five and fifty-eight. Ninety per cent are fathers with daughters. The fact that they agreed to anonymised in-depth interviews, which were recorded and transcribed, is indicative of their positive attitude to gender diversity. A qualitative content analysis of the empirical data was conducted and the findings were fed into the Global Women Career Lab, one of the world's biggest research projects on diversity, leadership and women's management careers. The FemCareer-Model (Al-Sadik-Lowinski, 2021), which provides a structured approach to the determinants of women's careers and leadership styles, was used for the analysis. It is explained in detail in the concluding chapter. This model helped to structure the qualitative interviews and provided a framework through which to analyse this complex topic. It is supplemented by findings from other international studies, so that the study participants' experiences can be placed within the context of earlier research. The research conducted for this book centres on men and women in management roles and how they interact and collaborate with each other. Although this research did not consider other groups, the book does reflect on some more general issues of diversity in companies.

Gender-diverse leadership: overcoming stereotypical expectations and gender conflicts

For centuries, the world of business has been almost entirely dominated by men, with only a handful of exceptions. Traditionally, men defined themselves in terms of their dominant role as the breadwinner for their family. Women were responsible for the family and home, and occupied a subordinate role dependent on male protectors. The stereotypes evoked and embedded in a given sociocultural context shape the division of roles in that society. This division corresponds to traditional role models that still exist all over the world, whereby men are responsible in the external world for their family income and for business and political matters, while women are responsible in the domestic sphere for the family and home. These stereotypes continue to affect how gender roles are perceived, including in the world of corporate management. The precise nature of this effect depends on social context.

Many women, including managers, continue to internalise sociocultural expectations about their roles and incorporate them into their professional identities. These beliefs influence their career decisions and behaviour in the workplace. However, some women have already shaken off traditional expectations and made inroads into what used to be men's territory. Maintaining their position in male-dominated leadership settings is often highly demanding.

Despite the changes of the past few decades, most men continue to define themselves in terms of their traditional role, and their leadership style expresses an identity based on masculine stereotypes. These traditional roles remain influential in many societies around the globe, as a result of which men are still overrepresented on management boards. All over the world, men either still identify with their traditional role or are only gradually moving to a new understanding of masculinity that has not yet firmly taken hold and achieved broader social acceptance. They define their identity in terms of success in the external world. Some men worry about losing what has until now been their core role. They fear they may be forced into a competition between the sexes with a whole new set of rules, or ousted by statutory women's quotas. These worries are expressed not just by men from countries like Japan that still have a sharp division of gender roles, but also by men from places where it is generally assumed those roles have already converged, such as the USA or the Netherlands. This illustrates the dissonance experienced by many men between, on the one hand, wanting to support women and live up to a new, modern idea of masculinity and, on the other, wanting the status quo to be maintained.

But understandings of men's and women's roles are changing – quickly in some places, more slowly in others, depending on cultural context. Both genders are undergoing a learning process. With some rare exceptions, it was only in the past few decades that women began breaking free of these traditional roles and making strides into areas formerly dominated by men. Women are learning, in a way informed by their socialisation, how to combine their work and family roles. Men are learning how to work with mixed-gender teams and changed rules, and – not always entirely willingly – are opening up their traditional spheres of power. In some cultural contexts this shift is already well advanced, while in others it is progressing very slowly.

> *Japanese CFO: Yes, that's my fear. That roles will completely switch. In my case, my wife is a housewife. To be honest, I would get very jealous if she were more successful than me. That would mean that I hadn't been at all successful in my career. If she earned more, she would ask me to quit my job and do the housework. I would be seen as a loser. Yes, to be honest, that is my fear.*

Both male and female managers' behaviour is influenced by how they see themselves and their roles. These self-conceptions are often the product of a diametrically opposed socialisation. Traditional understandings of roles continue to affect both sexes, with male-dominated rules of competition influencing the mixed-gender leadership teams that are now forming. Both men and women are going through a process of change and learning, and it is not uncommon for there to be conflicts between the sexes.

The generations of men who currently hold senior positions at companies and the many women in the middle of the hierarchy are still influenced, to varying degrees, by old patterns of behaviour. Change generally only leads to progress once the initial disruption and resistance has been overcome. Differences between men and women can be a source of conflict, or can be seen as an opportunity for diverse leadership. Before men's and women's strengths can be appreciated and productively combined, there first needs to be awareness of these differences. That requires mutual understanding, which this book will attempt to promote. Diverse leadership becomes stronger by harnessing the differences between the sexes and encouraging better collaboration.

Spanish CEO: I think that there are two basic arguments. One argument is more about ethics. We want to have a fair world. We need a world in which gender diversity is a reality. It's just a matter of fairness, of not condemning half of humanity to a secondary role just because of the sex they were born into. That first line of argument is about ethics. Then there's the fact that it's proven that diverse organisations are more effective, do a better job, have better growth and profitability.

The younger generations appear to find these changes easier to navigate. Young men want to have more involvement in their family lives. The relevance of traditional careers is being called into question. Researchers have attempted to predict what impact these changing attitudes to traditional roles might have on relations between men and women in future.

Company boards used to be almost entirely filled with men, and that remains the case in many countries around the world, especially if you consider the proportion of female CEOs. But the situation is changing. According to the 2021 Grant Thornton International Business Report (Grant Thornton, 2021), an annual report launched in 1992 that surveys 10,000 business leaders in twenty-nine countries, the proportion of female CEOs grew globally by an average of six percentage points in 2021 alone. The report also found that twenty-six per cent of CEO positions were held by women for the first time, up by fourteen per cent since 2015, while the proportion of female senior managers (including CEOs and the level immediately below) stood at thirty-one per cent. In 2004, that figure was just nineteen per cent. It took seventeen years to reach the thirty-one per cent mark, during which time progress often stalled. So the sharp rise in 2021 is striking. Women are well established in the middle ranks of companies in many countries, though by no means all. In Japan, for instance, women are still excluded from middle management. Or, alternatively, Japanese women are still opting for traditional support roles rather than management careers. Globally, however, a growing number of women are not content with being locked in the middle of the pack and want to participate at the top levels of business, politics and all other spheres of society.

Australian CEO: We need more guys to open the door for women. If there are one hundred people in a room and eighty of them are men, then it's easier to find a guy to open a door than to focus on the women.

One promising strategy to make companies fit for the future is to build diverse leadership teams. The vast majority of the men interviewed for this book see benefits to this approach. However, sustained global progress will only be possible with the support of existing male leaders and by harnessing their experience and insights. Only if men open the doors that women are pressing against today will female leaders get the chance to work side by side with their male colleagues in company boardrooms. To reach that goal, women also need to understand how to handle men's responses to these changes – which is something the men interviewed for this book can help with.

The structure of this book

The book begins by looking at how men explain the continued underrepresentation of women in senior management roles. The interviewees share their experiences from different sociocultural contexts around the globe. They also reflect on typical conflicts between men and women in management, including sensitive topics such as the #MeToo debate and the use of 'feminine wiles' in business settings. This is followed by a discussion of the notorious 'old boys' networks', which are often seen as bastions of male power designed to exclude women. The male senior managers talk about the distinctive strengths and leadership skills of successful women, as well as some of the skills they believe women lack. The female senior managers' experiences support many of these observations. The analysis concludes with the male managers' recommendations on how to improve gender diversity in company boardrooms.

Chapter two begins by considering the alpha men's views on why there are still fewer women in the higher echelons of companies worldwide, even though nowadays young women often start their careers better qualified than men. It's a complex topic; research has identified a whole host of factors that can facilitate or complicate women's careers, including social context, family–work balance and individual factors such as women's career orientation, career planning and leadership styles. When asked about the causes, the male study participants spontaneously look to the past and historical divisions of roles. They describe differences between countries that they have encountered over the course of their long international careers, which they are able to place within their respective cultural context.

The focus of the chapter then shifts to women themselves and the differences in their career planning, career orientation and choice of profession. The men consider discrimination, bias and stereotypes as possible explanations for these differences. Finally, they give their verdict on why women who make it to the top often struggle to stay there.

American CEO: Yes, but there's no doubt that if you're a white man, you're significantly more privileged and your opportunities have historically been greater.

The interviewees regard the persistence of traditional stereotypes as one reason why there are still fewer women on company boards, though (as mentioned earlier) they have witnessed changing attitudes in the younger generation. The men's explanation is that, traditionally, most women's roles were focused on looking after their home and family, and this remains the case in many parts of the world. Men's traditional role as breadwinner has stayed largely unchanged over time. According to the interviewees, the pace at which these stereotypical roles are changing depends on the sociocultural context in each country, but viewed globally there is a marked shift among the younger generations.

Both men and women are influenced by their social environment, which in turn influences companies. The interviewees claim that women have internalised stereotypes and, depending on sociocultural context, lack the confidence to pursue leadership roles. Bias and prejudices are present in management that influence male executives and encourage women to hold stereotypical views about 'career women'. The men believe that the times are moving in women's favour, including the changing social attitudes that are especially evident among the younger generation. Consequently, they do not see a pressing need for women to fight for equality, since changes have already been inexorably set in motion that are paving the way for more women to pursue their career ambitions.

Some of the men describe how male colleagues are still consciously or unconsciously defending their traditional rights and the domains of power that used to be their sole preserve and collective inheritance. They fear more and more women encroaching on the quintessentially male world of senior management. Men have often responded with incomprehension, hostility or worries about their own future.

German COO: I think that a very, very conservative view of society still prevails in Germany. A conservative view of the role of the family, which puts social pressure on women.

The traditional distribution of roles between men and women isn't the only explanation suggested by the interviewees. They also talk about how the gender imbalance on company boards varies from country to country: many North and East European and Asian countries, for instance, have more women in senior leadership positions than Germany, Japan or the USA. Over the course of their careers, the alpha men interviewed for this study have worked in over twenty-five countries between them, meaning they can bring diverse international perspectives to bear on the topic. They attribute the gender imbalance in part to historical, cultural, political and sociological differences between countries. They have observed that women are more confident about pursuing careers in some countries than others. Quotations from the interviewees are woven into a short round-the-world tour through selected leading industrialised nations, with a focus on sociocultural context and culturally distinctive conceptions of roles. Grant Thornton (2017) reports that Russia and China rank highly in a global comparison of the proportion of women in senior management, with France, the USA, Australia and the UK in the middle of the pack and Germany and Japan lagging behind other major economies. The interviewees for the present study also believe that, contrary to what is often assumed, China has greater equality for female managers than countries such as Germany or the USA. This belief is rooted in their observations of the number of women in management there and those women's focus on their careers. One historical explanation for this difference is the Cultural Revolution, which despite many negative aspects also brought about great advances for women's equality. In the men's view, this has made Chinese women stronger and more confident than women in France or Germany.

> French GM in China: Let's start with China. For instance, in our organisation, we have the largest number of women in operations management positions. Not only plant management, but in very technical, very difficult jobs. I think that's good, because typically, in our type of industry CEOs come from the technical divisions. China is very much advanced compared to the rest of the world in this respect.

Japan, by contrast, trails the other industrialised nations, despite historically having been a matriarchal society until well into the fourteenth century. The interviewees primarily attribute this to the strong focus on motherhood among Japanese women and in Japanese society as a whole. This isn't too far removed from the situation in Germany, where (in the German interviewees' experience) it is harder for mothers to pursue careers than in other countries and there is more social pressure on women to keep to traditional roles.

> Japanese CEO: To come back to your question of why there are so few female executives in Japan: I think it's entirely historical. The executives need to have decades of experience. In my generation, the number of female candidates who could achieve that experience was very small, but now things are more equal. If you look at the number at the moment, the number or percentage of women can't be changed rapidly, even though the government has encouraged that a certain percentage of managers should be female. I think the reasons for the unequal proportion of women at executive level are historical rather than due to candidate discrimination.

According to Grant Thornton's (2017) statistics, Russia has the highest proportion of women in senior management anywhere in the world. It has long been the norm for Russian women to work full-time. The proportion of women employed in industry and services stood at fifty-one per cent at the start of the 1990s. By contrast, the model of a full-time housewife didn't exist in socialist society. However, the dissolution of the USSR ushered in a political resurgence of gendered roles that drove women out of the labour market. At the same time, the switch to a market economy also opened up opportunities for women. The Russian interviewees explain that it was the women who helped liberate the country from chaos thanks to their agile, proactive approach.

By contrast with Russia, most French women in the 1960s–70s were housewives. But attitudes have shifted dramatically in the past forty years, accompanied by the introduction of hard-won equalities legislation. This change is reflected in French women's growing autonomy and self-determination, even if the interviewees believe French women are still less career-focused than Chinese or Russian women. In France, it's nowadays considered normal, even expected, for women to work, far more so than in neighbouring Germany. The proportion of women in senior management in France now exceeds that in the USA and is approaching the level in China.

In the USA, women's primary role before and after the Second World War was as housewives. During the war, women worked in 'men's jobs' for the first time, but afterwards quickly returned to the old division of roles. But this period nonetheless marked a significant shift in how America saw women's position in society. Although many American couples today are dual earners, women still shoulder most of the family responsibilities, which fuels prejudices about their career motivation. Legislators and companies have introduced policies that seek to eliminate discrimination, including against women of colour.

> *Dutch CEO: It is a fact that many women here work part-time, we are world champions of part-time, and that's not good for a career. Also, during Covid a lot of women were in charge of all the housework and they played a very traditional role.*

Alongside the sociocultural factors, the interviewees gave three other explanations for the lower proportion of women in senior management worldwide:
(1) Women are less motivated to rise up the ranks in hierarchical structures.
(2) Women are more focused on their families.
(3) Women want to balance their career with other areas of their lives.

This results in a 'pipeline problem', where there are simply fewer women available for companies to promote.

The interviewees also believe there is a problem in women's choice of industry: they tend to opt for careers in industries that match their interests, and neglect others. On top of that, women are generally more affected by discrimination than men. The interviewees admit they often promote people similar to themselves, though that similarity can encompass not just gender but also membership of certain groups (such as alumni of elite universities).

> *Spanish CEO: That's very true. I think that we all tend to believe we're fantastic – I mean, each of us. Then we try to replicate ourselves in the teams that are working for us. That's very human.*

In chapter three, the alpha men describe challenges and conflicts with women in management from their perspective. They observe that male and female colleagues behave differently in situations of conflict. The interviewees welcome the calming influence of women, which is absent in all-male teams, and report that, as CEOs, they often have to intervene in clashes between 'boys turned savage' that occur in teams or meetings where all participants are men. Women have a harmonising effect; according to one interviewee, their mere presence turns 'squabbling boys into productive men'.

The one thing the alpha men fear above all in their interactions with female managers is that they will be shown up by more capable women and so lose face. Some researchers even say that successful collaboration between the sexes in the workplace is only possible if men's anxieties are addressed (Hollstein, 2004). From their responses, it's clear that male managers crave recognition from women, not the same aggressive competition they're constantly engaged in with other men.

> *Dutch CEO: What we could discuss is the worries of men. 'Hey, I don't feel comfortable in a group of women. I feel intimidated, passed over, exposed, I feel outsmarted.' All those kinds of things.*

The next area of discussion is a sensitive one: the male study participants feel unfairly attacked by the #MeToo movement. Many of them are fathers with daughters, and they want to be supportive of women. They feel they're being unfairly lumped together with men who exploit their positions of power to sexually assault women. Many also claim that harmless behaviour that men engage in when they're 'alone with the boys' is now being viewed out of context and equated with actual cases of sexual assault against women by powerful men. All the men who participated in this study unanimously condemned such behaviour, but feel like they can no longer freely relax around other men and worry about being under constant scrutiny.

> *French CEO: There's always the risk of seduction. It's a slippery path where you can easily generate problems that you had no intention of generating. It's a risk. It's more of a thing with women than with men.*

> *American CEO: I believe the key is that men don't feel comfortable. They think that they can't talk openly, can't make jokes. The jokes have to be changed.*

The discussion then turns to a taboo topic that has received little scholarly attention: 'erotic capital', a term coined by the sociologist Catherine Hakim (2010). She defines it in terms of six elements. What makes Hakim's work provocative in the age of women's quota debates is that she takes a topic more normally associated with private, intimate contexts and relates it to professional life: do women use their erotic capital to move up the career ladder? This is a sensitive issue for the men, as they want to support women but worry about facing negative judgements. The relatively few comments that they made on the topic range from nuanced positivity and admiration to rejection of the claim that women take advantage of their erotic capital. Only one interviewee mentioned the possibility that men could use erotic capital too.

> *Russian CEO: It's not reality, just my imagination. If a beautiful woman comes to the negotiations, then all the men will just open their mouths and say, 'Oh, yes. Great. Good to have you here.' At some companies, especially in sales, it works very well. Because she's such a beautiful woman, she's able to get much better contracts than men or ugly women. But generally speaking, I don't think it makes a difference whether someone is a woman or not. All that counts is whether they're professional or unprofessional.*

What do the alpha men want from their female colleagues? They want loyalty. Because they have been socialised for roles in which they traditionally hold dominant positions, men expect women to recognise their authority in public settings. It is precisely because they value women's empathy and sensitivity that male leaders expect support and loyalty from women, especially in meetings and in the presence of other people. If women consciously or unconsciously prioritise winning an argument over showing loyalty to their male colleagues and superiors, they will be met with incomprehension and hostility – for instance, if they publicly criticise a decision that men regard as already settled. The men don't mention the consequences of such behaviour in the interviews, but we can imagine that they would withdraw support from women in such cases or else give them the same tough treatment they'd give another man in a situation of conflict.

> Spanish CEO: I've observed that men tend to follow the leader more blindly than women. In other words, men are less critical than women are, so when I conduct a meeting with only men, things go faster. There is less discussion, the agreements are made a little bit more easily because there is less need for explanation, less need for discussion, less need to create some consensus.

What do the alpha men from different countries think of women's quotas, which are intended to achieve parity between men and women in company boardrooms? Several European countries have statutory quotas, though the precise form they take varies considerably. Other countries make recommendations for certain types of company. The men are ambivalent about legally mandated quotas and tend to view them negatively, observing that they can restrict opportunities for younger, talented white men. At the same time, the men understand what the quotas are aiming to achieve and believe they can be effective in increasing the proportion of women in the short to medium term in sectors where there is otherwise no prospect of that happening. This ambivalence becomes especially apparent later on, in chapter six, when some of the men moot the possibility of quotas as a temporary measure to improve women's representation. Alpha men want women who aspire to rise up the ranks to drop the victim role and follow the same rules of career progression and performance evaluation as men.

> French CEO: No, it's the cultural, political, social environment in Europe now. The trend is the victimisation of minorities, whichever minority you want to talk about. You just focus your discussion on discrimination, on victimisation. You don't do anything, you just talk about it. I think in China there are now so many women who have access to top management positions that they've stopped discussing it.

The men see voluntary targets in a more positive light than statutory quotas. Despite the ambivalence towards statutory quotas, Japanese and German CEOs do see them as an effective measure, but they stress the need to combine them with clear quality and performance criteria so that targets and quotas don't become ends in themselves that negatively impact on diversity overall.

Chapter four looks at networks and relationships, which play an important role in managerial careers. Research on this topic links it to issues of power and managers' micropolitical competence. Through team games, boys and men learn from an early age to simultaneously cooperate and compete with each other. Bourdieu (2001) calls these the 'serious games of competition', which are played out in fields as varied as business, politics and science. Women in management are often excluded from, or unable to access, networks that could help them in their careers. In this chapter, the alpha men talk about how important building strong relations was for their careers and share their thoughts on old boys' networks. Not all the men believe these networks were important for their own advancement. They distinguish between internal networks in companies, close relationships with key decision-makers and relationships with market contacts outside the company. The interviewees are critical of male-dominated networks within companies that deliberately exclude women. Yet they still defend old boys' networks and the benefits that result from them where the networks in question are ones external to the company. They believe that women could achieve the same benefits with their own women's networks, though they acknowledge the constraint that these smaller groups would have less influence.

Meetings are the arenas of the modern corporate world, where participants come together to discuss business matters. But they're also about jockeying for position, visibility and power. Research has shown the significant influence that gender constructs have in organisational contexts, and specifically in meetings (Baines, 2010). In meetings, men are more likely to form alliances with other men, with a key role being played by existing ties that were originally forged outside the meeting and are then consolidated during it. This makes it harder to build new relationships with women. Stereotypes have a negative impact on women in meetings and make it harder for them to participate.

The interviewees want women to strike a balancing act in meetings, expecting them to simultaneously speak up more while also pacifying men's aggressive behaviour. They recognise the positive effect that women's presence has on male groups. Men, the interviewees have observed, are more constructive, mature and well-behaved at meetings where women are also present. The interviewees further believe that to achieve a positive influence, women need to concentrate on their strengths – specifically, communication and relationship-building – and be less reserved. A certain dissonance is evident between the interviewees' admiration for the women's strengths on the one hand, and the stereotypes and masculine norms that shape their expectations of how managers should behave on the other.

> German head of region: I think that if women were really women for once and men were more considerate, things would be better. We're getting there, but far too slowly. To reach that goal, women need to stay women and not become copies of us in leadership positions.

What qualities do the alpha men observe in highly successful women? What skills, abilities and personality traits do they want to see in women who aspire to leadership roles? These are the questions addressed in chapter five. In most studies on management, the success parameters and characteristics that are supposed to help managers progress in their careers are based on male leadership norms, behaviours and personality traits. Schein et al.'s (1996) 'think manager, think male' theory describes how traditional stereotypes about the sexes feed into the image we have of managers. The alpha men reward women whose decision-making style resembles their own with support and sponsorship. However, they believe most women lack the combination of decisiveness and risk-taking that they consider essential in leaders. They hold the rare few women whose leadership style does exhibit both these qualities in high regard, and are very supportive of them.

The men also believe women need to work on building their confidence and clearly communicating their career goals, as in their experience women often lack the ambition and resolve needed for a senior executive position and eventually a CEO role. These qualities must be paired with an understanding of company power structures and an ability to build strong relationships – two other areas where, in the men's view, women are often weaker than men. In summary, the alpha men see the key to women's success as a high level of confidence combined with ambition and clearly communicated career goals, which are qualities many women lack. The men's recommendations are at odds with the strategy adopted by many women, namely to stay invisible so that they can exert influence without facing discrimination.

> *French CEO: It could be a lack of confidence in herself. 'No, I'm not going to do it. I'm not going to make it.' Or sometimes the complex of not being as good as other people. They always think they aren't as good as other people around them, which most of the time isn't true. If you don't have self-confidence, you can't lead others.*

What specific steps do the alpha men recommend to get more women onto management boards? What can today's company leaders do to make gender diversity more than an empty aspiration? And how can mixed-sex leadership teams be successfully established? Chapter six attempts to answer these questions. Company culture plays a key role in helping more women get into senior management roles. As its own little microcosm, a company can do a lot to support ambitious women and build diverse leadership teams even in less favourable sociocultural conditions. In the men's view, building an inclusive company culture is a crucial step so that companies can then implement specific measures to recruit and develop women over the longer term. One core element of an inclusive culture is a guiding vision that gives women and their innate strengths a firm place at the heart of the company, alongside all other groups, and encourages people to openly challenge and dispel biases and stereotypes. An inclusive corporate culture will always trickle down from the CEO, but everyone in the company needs to be involved. Above all, it's important that everyone is aware of the benefits of diverse management teams and is committed to harnessing those benefits for their organisation. Only then can diversity be made a lasting reality.

But how to motivate male executives who have not previously championed the benefits of diverse leadership teams and only rarely throw their support behind women, if at all? The consensus among the interviewees is that the best way to persuade these men is by showing how they themselves stand to benefit from diversity thanks to improved company performance.

> *American CEO: At the end of the day, it comes back to winning and losing for a man. I don't think we will fundamentally change that for thousands of years, because I think it's an evolutionary thing, but I would try to. How does it help the male CEO achieve better results?*

Not all of the alpha men's male colleagues are yet persuaded of the benefits of mixed-gender leadership teams, or aware that promoting talented women could help them achieve their personal goals. The alpha men believe that hard facts about the long-term profits that diverse leadership teams will generate for companies make the most effective argument.

They also favour broadening the focus and talking about the benefits of diversity in general. In the view of the CEOs, striving for equal opportunities for all groups in a company is the best way to tackle the challenges of gender diversity. This expanded scope places less emphasis on the specific issues faced by women and instead considers wider problems. According to the men, solving these wider problems would automatically alleviate the problem of gender representation in management.

> *Australian executive: The big thing is, do those senior leaders who are male really understand what diversity is? It's not a numbers game of male vs female. Diversity is about different ways of approaching situations, and thinking and experience and knowledge, and understanding how you bring the most diverse group together to get the best result. I don't think you should be a senior leader if you don't believe that a diverse team is going to give you the best result.*

What other specific steps do the alpha men recommend to get more women into boardrooms? Their answers focus on two areas: creating female role models and sponsoring promising candidates. The men agree that having more successful female role models will encourage other women in a company to follow in their footsteps. The more visible success stories there are in a given company or sector, the easier it will be for women to imagine themselves in powerful positions. In Japan, more men need to experience having women bosses, so that they can grow to appreciate the qualities and benefits of female leadership. The interviewees believe that there are already enough women in leadership roles in China and certain other Asian countries. However, in industries that demand STEM qualifications, there are not enough talented female candidates in the pipeline. The men identify this as a specific area where there are opportunities to recruit and promote more women. The alpha men believe that sponsoring talented women is probably the most efficient approach. They imagine themselves steering the process and exerting their influence. They want to help women who meet their standards of good leadership (as discussed above) to secure promotions by adeptly positioning them on key committees. In some companies this still brings personal risks with it, but the men are willing to take a calculated risk if they believe in their protégés' loyalty and leadership qualities.

The alpha men agree: this is the century of women

'There's a special place in hell for women who don't help each other!' These words of former US secretary of state Madeleine Albright were widely discussed in the global press. What place will be allocated for male business leaders who don't help talented female managers and make their companies more diverse and future-ready? One participant in the present study, a CEO from the Netherlands, said that, in future, such men 'will run their company into the ground and get a place on the losers' bench.'

In 2021, an international survey of twenty-nine countries found that eighty-three per cent have achieved a proportion of thirty per cent women in executive teams (Grant Thornton, 2021). This figure is significant, as once the thirty per cent threshold has been passed women will gradually come to be seen as normal in all senior management roles. In 2004, the proportion of women on boards was just nineteen per cent. A handful of countries, including Russia and the Philippines, have almost reached the fifty per cent mark for women in C-level roles (Grant Thornton, 2017). Countries such as China, Lithuania, France and Malaysia have passed thirty per cent. Germany trails other countries and at the current rate of progress will not achieve parity on company boards until 2047 (Ankersen and Berg, 2021).

Some of the men, who until now have been firmly in the driving seat in their industries, fear that having an equal proportion of women in senior leadership positions will mean they have to give something up. But perhaps they could stand to gain something too. This was another topic the alpha men commented on, as they have had to make sacrifices for the sake of their careers. None of them was able to be as involved in raising their children as they would have liked. And none of them could permit themselves time off or break with the norms of traditional career progression if they wanted to achieve their goals.

Stronger participation by alpha women will require further changes to social norms and roles in many countries. In future, there will need to be more social acceptance of women who rise to the upper echelons of companies, just like there is for their male counterparts. Policymakers will need to support women with legislation and policies that facilitate the required social changes. Company boards will need to modernise and understand that they can't exclude half of humanity – whether that be for ethical reasons, because they want to meet their sales targets, recruit top talents and appeal to as broad a customer base as possible, or simply because they realise that executive teams function better when women are included too.

And last but not least, women themselves need to have clear career ambitions, they need to know how to complement men's strengths with their own, they need to understand where men are coming from and they need to be willing to build bridges with the men who currently hold the majority of management positions.

Dutch CDO: I think the biggest trouble, really, is on both the male and the female side. The two apparently don't meet in the middle, because when men think about diversity, it means they're getting more women into their corner, and the women on the other side of the spectrum maybe think, 'I need more opportunities on my side.' Both of them, willing or unwilling, consciously or subconsciously, are maintaining the divide, and they're not asking, 'How do we bridge it? How do we make a bridge from you to me?'

The mission of getting more women onto company boards, and so making those companies fit for the future, continues. The goal is to establish more diverse leadership teams that harmonise the strengths of men and women, as well as those of other groups, so that companies can keep going from strength to strength over the longer term. This mission is guided by a vision of a world where qualified, ambitious women will have the same opportunities as their male colleagues to contribute their talents on company boards.

In the remainder of this book, alpha men from eleven countries, whose career paths collectively span over twenty-five countries, share their observations on women in management. They come at the topic from a supportive, sympathetic perspective. Many of them are fathers of daughters, and they paint a self-critical, sometimes self-deprecating picture of their own roles. Their observations are critical and to the point, and will offer all readers plenty of food for thought.

2 How men explain the underrepresentation of women in top management

Why are there still fewer women worldwide at the top of companies, even though nowadays young women often start their careers better qualified than men? It's a complex topic: there are a whole host of factors that can facilitate or complicate women's careers. In this chapter, male CEOs and senior executives share their views on the causes of the imbalance in company boardrooms, looking to past experiences and historical divisions of roles. They describe differences between countries that they have encountered over the course of their long international careers. The focus of the chapter then shifts to women and differences in their career planning, career orientation and choice of profession. The men consider discrimination, bias and stereotypes as possible explanations for these differences. Finally, they give their verdict on why women who make it to the top often struggle to stay there.

Historical role divisions in a changing social context

Sociologists distinguish between men's and women's role behaviour and role expectations. Men and women are supposed to behave in a manner appropriate to their role, according to social expectations in a given cultural context (Eagly and Wood, 2012). These expectations are rooted in culturally variant ideas about each gender's characteristic qualities. Such influences also determine the behaviour of male and female leaders. The men interviewed for this study attribute the unequal proportion of women in senior management to this fact and believe it is crucial to any analysis of the situation. They also describe changes they've observed in recent years, which are working in women's favour.

> Australian CEO: I think it's only in the latest generation that it's really starting to shift. And I think it's going to continue to shift, because if I look at education and universities, the data that I've seen is that young women are more successful than young men in terms of academic attainment. We're building a better core of really good female future leaders. If you go back one or two generations, men had a stronger presence in universities.

The traditional allocation of roles is premised on strictly divided, naturally given gender roles that determine how each gender behaves. On this conception, men are breadwinners and head of the family, responsible for dealings with the outside world. The main hallmarks of men's role are strength, rationality, assertiveness, competitiveness and aggression. Traditionally socialised men expected women to recognise and defer to their authority, while women were traditionally cast as dependent on a male protector. The image of the woman who supports her husband at home after returning from work encapsulates this traditional division of roles. Women's primary role was to offer men comfort and solace when they came home to their family from their travels, from

https://doi.org/10.1515/9783111172651-002

war or from their daily work. Their duty was to manage the family and continually re-integrate their husband into the family home. They were responsible for social ties within the marriage and the family. Against this backdrop, women were labelled as emotional, passive, conciliatory and weak. Although women have always done work outside the home too, for many centuries this was always in a context of subordination to their father or husband. Their primary role in the family was expanded in times of war or social change that made it necessary for women to work in what were strictly speaking 'men's' domains. Men's traditional role as breadwinners has stayed largely unchanged over time. In this role, they are responsible for earning money, whether that be in business, the public sector, agricultural labour or the military. With few ex-ceptions, women only worked at companies during times of shortage and only in sup-port roles. For many years, the typical image of women in companies was as secreta-ries, assistants or typists – or, more occasionally, as heiresses. In the past, women usually only had the opportunity to manage companies if they were family-owned busi-nesses and there was no male successor or the daughter's husband wasn't up to the job. These traditional roles remain influential in many societies around the globe, in a va-riety of nationally and culturally dependent forms, as a result of which men are still overrepresented on management boards. All over the world, men still identify with their traditional role, and define their identity in terms of success in the external world. In this traditional role, men's main emotional bonds are with other men. Though these male–male bonds often take ritualised forms that limit their intimacy, they are still important and often stronger than men's relationships with women (Pleck, 1975). More modern men expect friendship and intimacy in their relationships with women, which they see as a source of emotional support that they need to cope with their daily ordeals. By contrast with the traditional expectation that women will defer to his authority in the family, the modern man expects women to salve his wounds and refill his emotional reserves. Boys are still usually socialised in childhood for a traditional male role, but in later adolescence and adulthood are measured against the standards of a modern men's role. Whereas in childhood boys are taught to develop their physical strength and sporting prowess and to avoid girls, in adulthood men are told they must form relationships with women as colleagues and emotional confidants. Men's modern expectations of women differ from historical ones, but they're no less consequential.

> German CEO: It's a challenge right across society. There are many factors involved. Because it's not just the men at work who shape the image we have of women or men. You also have a whole gen-eration of parents, female friends, relatives, sisters, brothers and so on. The family environment often has a big influence too. Especially fathers, for women.

> American CEO: Equality is not doing whatever you want. Jordan Peterson is a Canadian psycholo-gist. He talks about the need for responsibility, not the need for rights. None of us have any rights. The only way we frame value in our lives is by the responsibilities we have, whether that is to each other, to ourselves, to our family, to our employees, to our colleagues or to the person we share the bus with. We have no rights, but people feel they have rights. I think that giving someone a right actually changes the rest of society to acknowledge that right. If you force the rest of society to

be responsible for equity, then does it change faster? If you took any man, almost any man who has a daughter and said, 'Your daughter's life is going to be restricted by this and this,' I don't think they'd be happy about it, but when it's not their daughter, they seem to think that it's OK. I think that's bringing it all into responsibility.

Exceptions to traditional roles can be found in countries where, historically, women were able to participate in activities outside their family role or assume different roles altogether.

These include some of the world's very few matriarchies, such as the Mosuo in southern China, where woman have dominant status in society (Coler, 2007). The Mosuo do not have traditional family systems. Mosuo men stay with their family of origin and only occasionally visit their partners and children, and it is the women who control families' property.

Another example can be found in Japan. Until the dawn of the Muromachi period in the fourteenth century, Japanese society centred around women. Iwao (1998) describes how up to this period Japanese culture and politics were strongly influenced by empresses and female deities. People believed that women possessed supernatural abilities and could communicate with the gods, a power that men lacked. There were many female rulers in Japan between the third and eighth century CE, including six empresses. For much of Japan's history, women had considerable freedom and worked on the same terms as men. They dominated literature until the twelfth century and had the right of inheritance. They also had access to education and could freely choose their romantic partners.

In France too, as early as the fourteenth to seventeenth centuries there were already calls for equality and attempts at emancipation by individual women. Works such as Christine de Pizan's *The Book of the City of Ladies* and Marie le Jars de Gournay's *The Equality of Men and Women* were published. These early feminists opposed the principle of male superiority. The French Revolution gave rise to the first French women's movement, which saw Olympe de Gouges publish her Declaration of the Rights of Woman and of the Female Citizen. Other examples can be found all over the world. Despite this, traditional views of men's and women's roles continue to dominate.

French CEO: I've got two daughters, and I believe both of them could develop into very good, strong leaders, in their businesses, or wherever they start out. They've got, I think, the characteristics to do that. It's an interesting question for me, and everybody's still talking about it. Today, you can read a lot, you can listen to a lot of things on this topic. I think we can't ignore that historically there has been a certain level of, I don't know what to call it, competition between men. What we see today is the legacy of that. I think that's absolutely clear. This goes back to the constrictions of historical society, which probably have become values for a number of people. These values usually make it really difficult to transform things. I've got to believe that, for a number of people today, dealing with men is still more reassuring. There's a link to that physical strength. It's clear that whichever way we look at it, men have more physical strength than women. So when you look at a man, you're looking at a person who has more physical strength. Does this mean that this person is going to deal with this or that situation in a better way? I have to believe that some people have this mindset, because I think it's something we can't ignore.

Linked to these general expectations about typical male and female traits, there are also expectations about the kind of work men and women will do. The role of women involves socially oriented activities such as care, child-raising or domestic work. Men's role, by contrast, is primarily concerned with the world of business and commerce. Social positions are determined by role expectations. Women are socialised to see their role as being in the family, while men are groomed for careers in business and politics. These expectations can, depending on sociocultural context, make it more difficult for both men and women to pursue careers considered atypical for their gender. Several sociological studies have found that there is a high degree of consensus worldwide about male and female roles (Eagly and Wood, 2012). Researchers report that things that are routinely expected of men are regarded as abnormal if done by women, with both men and women condemning and sanctioning such behaviour. Probably the best-known study on perceptions of women managers was conducted by Schein et al. (1996). The 'think manager, think male' theory argues that one of the difficulties faced by women in management is gendered stereotypes about managers and executive roles. Schein et al.'s multi-year study found that the characteristics required to be a successful manager are attributed to men but not women. Depending on cultural context, both men and women believed women are generally less qualified to be managers, and good leaders were described as possessing primarily masculine traits.

Australian CEO in the US: It's also not because they don't want to, but because the whole societal system doesn't support it. One example is the way we look at sports. Consider university or college football in the United States, for example. I think the number of male and female students at college and university is similar, close to fifty–fifty, half boys and half girls. But we don't have half-boy, half-girl teams, we have girls' football teams and one hundred per cent boys' football teams. The level of competition in those football teams is super, super high. Right from school, or maybe even in the family environment before going to school, more emphasis is put on the boys' side of the equation than the girls'. There's a lot of competition between girls. If you look at a girls' football team, you might say their competitive edge compared with a male football team is less aggressive. Unless you look in detail. Women's football teams can be very fierce. Some guys' football teams are quite friendly and very OK with women, but not all of them. I think that's an example of people progressing and learning. Because that's our brain capacity. We learn to do better what we already do best by, for example, feeling a mistake as we make it, by being punished for it, or by being incentivised to do something. The applause you get from society for winning in a boys' team is much greater than the applause you get for winning in a girls' team or a physically disabled team. What happens next is you enter the corporate game.

This suggests that traditional role expectations have, like DNA, left their mark over long periods of time and across many generations, and continue to influence behaviour in management today.

What specific impact does this have on relations between the sexes in leadership teams? Academic studies have described the effect of role expectations, socialisation and social stereotypes on women themselves, who unconsciously internalise these expectations and stereotypes. This can affect their career orientation and motivation. Historically rooted stereotypes of women, like the image of the housewife so prevalent in Western cultures, define both men's and women's expectations of what women should be like. For instance, women are typically associated with emotional warmth, which is held in high social esteem by people of both genders. Women remain in or accept traditional gender roles because of the high social prestige attached to them. Men defend their traditional rights and the domains of power that used to be their sole preserve and collective inheritance. But now women are encroaching on the quintessentially male world of senior management. Men have often responded with incomprehension or hostility. Figures like that of the career woman don't fit with people's socially learned stereotypes, and so women who aspire to rise up the ranks are ascribed qualities such as 'emotionally cold'. Such labels often form the basis for men to discriminate against women. Women who have achieved success in traditionally male professions are regarded as unfair or dangerous rivals who threaten the way men have been socialised to see themselves. This perception is heightened if women stage confrontations with men in the presence of other people. In response, men use competitive strategies that they otherwise only deploy against other men, and not in their interactions with women.

Despite the steady growth in the proportion of women in employment in Western industrialised countries since the early 1970s, the gender stereotypes documented in academic studies have persisted over time, to a degree depending on cultural context. A number of researchers believe this is explained by the continued sharp segregation of the world of work by gender (Cejka and Eagly, 1999; Kite, 2001). Studies suggest that there is no prospect of any substantial change in the distribution of familial roles either. An international comparison shows that women still have primary responsibility for the home and child-rearing. This imbalance persists even if both partners work the same number of hours (Bianchi et al., 2000; Wagner and Brandstätter, 1994).

> German COO: I think that a very, very conservative view of society still prevails in Germany. A conservative view of the role of the family. Or rather not of the role of the family, but there's a conservative understanding of the family whose division of roles puts social pressure on women, along the lines of, 'You have to wait three years, six years first.' With just two children, that's then six years gone, give or take. And not every family divides the work up the way they could and should. Though the word 'should' depends on the parameters the family sets itself. I have to say that my family isn't the best example, where I could say that my wife kept working. We were working under other constraints, simply because we moved around so much.

The proportion of women in leadership roles varies from culture to culture

This section begins by considering the men's explanations for why some countries have more women in senior management than others. Historical role models remain influential across a range of cultures. Over the course of their careers, the study participants have worked in over twenty-five countries between them, meaning they could bring diverse international perspectives to bear on this topic. Below, quotations from the interviewees have been woven into a short round-the-world tour through selected leading industrialised nations, with a focus on sociocultural context and culturally distinctive conceptions of roles.

In many industrialised nations, women now have equal or even better education than their male colleagues, and a growing number of companies publicise their diversity targets and policies. Despite this, an unequal distribution of women in the most senior management positions persists in most countries. This imbalance varies from place to place. Many North and East European and Asian countries, for instance, have far more women in senior leadership positions than Germany, Japan or the USA.

In the literature, various explanations have been put forward for this phenomenon, some but not all of which point to historical, cultural, political and sociological differences between the countries. With some adjustments, these explanatory models can be applied to a whole range of contexts.

According to a global study by Grant Thornton (2021) that covered twenty-nine countries, the average proportion of female senior managers worldwide stood at thirty-one per cent in 2021. Eighty-three per cent of countries included in the study had achieved the thirty per cent mark. In 2004, that figure was just nineteen per cent. It took around seventeen years to pass the thirty per cent threshold, during which time progress often stalled or, as in 2018, was even rolled back. There has been a total rise of six percentage points since 2017. The study analysed senior management roles, also known a C-suite positions, which include both the CEO/board and the hierarchical level immediately below. In summary, researchers have observed a global increase in the proportion of women in management in recent years. The rise in the number of female CEOs is striking, as for many years it lay at a relatively low level. The proportion rose globally from fifteen per cent in 2019 to twenty-six per cent today. The participants in the present study attribute this development among other things to the 'flexibilisation' of the labour market during the global pandemic.

The statistics show more progress in some regions of the world than others. According to the Grant Thornton report, Africa leads the way with thirty-nine per cent women in senior executive roles, followed by the ASEAN region on thirty-eight per cent. Overall, APAC only achieved twenty-eight per cent, likely due to Japan and South Korea. In 2021, the European Union improved by four percentage points to thirty-four per cent. North America achieved a figure of thirty-three per cent, with South America slightly ahead at thirty-six per cent.

Spanish CEO: First and foremost, there's the culture of most countries in the Asia-Pacific region. If you put aside north Asian countries, i.e. Japan and Korea, where you have exactly the opposite situation, the role of women in these societies is extremely important. The role of women in business is very important. You can't imagine how many female partners, how many female customers, how many women there really are in this business environment. That's part of the reality in China, in Vietnam, in Thailand – even in Indonesia, which is maybe a little bit less advanced on that front.

The same goes for the culture and the history. So why has the culture pushed women to these kind of positions? I don't know, but it's the reality.

Until 2017, the same report gave individual figures for major industrial nations. The global rankings for the proportion of women in senior management were topped by Russia (forty-five per cent) and China (thirty-eight per cent), followed by France on twenty-eight per cent, Sweden on twenty-seven per cent, the USA and Australia each on twenty-three per cent and the UK on twenty-one per cent. Germany and Japan trailed behind the other leading economies, on fifteen and seven per cent respectively. Contrary to what might be assumed, the report shows that smaller countries like Lithuania and Poland and certain Asian countries, such as the Philippines and Thailand, punch above their weight when it comes to women in management. Of course, statistics can be presented and interpreted in different ways, depending on your assumptions and interests, but one thing seems certain: the progress in lower and middle management ranks is remarkable when you consider that women have only been able to work in management at all since the mid-twentieth century. But companies around the world are still struggling to make progress in the top echelons, even if the overall direction of travel has been positive in many countries – especially in 2021, the second year of the coronavirus pandemic. Based on their analysis of different countries, the senior managers interviewed for this study conclude that the times are moving in women's favour.

> *French GM in China: Let's start with China. For instance, in our organisation, we have the largest number of women in operations management positions. Not only plant management, but in very technical, very difficult jobs. I think that's good, because typically, in our type of industry CEOs come from the technical divisions. That means they are able to grow within the organisation. China is very much advanced compared to the rest of the world in this respect. The second country is the US. I think women have a much stronger position in society there than in Europe. Though not when I was there, which was thirty years ago. It wasn't yet reflected in the orga chart. It was very much male-oriented. Although at that time, actually, when I was there, it was very funny because there was this positive discrimination. Very, very strong. I remember I had a friend. She was a Venezuelan woman. A woman from a minority. Her plan at first was like this: she wanted to rise up the ladder, and she became a VP in three years or something. If you become a GM in the US, you get a number of things that you don't find in other places around the globe. The US is a bit more advanced, with better positioning of women in society. When I was over in Europe, I was with a Swedish company. It was also quite interesting to see that in Sweden the position of women was really good.*

Interviewees who work in the APAC region often mentioned China as a positive example of women's representation in management. In China, sociocultural conditions for women and their careers are caught between two diametrically opposed influences. On the one hand, as noted earlier, Coler (2007) describes how one of the world's few matriarchal cultures, the Mosuo, is to be found in China. On the other, a far greater number of authors, including Granrose (2005, 2007), Warnecke and Blanchard (2010) and Li (2000), have described how male-oriented Confucian traditions have heavily influenced the country's culture and the roles of women. Counterposed to these influences are policies designed to achieve equality across a range of areas. In 1950, the Chinese government passed legislation that paved the way for improving women's status: 'Women shall enjoy equal rights with men in political, economical, educational and social life.' (cited in Li, 2000) A phrase from a speech by Mao Zedong, 'Women can hold half the sky', became a slogan for the Chinese equality movement. In today's China, dual-income households are a socially accepted norm. The high proportion of women in employment, which far outstrips other industrialised countries in the West and the global average, can be seen as the result of the last fifty years of action by the state. The Cultural Revolution was a globally unique phenomenon in helping to advance gender equality. Feminist theorists have described how, women's issues were 'masculinised', and women were treated as identical to men despite often having different life circumstances. According to Yang (1986), the slogan 'Whatever men can do, women can do too' and uniform clothing for men and women were expressions of the views that prevailed at that time. Women were employed in all sectors just like men, including roadbuilding and construction in general.

Authors such as Ren (2010) see more equality of opportunity in China than in Western nations and describe a continuous decrease in inequality since the establishment of the current Communist government in the mid-1980s: 'Chinese institutions are seen to have a higher level of gender equality than Japan, the UK and the USA; with permanent full-time work being the norm for all adults irrespective of sex; and a high degree of egalitarianism in family roles' (Ren, 2010). Opposing positions point to the underrepresentation of women in senior government roles, which critics claim shows that Chinese women still don't have as much power as men.

Chinese CEO: I see successful women everywhere. Yes, in senior positions. It's equal. If a woman wants to achieve a senior position, she can; it's possible here. Sometimes, we joke and ask whether we need more men in HR and finance. Everywhere, you have women in these areas. In my executive team, there are forty-five per cent women. To be sure, it also depends on the industry. Perhaps it's different in state-owned companies. But there too I know some very powerful women.

Chinese CEO in Hong Kong: In my organisation in China, I have maybe around thirty-five per cent women at MD and VP level. People will think that the transportation industry will be male-dominated. No, I have quite a lot of capable women working for me. I don't have the figures for individual countries, but overall. At our headquarters in the US, the situation is more or less the same. Right now, our chief commercial officer is a woman, and then our chief marketing officer is a woman. My boss is actually a woman as well. You can see that, really, particularly for [company F], we are focused on developing gender diversification of the team; it's important. Not only women versus men, but also people from different countries, different age groups. I would say we are fortunate to have a very good culture that promotes diversity, offers equal opportunities to everyone.

Chinese CFO: In my view, maybe that is the legacy. In some countries, women may not be given an adequate education. They are disadvantaged but, in my view, that situation is changing. The second thing is that some people within a company may have the misperception that men are more dedicated, and women are more concerned with their family. That kind of prejudice may prevent women from climbing up the corporate ladder, but I would say that's changing as well.
Third, I think that culturally, like in the north of China, and historically, people may have reeled off the idea that women should stay at home. If they're working, that means their family has some is-

sues. I'd say the current culture is also changing. Right now, maybe, the reality is that in the north women are still less represented at corporate level, the men are playing a dominant role, but I can see this is changing.

Japan can be taken as a contrasting example to China when it comes to equality for women in management. The Japanese CEOs explained the social context: although the number of well-educated Japanese women has risen steadily in recent years, Japan trails behind other leading economies when it comes to the proportion of women in leadership roles. Women are a rarity in Japan's business and political elites. A 2017 study by the World Economic Forum ranked Japan 114 out of 144 countries. It has remained in last place among industrialised nations for years without any notable change, despite the fact that Japanese women have the highest life expectancy, literacy and level of basic education in the world.

Japanese CEO: In my time, when I was at university and joined the company, the government had just introduced an equalities law. It meant that companies had to treat women and men equally. That was in the 1980s. Still, from that time, for a couple of decades, some women were happier to just do all the household jobs, have babies and then raise them. They tended to see that as the female role. Men too. I think that was a perception on both sides. Some people on both sides were very happy at that time, actually. Women never complained about it and nor did men. But the government encouraged women to work more, and go out from their homes. There were several reasons for that. They needed more manpower and the women were very much underused. Lots of talented women were underused, that's a fact, so they were encouraged to work. Women's attitudes changed too. Now, my daughter is twenty-nine years old, and after graduation she joined some company doing the same work as men. Of course, she thought about her career. The only difference is giving birth: would a man take care of the baby? It's hard. It'll probably take ten, twenty more years of hard discussion, hard debate on this topic. Now, maternity and paternity leave, that's also become very popular and no longer seen as unusual.

When it comes to fully including women in business and politics, Japan often fares poorly compared with other countries. One reason may be that, although Japanese society was centred around women until the fourteenth century, it was subsequently dominated by men. *Amaterasu-ō-mi-kami*, the 'great divinity illuminating heaven', is the most important deity in the Shinto religion. She personifies the sun and light, and is regarded as the founder of the Japanese imperial family. It was once believed that women possessed the supernatural ability to communicate with the gods, a power that men lacked (Reischauer, 2020). For much of Japan's history, women had considerable freedom and worked on the same terms as men. They dominated literature until the twelfth century and had the right of inheritance. They had access to education and could freely choose their romantic partners. Until the eleventh century, since society was women-centred, it was common at all social levels for the husband to live with his wife's family after marriage, or to live separately from her and be allowed to visit her only on certain nights. This female supremacy continued for a considerable period of time among ordinary people such as farmers, fishers and traders in rural areas, in which about eighty per cent of the Japanese population lived at that time. During the Meiji period, laws and ideology gave rise to a hierarchical, traditional family structure, in which every member took on a specific role dictated by age and gender, and this characterised the family in Japan up until 1945. The education of women was focused on their role as housewives and mothers. Japanese women were expected to live by the three obediences (to father, husband and son, depending on her current phase of life) and four virtues (conduct, speech, works and comportment). Iwao (1998) explains the traditional image of women was that of the *ryōsai kenbo*, the 'good wife and wise mother'. The women of the pre-war generation, those born around 1935, accepted this ideal and concentrated on housework and bringing up their children. They supported their husbands, who were the breadwinners. They were brought up according to these values and with the awareness that men were deemed superior.

> *Japanese CEO: To come back to your question of why there are so few female executives in Japan: I think it's entirely historical. The executives need to have decades of experience. In my generation, the number of female candidates who could achieve that experience was very small, but now things are more equal. If you look at the number at the moment, the number or percentage of women can't be changed rapidly, even though the government has encouraged that a certain percentage of managers should be female. I think the reasons for the unequal proportion of women at executive level are historical rather than due to candidate discrimination.*

After the Second World War, the new 1947 constitution redefined women's rights, placing special emphasis on gender equality. Women's suffrage had been granted in 1945. In 2014, Japan's then prime minister Shinzo Abe introduced his 'womenomics' strategy, with a target of thirty per cent of managers being female by the year 2020. Many commentators have noted, however, that there was a lack of more precisely focused policies to support the implementation of this strategy. As a result, in 2017 Japan still only had seven per cent women in senior roles (Grant Thornton, 2017). The next lowest-ranked country was Argentina on fifteen per cent, and the only country with a lower figure (in a separate study) was Pakistan on three per cent. More recent data from 2021 does not show any notable progress in Japan.

> *Japanese GM: It depends on the country. It depends on the company as well. Our company was based in Scandinavia originally. Many female executives were very active and present. I had no impression of underrepresentation of senior women executives. But in Japan there are very, very few women in executive positions in any part of the industry, in any company. When I started my career in the US back in 1997, the situation was already different. Both wives and husbands worked. That was the normal situation. I think part of the reason is the employment situation in the US because of the layoffs that were common in the US after the eighties. In order to secure a family income and a healthcare insurance programme, both husband and wife have to work. Otherwise, it's quite a risky situation for their lifestyle. That's a US reality. I think that helped a lot, as it was a necessity for woman to keep working in a company setting. Women are very ambitious in the US compared to the situation in Japan. Perhaps because of education. My children's education was very fair and gender-neutral, that's my impression. Education is key to promoting ambitions among women.*

Russia illustrates the impact that policies can have on the division of men's and women's roles, as well as the ways in which social and political norms can interact. According to Grant Thornton's (2017) statistics, Russia has the highest proportion of women in senior management anywhere in the world. PWC (2013) reports that Russian women are most likely to be chief accounting, HR or financial officers. Women were given the vote in Russia immediately after the Communist revolution in 1917. That made the Soviet Union the first major European country to do so, long before many others and a whole twenty-seven years before France. The USSR's first constitution in 1918 proclaimed women's equal role in Soviet society and guaranteed women the same political, economic and civil rights as men. Historically, the USSR had the highest women's employment rate in the world (Ashwin and Yakubovich, 2005; Rzhanitsyna, 2000). In the Soviet Union, it was the norm for women to work full-time. The proportion of women employed in industry and services had risen to fifty-one per cent by the early 1990s. Even in physically strenuous agricultural occupations, women accounted for forty-five per cent of the workforce in the late 1990s (Goskomstat, 2006). In the public arena, the role of women was far more firmly established than in Western economies. They worked as crane operators, car mechanics and miners. Despite excellent state childcare facilities, the USSR still had what Western gender researchers call the 'working mother's contract'. Society expected women to bear the burden of job, children and household alone. Full-time housewives were an unknown phenomenon in socialist society. To improve women's rights, a comprehensive childcare network was built, including maternity homes, nurseries and all-day schools. The childcare provision was geared specifically towards the needs of women in full-time employment. During the restructuring of the perestroika era in the 1990s, conditions deteriorated for women. The economy underwent a complete restructuring after the collapse of the Soviet Union in 1991. The economic liberalisation was accompanied by a deleterious effect on the positions of women in the labour market. There were mass layoffs, primarily of women, as they had previously been employed mainly in 'light industries', which were the ones more seriously affected by the restructuring. In 1992, seventy-eight per cent of those officially registered as unemployed were women. In the redistribution of property and capital which occurred around that time, women stood virtually no chance against men and were left empty-handed. Viewed through a historical lens, overcoming the challenges of the perestroika period was nothing new for Russian women. During the country's numerous wars, women had always had to rely on themselves and had helped to rebuild the country on several occasions.

Russian CEO: In the past, the previous generation's mindset was that a woman's primary function was to be a mother and to keep the house in good order and to help with raising children. I would say that lasted till the 1990s, 1995, when the Soviet Union collapsed. After that, the new generation didn't have this mindset. Why? Because in the nineties, it was a total disaster in the country. If you didn't take action yourself, you wouldn't have anything to eat, and it destroyed the mindset that someone has to do this or someone has to do that, and we changed the rules of the game. Because in some families, women were more proactive. They did business more proactively. Some people still had mindsets in the nineties to 2000s about what women should do or men should do or whatever. Then the generations totally changed. For example, last week, I was holding my seminar at the Russian Presidential Academy, which is a university-like institution for people who will be working in

CEO posts in the future. I was really surprised, because fifty to sixty-five per cent were women. I think it very much depends not on men or women, it's more about the culture of the company itself. I think there are several different styles of leadership, like an autocratic style of leadership, a democratic style of leadership. That really depends on the person's mindset, not their sex, because I've seen autocratic women managing companies and democratic men in the office. What I've witnessed in some big corporations is that the whole pyramid of the company depends on the leadership style of the leader. For example, at one Russian bank, it was about results, not gender. If you walked on the floor where the CEO and the C-levels were sitting, it was almost half men and half women.

The dissolution of the Soviet state was marked by a period of political consolidation of gender-specific roles. With perestroika, the value system changed and women came to be seen as a group requiring protection, and one whose first priority should be the family. Gorbachev argued in 1987 that women should be allowed to return to their 'exclusively female vocation'. In order to encourage gender differentiation, the HR departments of governmental organisations promoted flexible working hours, working from home, reductions in working hours and generous leave for pregnancy, childbirth and the care of young or sick children. These support systems were aimed solely at women. Because of these welfare regulations, female workers consequently came to be classified as more costly than men. Under these regulations, certain types of work were officially forbidden to women. However, the transition to a market economy also offered women certain opportunities, as described by Sperling (1999) and Ardichvili and Gasparishvili (2001). Many women took the initiative and set up small enterprises during this period, some of them even doing business with neighbouring countries. Women who had formerly been lecturers, factory workers and teachers showed that they had entrepreneurial flair and that they could adapt to the new era and seize opportunities. It is probable that the many important female entrepreneurs in Russia today are the result of this phase.

German CFO: To get back to the countries: in Russia, there was this 'babushka syndrome'. We had lots of female senior brand managers and category heads who had children, but it was their mother or mother-in-law who was back home looking after them. Russian culture bears a strong feminine influence. If only due to the twenty-six million war deaths, of which I believe eighty per cent were men. There were simply no men.

In France, as early as the fourteenth to seventeenth centuries there were already calls for equality and attempts at emancipation by individual women. The history of French women is marked by intense conflicts and battles. The country's sociocultural character has been profoundly shaped by powerful male spheres of influence, which men try to keep women out of. The French CEOs interviewed for the study compared the situation for women in senior management in their country with that in Asian countries. Perhaps more than in other countries, the French business world is directly interwoven with the world of politics, which in France was long the exclusive preserve of men.

France was one of the last European countries to give women the vote, only doing so in 1944. Yet French women were the first in Europe to demand their political rights through petitions, at meetings and on the barricades. Equality legislation was passed in

1946, shortly after French women received the vote, though implementation of that legislation took longer; for instance, it was not until 1965 that French women could work without their husbands' permission. Only after that period did French women acquire the right to make decisions about their own bodies, their bank accounts, their married lives and their choice of profession (Hervé, 1995). Even in the 1960s to 70s, most women in France were still housewives. Key legislation on workplace equality was passed in 1982. Attitudes have shifted dramatically in the past forty years, which is reflected in French women's growing autonomy and self-determination. In France, it's nowadays considered normal, even expected, for women to work. This has been helped by government family policies, which have extended the childcare system to enable women to work full-time. This change only happened in companies after the introduction of statutory quotas. One important step towards increasing the number of women on the boards of major French companies was the passing of the 2011 Copé–Zimmermann Act, which set a target for 2017 of forty per cent women on the supervisory and administrative boards of French companies with over 500 employees and in the civil service. The proportion of women in senior management in France now exceeds that in the USA and (by a wide margin), Germany, and is approaching the level in China.

French CEO in Thailand: Thailand is a very special case, because here you have many well-known, successful women in the press, in magazines, on TV. Many women who are CEOs of companies. That's very specific to Thailand, I think. So the complex of women's inferiority to men is probably lower than in other parts of the world. Of course, the education at home, plus also the school system, has an influence. I would say that now the education system in France is the same. Whether you're male or female, you're educated the same way. You always need to show strong self-confidence in any situation. You need to be a good speaker, good-looking, tall, strong. It's true for men and women, the stereotype of the leader. Like you can see in all the books. And you try to be like that, you have been taught to be like that at school. The education system is what makes the difference here. The education system is based on experience, respect for senior people. So you don't interrupt people who are older than you, like you do in Europe, where you spend all your time interrupting your teacher, asking tricky questions to your professor, trying to put him in a trap and so on. Here it's much more respectful. You respect people who have experience, you respect their seniority and listen much more. They're much better listeners here. They have very good listening skills that we don't have in France. That's because we have been taught to speak all the time and be the best of the best. Number two: creating a favourable environment. Here that isn't an issue any more. We don't discuss gender or diversity all the time. We don't discuss those things here. In France, you spend your time talking about it, but you don't actually do anything. You just speak about it and don't make a decision. When it does finally come to making the decision, you're very cautious, or you make your choice and most of the time it's a man and not a woman.

Germany still lags behind other countries. Despite sixteen years with a female chancellor at the helm, the proportion of women in senior management has stagnated at around eighteen per cent (Grant Thornton, 2017). Only thirteen per cent of board members at 160 listed companies are women (Ankersen and Berg, 2021), though that is a slight improvement over 2016 when the figure stood at just six per cent. So things are changing in Germany too.

The prevailing image of women in German society and culture can be summed up in the words 'housewives and mothers'. According to the German interviewees, this historical view of women can be traced back to the period before and after the Second World War, and it continues to affect how women in management are viewed to this day. Historically, German society – just as in many other countries – was organised along patriarchal lines, and women were frequently deemed neither independent nor capable of making decisions. For a long time, women in Germany were not permitted to work without the consent of their husbands or fathers, were not in control of their own money and had no legal rights with regards to their children. A woman's primary role was that of housewife. The first major German women's union was founded in 1865. The focus at that time was on educational rights for girls and women. Women were given the vote in 1918, twenty-six years earlier than in neighbouring France. During the National Socialist era, women were primarily seen as being there to assist their husbands and the rights that the women's movements had fought for were effectively reversed. Women were supposed to concentrate exclusively on their roles as mothers and to bear as many children as possible.

After the war, the role of women in Germany developed in two very different directions: in West Germany, with its system of traditional gender roles in which women were primarily seen as mothers, and in East Germany, where the emphasis was on employment for women. These divergent paths had major implications for gender equality.

In the Federal Republic of Germany (FRG) in the west, traditional role models were maintained well into the 1990s. Despite equal rights being constitutionally recognised in 1949, the legal framework proved utterly inadequate to dismantle the traditional model. It was not until 1957 that the 'obedience article' (*Gehorsamkeitsparagraf*) was abolished, and not until 1958 that the Equality Act was passed. This was the first time that husbands had been denied the ultimate right to make decisions on all marital matters. *Hausfrauenehe* ('marriage with a full-time housewife'), in which the husband bore the main responsibility as breadwinner, was abolished in 1977 with reforms to marriage and family law.

German CMO: So, to take up the thread again, I think that social attitudes in Germany are far more conservative than in other countries. There's greater social pressure than in other countries. As a result, women simply press the pause button. And even if that pause is only six years, because of how quickly our world moves, how much things and organisations change, that automatically makes it difficult to come back on board, to keep up with these changes. There are plenty of examples where women say they just won't have children and get right on with their careers. They're not necessarily the ones who people find it easiest to tolerate, I should say. So I think organisations need to work on ensuring that they aren't disparaged as careerist bitches. There needs to be a change of mindset in the companies to create more opportunities. I think many women still feel like they're discriminated against when they show the same mettle as men, like it has completely different connotations when a man does the same thing. And I should say in my experience these things are very different in Germany than in Australia or the UK. I'd class Austria as even more socially conservative and resistant to change than Germany. Resistant to change from the men's point of view: 'We don't need to expand our circle. Why should we? We're getting on fine by ourselves.'

In the early German Democratic Republic (GDR) in the east, society was organised primarily around the gainful employment of both men and women. An additional aim of women's employment, other than making use of their labour, was to achieve gender equality. Policies relating to gender and family were geared towards promoting work–life balance for women. The 1949 GDR constitution not only enshrined the equality of men and women but, even at that early date, laid down additional legislation with regard to equal pay and the reconcilability of work and family life. Women's needs were given priority. With Germany's reunification in 1990, the FRG's constitutional, legal and social framework was adopted throughout Germany. The ending of the period of separation brought together two different political and economic systems and two sets of people who had different experiences and ideas about family and society, equality and gender rights. But society in the western regions of the country remained essentially unchanged, including people's attitudes towards these important matters.

> German CEO: Yes, that's an interesting question. I prefer to argue from the perspective of 'Why does it work in other countries?' Like the UK, for instance. Though I don't know the figures for the UK; I argue based on my own experiences of the UK or, say, Australia. I think that in those places, compared with what I've experienced in Germany, it's far more normal and matter of course for women to keep working without taking a break. It's more equal, more emancipated. Of course, that also has a bearing on their marriage or their relationship. The reason might be that those countries have better childcare provision. That's certainly true in Australia. There, it's the most normal thing in the world for kids to go to crèche at the age of six months or one year. It was the most normal thing in the world when my child went to crèche at the age of one, and my wife could carry on working as usual. I think that in those countries, not so much now in Austria but certainly in the UK and definitely in Australia, it's more socially acceptable for women to go back to work. Indeed, there's even a certain expectation that they will, and it's a given that their employer will let them. And there are companies, including in Germany, that really embrace it. Like recently [company XY], where it's the most normal thing in the world for women to return from maternity leave, for the father to then take paternity leave, for women to be able to work, so that mothers with children can be accommodated. And not every family divides the work up the way they could and should. Though the word 'should' depends on the parameters the family sets itself. I have to say that my family isn't the best example, where I could say that my wife kept working. We were working under other constraints, simply because we moved around so much.

Surveys on perceptions of gender diversity in different countries show that Europeans and Asians think the figures for the USA are more favourable than they are in reality. Despite all efforts to achieve gender equality in the workplace in the USA, women there face barriers and challenges to being accepted as leaders. Sander and Keller (2021) report that only twenty-one per cent of C-level roles are held by women. Women, especially women of colour, are a minority at senior level all over the USA according to Grant Thornton (2017). However, between 2015 and 2020 the proportion of women at senior VP level rose from twenty-three to twenty-eight per cent, and in the same period the proportion of women in all C-level roles rose from seventeen to twenty-one per cent. Twenty-three of the 500 largest US companies have a woman in their senior management team. Ankersen and Berg (2021) put that figure at over thirty per cent for the thirty largest companies on the main American stock index. For every hundred men who receive a promotion to board level, eighty-five women do, falling to fifty-eight for Black women and seventy-one for Latina women. Men hold sixty-two per cent of middle and senior management positions. The thirty-eight per cent held by women comprises thirty-one per cent white women, four per cent women of colour and three per cent Asian women. The USA's first Black woman CEO at a Fortune 500 business was appointed at Xerox in 2009. During the Covid pandemic, two million women dropped out of work, far higher than the rate for men. Despite that, the number of Fortune 500 companies with a female CEO hit a record high of forty-one, including two Black women (Hinchliffe, 2021), equivalent to eight per cent of the total. In 2009, that figure stood at three per cent (Zweigenhaft, 2021).

> *American CFO: I've seen quite a few very talented women. Recently we had another one. We had developed her a lot. And she got to C-level. Now she's on maternity leave, because of her second child. I don't know if she can catch up. We traditionally believe that mothers will concentrate on their kids first.*

US women were granted the vote in 1920, which paved the way for further legal reforms to improve their situation. However, substantial improvements to women's working conditions were not achieved until the 1960s. Although the country had already been dependent on women's support in the workplace during the First World War, the traditional cliché of the housewife persisted. Housework and raising children were seen as the highest priority for a traditional woman. The Second World War marked a dramatic shift in how women's roles were seen (Heinemann, 2011). When the USA entered the war, it caused a huge labour shortage, and arms production struggled to keep up with demand. Women were recruited to do vital work for their country. Domestic industry was reliant on women and they were increasingly allowed to do what were traditionally considered men's jobs (Jeffries, 2018). In 1945, when the end of the war was in sight, a phase of enormous restructuring began in the USA. Millions of women withdrew from the world of work and returned to their original role as housewives. But the war was nonetheless a major turning point in how women's role in society was perceived. The 1964 Civil Rights Act prohibited discrimination against women. Until then, women in the US only earned around sixty cents for every dollar earned by men. Although many American couples are now dual earners, women continue to shoulder most of the family responsibilities. This fuels prejudices about their career motivation, based on the generalisation that all women will have less time to commit to their career.

In the 1960s, the US was rocked by social change. One result was a strong women's movement. Influenced by the success of the Black civil rights movement and other progressive currents, a host of lobbyists and organisations campaigned for full equality for American women. They didn't just want to fundamentally transform American institutions, customs and values, but also to revolutionise traditional conceptions of men's and women's roles.

Despite all the changes, it was a long time before (some) women were given statutory, albeit unpaid, maternity leave, and they have to return to work twelve weeks after giving birth if they want to keep their job. In 1976, the Supreme Court ruled in a case brought against General Electric by a female plaintiff that excluding pregnancy-related conditions from an employee benefit plan did not constitute gender discrimination. This ruling reflects the common management practice at that time of discriminating against married women, and firing any women who became pregnant (Mathe et al., 2011). Only in 1993 were both parents given the right to twelve weeks' unpaid family or sick leave. Since then, many other legal measures to combat gender discrimination have been introduced in the USA. Companies have responded with initiatives to promote women's professional development, focusing on issues such as work–life balance and protections for women of colour.

American CEO: We do a lot to develop women in the company. Several initiatives. And we have KPIs to develop colleagues of colour. In the past it was difficult for mothers. They had no protection like in other countries, and the culture was that mothers wouldn't continue pursuing a career. That wasn't the official view, but it was tradition, and there is still a lot of bias. But we have success stories. Just recently, a woman took the lead of an important Fortune 500 company.

Australian executive: Australia is probably more similar to the US, where gender diversity and strong female leadership are really embraced and there's a strong desire to ensure equality. Again, it's still catching up from previous generations. I could talk to my sister. I have sisters who are very senior leaders. In our organisation in Australia, our general manager is actually a woman, so I've always had strong female leaders around me. India is very different, above all because of how gender is seen differently in their religion and culture. The mother is the figure at home raising children. It's very different. There are very, very few women in senior roles. Very few, and they're an exception. India is still a long way behind Western culture and Western expectations.

Men believe women don't focus enough on their careers and make mistakes in their career planning

One explanation for the inequality between men and women in senior management is known as 'deficit theory', which argues that the causes of the inequality lie in the women themselves (Regnet, 2017). Some of the men's responses in the interviews echo this theory. Deficit theorists investigate women's qualifications for senior management tasks, their typical patterns of behaviour in management roles and the way they approach career planning. Many studies conclude that women are often not strategic enough in the way they build their careers, or do not set their sights on top-flight careers. The alpha men made observations along similar lines, and tried to explain why women are less interested in career advancement than their male colleagues.

Japanese CEO: Of the relatively few women we have, many don't want to be promoted. I respect that. It's a bit of a waste if she has great skills, but it's her choice. There's always a reason in life.

Career orientation and career motivation are key components of career success. Career orientation 'integrates individual career desires and motives', influences a person's 'choice of profession' and the 'values they apply in their work' and is linked to the 'specific conceptions they have of their career' (Geisler, 2009). That means a person may have different career goals depending on their career orientation. Career orientation is determined by values, motives and specific goals. Richardson (1974) conducted an empirical study showing that career orientation can be regarded as a multidimensional construct, of which work motivation and values are central elements. For one person, financial incentives and a high level of responsibility might be the key factors in their career decisions, for others it might be personal development and the working environment. Wottawa et al. (2011) conclude that young men primarily describe their career goals as power and money. Young women, by contrast, mention ethical values and doing something they enjoy as their main motivations. Women are more motivated by social acceptance and a desire to avoid failure. Other researchers believe that men's and women's career motivations are similar, but that as a result of their different socialisation and structural opportunities they differ in career planning and decision-making (Astin, 1984).

> *German head of region: It comes at a price, of course. Perhaps women are simply smart enough to realise that the price they'd have to pay to get onto the board is too great and that sometimes it's better to say no. I once had a very nice female colleague, a CFO in Russia, who was responsible for two hundred people. She was still doing it ten years later, because she enjoyed it. The company was her family. And perhaps it's this desire for recognition ... That's changing now too, of course. My generation, and my father's generation from after the war, were taught that children had to do as they were told. I can see that the generation coming up now are different, more easy-going. And perhaps women realised that earlier on; perhaps women want to see things through and not always move on after two years once they've ticked something off their list. Fast track, stress assignment. I'd definitely look at whether women perhaps see things more holistically and say, no, I'm not done yet, why should I move on? I'm enjoying what I'm doing now, I want to help people, I want to protect their jobs. And there you can see a maternal aspect coming in again.*

The interviewees gave three deficit-based explanations for the lower proportion of women in senior management worldwide: (1) women are less motivated to rise up the ranks in hierarchical structures; (2) women are more focused on their families; (3) women want to balance their career with other areas of their lives. This results in a 'pipeline problem', where there are fewer women available for companies to promote.

According to the men, women in societies that place a very strong emphasis on the role of mothers, such as Japan, are less career-focused. Barsh et al. (2012) found that women want to advance in their careers, just like men, but don't aspire to the highest roles in companies. According to their research, only eighteen per cent of entry and mid-level women had their eye on a C-suite role, compared with thirty-six per cent of men. The authors attribute this to many women prioritising family. Prejudiced attitudes in companies about women juggling motherhood and careers also play a role, alongside structural barriers and a lack of motivation by women to progress to C-level positions.

Japanese CEO: I think it's deeply rooted in cultural and social values and traditions, but ambition itself was very low among all those female employees. In Japan, men and women are almost equal in number in early-stage education and higher education. Women also go into the labour force after finishing education in the same numbers as men, but for certain reasons they drop their career in maybe their late twenties or mid-thirties. Part of the reason is definitely that they get married and have kids, but the biggest reason is a shortage of childcare programmes in Japan. That's one reason, I think, but again, to go back to my original point: the ambition of women itself could be the problem, and the pressure of society's values, traditions and expectation by the parents.

Women's focus on family as a career damper

Most of the alpha men's explanations for the imbalance in leadership roles can be categorised under this heading. The interviewees have observed that many women interrupt or break off their careers for family reasons. Under the rules of career progression that currently prevail, that makes it impossible for them to reach senior management posts, such as CEO. The men themselves often have a family set-up where their female partner supported them and took primary responsibility for raising the children.

Spanish CEO: We're a very traditional couple. One year after we got married, my wife decided to focus on the kids, in part because my career was heading in a more promising direction. She decided to stop and devote herself to the family. Frankly speaking, we were and are extremely happy. My kids saw that, but they were not taught that this was the only possible model. On the contrary. This was one possible model that sometimes works and sometimes doesn't. It depends on the people. I see that in the new generation. In the past it was clear that the person who had to sacrifice their career for the sake of the family was the woman. That was in all our minds. I have to say that in the last five, ten years, things have changed quite a lot. In my team, I have at least two women who have decided with their partners that the professional priority would be given to the career of the wife instead of the career of the husband. That priority was in the past systematically given to the man; now things are changing.

German CFO: I couldn't get help with childcare during our tour. In Australia, we were so far away from everyone. My mother wasn't there, nor were my parents-in-law. Even if they'd wanted to, they couldn't have helped with our family. My wife automatically took on the role of managing the family during these relocations. It took two years for the family to get settled in, and then in the third or fourth year we'd be off again and it all started over from scratch. My wife did work on and off, at an NGO, at a school, that sort of thing.

French CEO: Especially when I was younger, I had some long days at work. I understood that was part of my career development. It was absolutely not so I could avoid dealing with the kids. I'm a hundred per cent clear about that. Actually, I was always concerned with how life was going for my wife and for the kids. It was only OK when I had a certain level of assurance. We had a clear repartition of roles. I could not have done what I've done without my wife, absolutely. Then we had our first daughter in the US. When we came back, we really had to make a decision. I strongly believe that the presence of the parents is fundamental for children's growth. I try to do as much as I can during the weekends. Obviously, during the week, like I said earlier, I was very busy or on business trips.

Career women with families have a variety of sub-identities: they are wives, mothers, professionals. Hall and Hall (1976) describe how people engage in different social roles and thereby form various sub-identities. According to their theory, career success is attainable only if managers invest in and centre their career role. For women, by contrast with men, this means greater focus on making the roles compatible. Support from family and arranging childcare are of particular importance.

Family responsibilities can mean women invest less time in their careers, which are often interrupted when they become mothers. This role conflict can fuel prejudice against women by employers, leading them to automatically assume women will take career breaks and to view these breaks in a negative light (Rothbard, 2001). In many Western countries, the more children women have and the more highly educated their partner, the less time they will invest in their careers. The amount of paid work they do for companies is inversely related to the amount of unpaid work they do at home.

> *French CEO: We recruited her and then I spent a day supervising her in her new job. It was the day of our annual inventory, which is quite an event. Then at six o'clock she said, 'OK, I'm going, I have to start my second day of work at home.' I was surprised, because in my world everyone would stay longer for this important day. I only realised later, after my divorce, that I was an idiot. She became my role model for me as a single father. Having more women in the company helps us to overcome prejudice.*

Conflicts generally occur when women have no choice but to juggle both roles at once. In societies centred around motherhood, women tend to choose jobs that give them the flexibility to meet their family responsibilities. Many also prioritise job security (Kim and Parish, 2020). Despite that, many mothers still have high career motivation. In one survey of over 1,800 German women, forty-two per cent said that family and career are equally important to them (Ziegler, 2011). Only two per cent of respondents ranked career higher, while fifty-six per cent put family first. Women in China and France differ from women in other countries in terms of their self-reported career orientation. These are cultures where it's accepted for mothers to work full-time and where women remain focused on their careers even after becoming mothers (Al-Sadik-Lowinski, 2020).

> *Dutch CEO: It is a fact that many women here work part-time, we are world champions of part-time, and that's not good for a career. Also, during Covid a lot of women were in charge of all the housework and they played a very traditional role. But I can see that highly successful women will really change that. I look back wistfully at the situation my wife, who works full-time, and I had in China. It was ideal. Things are much more complex now here in the Netherlands, with coronavirus and elderly parents. And a lot less support.*

Globally, women in senior management roles are more likely to remain single and childless so as to avoid being doubly burdened. A German study found that twenty per cent of all female managers were single and seventy-one per cent did not have children (Holst et al., 2015). A Swiss study (cited in Hollstein, 2004) reported an even higher proportion, with a third of female managers found to be single. Studies comparing the careers of unmarried, childless women and married women show that mothers are still worse paid and regarded as less competent than women without children (Powell, 2011). The phenomenon of mothers earning less than childless women has been dubbed the 'motherhood penalty' (Budig et al., 2012). Budig et al.'s study, which covered twenty-two countries, showed that mothers not only earn less than men but also, on a global comparison, significantly less than childless women. One significant influence on careers is absence due to maternity leave. Seventy per cent of female respondents in another study said that maternity leave had damaged their career, and thirty per cent that they had not taken all the time they were entitled to for fear of the consequences (Thompson et al., 1999).

> American CEO: My daughter just resigned from [company P] after twelve years to spend time at home. She was very happy with that decision. She has three kids, all under the age of five, and a husband who's gainfully employed, but it was incredibly hard for her to make that decision. She was really tortured about it, mostly because of what society expected of her, at least among her female peers at [company P], her friends, her parents. It was an interesting journey, and she'll likely do something professionally at some point. She may be an elementary school gym teacher, because she thinks that'd be a lot of fun and very fulfilling, and compatible with her needs. I said she'd had a good ride there in marketing. Twelve years in marketing is pretty good because they like to throw people out pretty quickly at that company.
> Eventually, she took six months of maternity leave and went down to two, three days a week. She made choices that she knew would disadvantage her, because the company was waiting for her. She was very highly rated all throughout her time there, but in order for her to get back on the fast track, she needed to be full-time, she needed to be able to relocate, she needed to do all these things that she just wasn't willing to do, and it wasn't important enough for her to rise to a higher level. I kept asking her, 'How badly do you want the next job?' She said, 'I want the next job so I can say I got the next job.' I said, 'OK, I understand that, but do you really want to do the next job?' She said, 'Not really.' She's a very achievement-oriented, goal-oriented young lady. When she joined, I said, 'Nose to the grindstone, they value people who put in the work. Your ability to write and to speak effectively are important, your network is very important, your ability to get others to support you, you're the boss. Actually, she worked for one of the women who's now risen up to a pretty high level, she's in the top ten. She just got one of the division president jobs. That woman, by the way, was married with little kids, worked seventy hours a week, and couldn't get her head around why my daughter didn't want to do that. She was very supportive of her early in her career, but then she lost the support of this mentor because she just saw the role of the company in her life differently than this person who lives and breathes the company and has no outside interests.

> Australian executive: There's also group pressure in the family, when grandparents and parents speak to men differently than to women. This provokes conflicts. When women feel that the company environment pressures them in the same way as the family environment, they may feel a big career isn't something a woman should aim for.

> German head of region: Women are just as smart and just as good managers. But I think for many of them the mother aspect comes to the fore when they have children. They step back, because they

don't have super high mobility, because they want to keep the family together. I think that's due to a certain sense of duty, and many take it very seriously. But, for instance, I've got a lot of strong women in my team who aren't at all mobile because they have young children, in Warsaw or Bucharest or wherever it might be. Which I admire. In my eyes, the real power women aren't just the showy role models. I'm not remotely interested in them. Self-important, loud, massive ego, unrelenting. The women who really succeed in managing family and career, including at more junior levels – them I have respect for. There are so many of them with young children, who switch the laptop back on at ten at night, who get up again at five because the baby wakes them up. And yet still manage to be better than the men: that I respect.

I think you simply need to allow a lot more women to grow up from the bottom, who'll then really know the company. That can be done by stretch assignments, which could come from the board. Then you wouldn't need to always hire someone external because you haven't done enough to promote women's development. And the problem – and this really has to stay between us – is that unfortunately the type of women who tended to be promoted were ones that absolutely nobody wanted to work with. Some of them were so career-focused and would stop at nothing to achieve their goals. There are positive female traits, like sensitivity, motherliness, empathy. But there are negative ones too, of course. I think the big disadvantage is that we're still very much stuck in the quota mindset. And even on boards, women are squeezed into these very familiar niches.

Japanese CEO: It depends on the availability of support. As I mentioned before, in Japan childcare programmes are very poor. No nannies in general, because Japan shut down the border to foreign workers. People can't bring in nannies or babysitters from any other country. That's important given the current ageing population. There's a general shortage of labour. No one wants to be a baby- sitter or work for a childcare centre. If plenty of services were available in an easily accessible en- vironment, then having kids wouldn't be a big obstacle. These days they don't have any hesitation at all, that's my theory. Even if the mother-in-law may disapprove.

German head of region: I had an ex-girlfriend in France. She and her husband worked and the kids stayed at after-school club till five. We don't have those kinds of options in Germany. In America back then, my company built its own kindergarten. It even had video surveillance. And in America we have lots of very successful women VPs. I think we have more women than men. That's due in part to the childcare provided by the schools and kindergartens.

Japanese CEO: After our marriage, I got a job in the States. That was thirty years ago. Our company asked my wife to quit her job and follow me. She was hesitant to stop her career as a pharmaceut- icals researcher but finally the company persuaded her. When I came back to Japan she also returned to our company. After seven years she was in middle management, not a director or VP. In this work- ing environment, women sometimes have to leave their careers and follow their husband, even if the woman wants to continue in her role. That's typical Japanese thinking. Well, sometimes a woman gets a job outside Japan and her husband follows her. If she earns more, he should probably quit his job.

The pipeline problem: women tend to choose typically female degrees and industries

Are women strategic enough in their career planning? Certain industries are often said to have a 'pipeline' problem due to a lack of talented female candidates. While a large number of women work in sectors such as services, consumer and luxury goods and healthcare, very few are to be found in better-paid STEM industries (Fietze et al.,

2011). The pipeline problem must be viewed in context, comparing different STEM fields. On average, across the world women are less likely to study STEM subjects at university, and consequently are underrepresented at all management levels in STEM industries. Women are also disproportionately likely to leave STEM fields. After twelve years, around half of all women leave computer science and engineering, compared with just twenty per cent in other fields (Correll and Mackenzie, 2016). According to the 2020 Women4Stem Report (Women's Forum for the Economy & Society, 2021), whose respondents included 1,500 women in STEM jobs from twelve G20 countries, women only represent a quarter of the STEM workforce, fourteen per cent of STEM managers and nine per cent of STEM CEOs. The alpha men interviewed for the present study shared their views on the segregation of the labour market along gender lines. In their opinion, one of the main causes of this segregation is the pipeline problem that occurs in industries where, traditionally, engineering qualifications are needed to progress up the career ladder. They have noticed that women tend to choose industries that match their interests and neglect others where they could advance more quickly, and hence are squandering potential career opportunities. The problem for CEOs is that they get a lot of highly qualified male applicants for executive roles, but only very few applications from women, if any.

> French CEO: We have fewer female graduates from engineering schools, so we have fewer candidates to enter the company, and then we have fewer candidates for higher levels.

> Spanish CEO: Well, if I look at the sector that I know best, it's not one that's very attractive for women. It's much more of a male universe. Maybe it's a matter of education, but what I often see when we are recruiting is that we get far more applications from male candidates than from women. My conclusion is that our industry is not really the first priority for women, who prefer to work in other industries. My daughter is an example. She was looking for an internship. I told her, 'OK, come to us.' She said, 'Never ever.' For sure, there are a lot of exceptions, but generally speaking, women and our industry are not something that combine very well.

Some studies suggest that self-fulfilling prophecies are at play here. Women may tend to choose the kinds of jobs that society expects them to. That would explain why disproportionately many opt for the social and health sectors. It would also explain why in many countries women in senior management will tend to be in departments that diverge less from female stereotypes, such as human resources, public relations or marketing. Many management experts regard such roles as career 'dead ends' (Wippermann, 2010). The interviewees see this as a problem in the choices women make. Another factor is discrimination, which generally affects women more than men.

A study on gender equality in the Chinese tech sector (Celik, 2020) reported that women make up around fifty per cent of China's tech workforce, which is higher than in Europe and the USA. However, women are underrepresented in R&D and at executive levels, and overrepresented in HR and marketing. Although Chinese women are highly committed to pursuing careers in the tech industry, many believe there is a glass ceiling that prevents women from advancing to senior management roles.

As regards the relevance of STEM qualifications for obtaining boardroom positions, another study (Ankersen and Berg, 2021) found that in some countries those positions most commonly go to graduates of business and economics subjects, as compared with just twenty-six per cent being held by engineering graduates. That casts doubt on the pipeline problem and, given that women are well represented worldwide in business and economics subjects, the thesis that female STEM graduates will necessarily make it to the top.

French CEO in Asia: There aren't enough women now in the position of having access to C-level positions, because of the pipeline problem I was talking about. If you have the same number of men and women, then there's no reason why there wouldn't be the same percentage with access to senior levels. There aren't enough women. For many reasons. Probably because when they get married they stop working, when they get their first child they stop working. Plus sometimes the image of the perfect mother, who stays at home preparing nice flowers and decorating the house, has an effect. That sort of thing. If you exclude this category of people and focus on those who really want to express themselves through a professional career, who want to be successful, who need money, want to be able to stay at a nice hotel during their holidays and drive a nice car, like many women you meet in China ... If women are in competition with men, they have the same chances to succeed as men, I think, but there's not enough of them. There's a bigger number of male contenders.

French CEO: I think, obviously, we're going to have very technical profiles in our teams. Today, it's still an issue that we have only, let's say, about twenty to twenty-five per cent women at engineering schools. Women aren't so interested in technical matters, and that's obviously a difficulty for industry and companies.

Men, too, can see that prejudice and discrimination are barriers to women's careers

In the past, the typical manager was male. Even today, in many parts of the world women still encounter gendered expectations of what a top manager looks like – expectations that they can't fulfil because they're not men. The phrase 'think manager, think male' (Schein et al., 1996) describes the globally observable phenomenon that people's mental image of a manager is someone with traditionally masculine qualities, whereas the qualities ascribed to women are not those generally deemed necessary to thrive in top management. Gender stereotypes posit differences between men and women in ways that still reflect traditional divisions of roles. They also describe typical behaviours that society expects from the two genders. The resulting 'unconscious bias' contributes to discrimination in hiring, pay and promotion decisions.

Japanese CEO: I would say most people may feel some pressure. Part of the reason could be they're simply afraid of working for a female boss. They've never experienced that. Part of the reason could be gender bias. As mentioned before, they have a stereotypical mindset. Women are better at taking care of the family and children, not necessarily in the workplace. It's a stereotypical bias, but highly influential among women.

These prejudices are especially deep-rooted in Western countries, and many women harbour them too. Some commentators speak here of a self-fulfilling prophecy: based on their socially learned roles, women themselves believe they won't make it into senior management, as that's reserved for men, and so limit their ambitions right from the outset. They also apply these internalised stereotypes to other women and block their progression. This creates a dilemma for women with career ambitions. They can reject all existing role models and risk being seen as unlikeable, which is how women are penalised for acting in ways typically associated with men. On some male-dominated boards in Germany, for instance, women are singled out for criticism and made to feel insecure by snide or 'humorous' remarks. This behaviour can also be directed at other men who, for whatever reason, aren't part of the group that behaves this way.

> American CEO: An alpha female may have women on her staff who are more, if you will, nurturing, a little more thoughtful, a little quieter perhaps. She might say, 'Hey, you need to be more aggressive and assertive and so on.' Yes, I think that could be challenging for up-and-coming female leaders.

In the interviews, the men only occasionally mentioned cases of men discriminating against women. More often, they spoke about how women's careers can be impeded by discrimination and prejudice from other women. In a few cases, the men themselves expressed stereotypical views of women and criticised those who act in typically male ways.

> German executive: I'm now going to say something very provocative. The women who've fought their way to the top are sometimes utterly unbearable. Because they're so careerist. Not all of them, but there are some who were absolutely determined to get themselves promoted. Personally, however, my female bosses have always been better than the male ones. Perhaps I'm overstating it, but interestingly many women used to adopt signifiers of masculinity: short hair, black suit, white shirt. They kept getting more and more masculine. I feel like you don't see that as much any more, in part due to the digital world. Because in today's digital world, teamwork is more important than deep-voiced sales patriarchs. There's a certain group of women I hold in the highest regard, but then there are others, often from East Germany, who just wanted to get on in their career, no matter what. The women in that mould were very obstructive, aggressive, single-minded. I've met so many like that, I could give you ten examples. Trouser suit, white shirt, short, dyed-red hair. And they were trying to act like men, instead of being themselves. I've seen a lot of East German women who were still straight out of Eastern-style Communism. And sometimes they're from very humble backgrounds. All that mattered was their career. Often at the expense of a family life, they were very often single. In my own experience, my female bosses have often had more human sensitivity and perspective, they were better at motivating and understanding people than their male colleagues.

> Australian CEO: Both on the male and on the female side, you'll find similar mechanisms that either applaud successful women or don't. Some women think, 'That's not what you're supposed to do. That's not the attitude you should have in this company.' There are a lot of men who think the same, 'You're a girl or a woman. You're not supposed to have this typically male career track. You should be an assistant rather than a leader.'

> German executive: I think the biggest problem is that there are still limits to the acceptance of women on these top executive committees. And there are people, including me, though we're the ex-

ceptions, who appreciate the benefits of having women there too. Because it dilutes the machismo in the boardroom a bit, and I find it nice having less testosterone in the air. Instead, people focus on the business at hand, moderate the way they speak. There's a different atmosphere. I think the women I've met have all suffered from this alpha male behaviour. Things would have been very different if we'd had a female chair.

But if it's like it was at [company X], where there were only one or two women out of eight people and pretty much the whole supervisory board was filled with white men, then it's very difficult. I was constantly aware of this irritating, completely unnecessary banter. And a lot of people soaked it up, and we were targeted too. There was one colleague of mine who always got teased a bit, because he was homosexual. There was always an undercurrent of these odd, unnecessary remarks. You don't need that. And if you become the target of this banter, then it's tough and at some point you'll have enough. And you often see people saying they'll go and look for something else. Or they'll be shuffled off to somewhere else in the organisation, the advisory board or the supervisory board. So I think it's good that you're writing about it. But there's still a huge amount of work to do.

Men observe that many women lack self-confidence

Studies show that women tend to be more critical of themselves than equally qualified men. They underestimate their performance and abilities, and take a more critical view of their accomplishments (Regnet, 2017). They often attribute successes to favourable external factors, such as good luck or support from mentors (Al-Sadik-Lowinski, 2018). In a study by Bosak and Sczesny (2008), female students described themselves as less assertive and dominant than their male counterparts. Many women internalise social stereotypes without subjecting them to a reality check. Female managers likewise rate their own leadership effectiveness significantly lower than men do, according to a meta-analysis of US and Canadian studies (Paustian-Underdahl et al., 2014). Due to their lower self-ratings, women are less likely to actively take charge of their own career and put themselves forward for C-level positions (Athanasopoulou et al., 2018).

Chinese CEO in Hong Kong: I would say, first, that they look down on themselves. In fact, they have the capability, but they think they don't. You really need to have confidence in yourself. That is one of the reasons I can see that women may not be that capable of working in the corporate world. For me, that is the major, major reason. Other than that, I think that if they are confident in themselves, like every one of us, if they work hard, are open, are aware of how to improve themselves, then women and men are the same. As I said, their confidence level is not high enough, so they shy away from those opportunities. Quite frankly, in our company, we have to promote by policy, but the managers will not promote someone if he or she does not raise their hand to bid for the job. If the women are too shy to raise their hand, their development opportunities will definitely be less. I believe, particularly in locations like Thailand and the Philippines, that some of the women are very capable but they may be shy to promote themselves. If that's the case, they lose quite a lot of opportunities.

It comes more naturally to men to promote other men

A report by the AllBright Foundation (Ankersen and Berg, 2020) describes the 'Thomas cycle', so called because at the time of publication that was the most common name of German executive board members. The 'Thomas cycle' refers to the phenomenon that the men on company boards tend to recruit new members who are similar to themselves, and so the boards end up largely homogeneous in terms of gender, age, background and education. Several other studies have likewise shown that men tend to promote men similar to themselves. The interviewees confirmed that they had observed this elsewhere in the world too.

> Dutch CEO: *They started to hire the same smart, white men in suits, and they have similar jobs and in the evening they go to the bars, and in the end that didn't work out well. There are biases which need to be identified, and then things need to be changed. I believe this is the right time to do that.*

> Spanish CEO: *That's very true. I think that we all tend to believe we're fantastic – I mean, each of us. Then we try to replicate ourselves in the teams that are working for us. That's very human. It's like you want your son to be like you, you want your young son to look like you; but that's a mistake. Yes, we tend to believe that our profile is a successful profile and the more profiles like our own are in the company, the better it is for the company, which is probably wrong. Certainly, that explains to a certain extent why men in power often decide to go for men instead of a woman. We tend to believe that we're wonderful, and in our eyes any kind of model that looks like us is better. For sure, a man can recognise himself more easily in another man than in a woman.*

> Dutch CEO: *On the negative side, many men in leading positions like to hire people who are similar to them. Who look like them, who they feel comfortable with. And that's a bad thing because it's bad for creating an inclusive workplace. It's bad for innovations. At the top, I think we need to be a lot more diverse, and that's a conscious choice. You need to be very aware of it and you need to make conscious decisions. If men keep hiring men that look the same, with the same suit and the same tie, you won't get the same result you've always had. We want to do things differently. More sustainably. You see that a lot of companies that are doing that, are more innovative, are actually doing things the right way.*

Few previous studies have analysed whether women in top management also tend to promote other women who are similar to themselves. One theory that suggests the opposite is known as 'queen bee syndrome', which refers to women who've made it to the top then obstructing other women's careers. One explanation for this behaviour is that, in order to avoid further discrimination, these exceptional women want to avoid being lumped in with the discriminated-against minority group, and so act more like men instead.

Promoting 'people like you' doesn't necessarily mean promoting people of the same gender, however; it might also mean promoting people who belong to the same group, such as fellow graduates of certain elite French universities, regardless of their gender. Women who belong to one of these elite groups can benefit from a network that largely removes gender barriers.

French CEO: I've met several people who want to promote someone similar to themselves. In France, it's about your university. If you're an engineer from ESSEC Paris, you'll hire an engineer from ESSEC Paris, no matter whether they're male or female.

Men's thoughts on why women don't stick around in top jobs

The attention of international research has only recently turned to the question of women CEOs' staying power (or lack thereof) compared with their male counterparts. However, as the number of female CEOs has risen, there have been a lot of studies on the influence that a CEO's gender has on a company's performance, with some suggesting that companies with female leadership perform better (e.g. Krishnan and Parsons, 2008). Catalyst (2004) analysed the profitability of Fortune 500 companies from 1996 to 2000 and found that more diverse companies have better financial performance. There are also, however, studies showing negative correlations between company performance and having a female CEO. This topic remains an avenue for future research.

British CEO: No doubt about it, in the corporate world the competition is very tough. When the CEO leaves, particularly if it's very sudden, there will be a lot of stories about it. I think that applies both to female and male CEOs leaving their jobs, but you had a very good point. Why does the former seem to be more visible? Mainly because the number of women at C-level is lower. People seem to magnify it, and they're always saying, 'Oh, the percentage of this is high.' Of course, if the number of CEOs is low, even one or two departures will represent a very significant percentage.

Worldwide, female CEO role models face intense media scrutiny, especially those in their country's biggest listed companies. Because they are so few in number, their success or failure is treated as synonymous with that of all women who strive for top jobs. A few of the alpha men reported cases, primarily in France and Germany, of company boards systematically excluding women, of women being kept out of the loop or of people undermining women by bypassing the company's reporting hierarchy. These cases illustrate that women who make it onto boards traditionally filled with men sometimes face stiff resistance from male colleagues, especially if they've been appointed from outside the company.

Spanish CEO: We've seen several female CEOs and C-level executives 'giving up early' (the SAP CEO in Germany, Deutsche Bahn and others) and big media reports and articles about it. In France there was also Isabel Kocher at Engie. In Europe, these women are under a lot of scrutiny. What is your view on this: is it the same for men or could there be other specific reasons – pressure, competition, being pushed out by others? In my eyes, there's no difference between men and women in that specific respect. Probably it's just a false perception, as the media tends to give more coverage to the female cases, failures and successes. Personally, I am not aware of any statistics supporting the idea that at the highest level women are less resilient to pressure.

The interviewees do not see any difference in performance between male and female CEOs, but believe that because the latter are still a small minority, they are more exposed and subject to a lot more scrutiny. If a female CEO isn't able to hold on to a top job, then as a role model she will come in for a lot more criticism than a man would in a comparable situation. Another factor the men identified is that female executives who are hired to the top team from outside the company often fail because they don't understand the existing rules and power dynamics within the company. Their attempts at reform will fail unless they can quickly build up strong relationships to help them better understand the organisation and secure their position.

Dutch CEO: Women, for sure, don't walk away from responsibility, but if they don't want to be part of the group – 'It's too hard, it's too tough, I don't want to be part of it' – that's more of a culture issue than a female issue. Then men say there aren't enough women to be promoted. Actually, our prime minister said it once, 'I don't care if they're female or male, they just need to be the right person, and I didn't see the right person and for good reasons.' He was slammed in the media, because he hadn't looked at a wide enough range of people. Competences, that's complete nonsense as well, of course. I think in many companies, there should be more women than men because of the qualities we need. Then you need sponsorship. For sure, without a sponsor, without a mentor, I wouldn't be CEO of this company, I wouldn't have the support. If many male leaders are leading the company, if you aren't connected with them and they're not sponsoring you, then you won't make it. You also won't have the protection you need. When I became CEO, of course, there were many people who were a little bit jealous of this or that, and if people feel you're protected, they won't touch you. If they feel there's an issue and I don't have the support of the owner family, then it will be very tough on me and sometimes I will lose that battle.

German executive: So there was this woman from [American company X]. I won't say her name but I was very impressed by her. I thought she was great. Now, of course, I can say I saw it coming. [Company Y] is a prime example. White as white can be, full of white German men. It had all those little games, those cabals we talked about at the start, those old boys' networks where everyone helps each other out, gives each other jobs. Who let each other get away with blatantly breaking the most basic rules, 'Let's keep it nice and polite'. That attitude of looking the other way, you scratch my back and I'll scratch yours. And then suddenly someone comes in who isn't part of all that. And then organisations like Y have an allergic reaction. There was no way it could turn out well. The organisation wasn't ready for it, and at the top the poor woman was cut out of the loop. I can guarantee that she slept badly, had stomach problems, that she broke out in hives, because she mentally couldn't hack it, and thought to herself, 'I don't need to put myself through this'.

German executive: They wouldn't let her into their old boys' clubs. The supervisory board chair and CEO talked to her direct reports without her, and without letting her know. The direct report then thought, 'OK, I agreed that with the CEO, or the co-CEO, so it's all fine'. They used underhand tactics and bamboozled the woman, so that she wasn't involved and didn't know about meetings. We all know these games. They've been around for a long time. Consider another example, those goings-on at [company Y], with that woman who was meant to join the board. I don't know who ended up getting the position, whether it was a woman or a man. But I'd bet it was a man. That was another of these power games. She wouldn't have survived there. You have to look at it objectively. I mean, she might be smart, might pack some punch, she's from McKinsey, doesn't have a family. Would she have managed it? On the one hand, she'd probably have had the staying power. On the other hand, there were the dynamics you get at somewhere like Y. All white, all male in the old clique up at the top, with the family still in there. I can only say, 'Forget it. It'll be extremely tough.' That particular top manager would really have had to be prepared for a frosty reception.

The men's explanation for the dearth of women in top management: women lack career ambitions due to sociocultural influences and expectations

The alpha men attribute the imbalance of men and women on company boards to a combination of historically ingrained roles, social norms regarding leadership roles at global companies and the traditional advantage enjoyed by their fellow men. In recent years, however, this advantage has ebbed away. Due to their international careers, the men are in a good position to assess the impact of cultural and contextual factors on women's careers. In their view, social attitudes to female leaders vary from country to country, as do the way that women in C-level roles see themselves. Germany and Japan come off poorly in the men's accounts, and even France lags behind Asian countries such as China, Thailand and Malaysia where female executives are already seen as part of the norm. European men rate the USA and some Nordic and East European countries as more progressive.

One main factor that the men see as responsible for the lower proportion of women in top management is women's low career orientation, which is due in part to their socialisation. Most women choose family over a high-flying career. The alpha men take it as axiomatic that it's impossible to achieve a balance between the two in the modern corporate world. Even today, you can't take long periods of parental leave if you want to have a top-level career. Our current career models don't allow for any deviations from the standard path, such as career pauses or breaks. The alpha men talked in detail about their own family situations, including the unstinting support they receive from their partners. They know alpha women who have similar family set-ups, except with the normal gender roles reversed: the husband takes the traditional female role so that the wife can focus squarely on her career. Among the younger generations, the alpha men have witnessed an erosion of conventional roles, which they believe will fundamentally transform traditional structures over the shorter or longer term. They conclude that the times are working in women's favour and so there is no need for a 'battle of the sexes'. In the male CEOs' experience, women often choose to study subjects that are traditionally female-dominated, and later pursue careers in typically female industries. In certain industries, this results in a 'pipeline problem'. Male CEOs from heavy industry note that there are often simply not enough women in the talent pool who could be potential candidates for C-level positions. Examples of men systematically discriminating against women were brought up in the interviews, but only very occasionally. Examples of women discriminating against other women were more common. Despite that, the alpha men acknowledge that women generally have it harder to rise through the ranks than men, though men also need a thick skin to make it to the top. Another factor they suggested may explain the differences between men and women's career trajectories is women's relative lack of self-confidence. Regardless of gender, confidence and assertiveness are two qualities a manager must possess if they are to have a shot at reaching the top. If women do make it, they will face the same pressure as male leaders. Some of the interviewees who are based in Germany mentioned situations where women were systematically forced out of senior positions. Women who want to succeed in top management still need to have a great deal of energy, strong nerves and physical and mental resilience. They need to be driven by a powerful ambition. And they need a knack for strategic powerplays and alliance-building so that they can fend off any attempts to force them out.

Alpha women are more likely to see discrimination as a reason for the imbalance in company boardrooms

Female executives from several countries were also interviewed for this study. When asked about women's prospects for making it to the top, their answers did not fundamentally differ from the men's: they attributed the underrepresentation of women to the way they are socialised, to prejudices in society, to reservations about having mothers in leadership positions and to a lack of solidarity among women. The main difference from the men's responses was how often they mentioned examples of prejudice and discrimination, by both men and other women.

Social stereotypes and relations between the sexes impact on women's advancement

The female interviewees' perceptions of equality of opportunity varied significantly from country to country. Opportunities for women in Japan were rated as very poor, while China came out best among the leading industrialised nations. Russia (the country with the most women in senior leadership roles), France, Germany and the USA were ranked in the middle. In countries that have very low proportions of women at senior level, such as Germany, it's vital for women to shake off their socialisation and set clear career goals.

> German CEO (female): Germany is definitely in the dark ages as far as gender rights and gender equality are concerned, in my opinion.

> German CEO (female): I think that where there's a will, there's a way. You can do it. The bar is high, but it's not so high as to be impossible. But I do believe that the general state of affairs, the hurdles you have to overcome, the prevailing images, are still really firmly rooted and the environment we live in is still pretty backward. And then there are all these issues, like men taking parental leave, that's still criticised. The available childcare options are still relatively poor in my view. What also makes me give it a five is the stereotypes that are really prominent in my male colleagues' minds.

> Japanese company president (female): We're exceptions. Do you understand? Most women in Japan don't even think that they could become managers. I even mean the lower and middle levels. It's not yet available as a possibility in their worldview. But I've never seen any limits for myself.

American CEO (female): It's not usual yet to rise to C-level as a woman here. It's even more difficult to become CEO. There are many reasons. Women of colour had no chances until recently. Now we have two women of colour who are CEOs in the Fortune 500. And the media celebrates it, but actually it's a shame.

Another important aspect, in the women's view, is the relations between the sexes in the workplace, which can lead to conflicts. Part of their strategy to solve this problem is to engage with men's concerns. Women need deliberate strategies for dealing with male executives who can help them achieve their larger goals. It is also crucial to understand what men appreciate in women, and what will provoke or upset them.

French CCO (female): I think that we see them as intellectually equal in society, but not in reality. If you look at people's actual home lives it's not true. Everyone still has these clichés, I mean about women and men. Men are still men and they have to be strong and in charge, and women are still the ones who take care of the house. Things are changing, but we haven't totally stopped thinking like that. I don't think France is too bad really. Because we do everything we can in France to enable women to work. What is still a problem in France is the status of men. Many of them don't want that to change. They don't want society to change. Some men think women are taking away men's rightful place in the world. When we see what happens in politics when a woman comes into the National Assembly and talks about the sorts of things that really happen in a country like this, it's scary. I think an important cultural thing in France is the relationship between men and women. I mean on an intimate level. It makes men see women like prey. Men chase women as if they were prey.

Dealing with discrimination saps women's energy

Several of the alpha women talked about discrimination and prejudice against women in senior positions. These prejudices are linked to stereotypes that still associate successful leadership with masculine qualities. Whereas men are automatically trusted to be good leaders simply by virtue of being a man, women have to work twice as hard to earn this trust. Discrimination was mentioned by women from all countries. The German and French alpha women reported numerous cases of discrimination against themselves or female colleagues, which they saw as men deliberately targeting women. The discrimination can be broken down into the following categories: discrimination regarding women's professional competence; sexist remarks; and discrimination regarding pregnancy and motherhood. This discrimination occurs in both private conversations and public settings.

The French women openly discussed a topic that is often taboo among women, and was earlier touched on by the men: namely, that across various cultural contexts, alpha women continue to face discrimination not just from men but also from women. Reports of women who attempt to obstruct other women's careers are not uncommon.

The women described how they were able to succeed by working harder, achieving better results and using their own personal coping strategies.

German CMO (female), working in the US: I can tell you a lot of stories. And I'm sure a lot of other women could too. So anyway, when I was at [company XY], the discrimination was huge. One person told me about an appraisal interview were the other person made remarks like, 'Your performance fluctuates, like when you have your period for example.' Isn't that awful? And a colleague of mine was told, 'You're capable of doing the job, but I only want a man on it.' That was discrimination in its purest and most outspoken form. When I got married, I told no one. Because then everyone would have immediately thought I was going to have children and that would have been my career over. But it didn't only happen at XY. It happened at YZ too. I was sitting with my boss. That was after I had quit college. He told me that evening that women don't really want careers. They just want to go on nice foreign trips. That was the conversation. And women who have careers, they're all harridans. Time and again you come up against these really powerful prejudices and even verbal putdowns. And later on, when I was managing director in Spain, I thought about returning to Germany. I had two or three job interviews in Germany, but they were all pretty brutal.

French CEO (female): Never hesitate to articulate where the obstacles lie, because it's precisely these very real obstacles that hold women back. And sexism especially. We haven't talked much about that. Sexism, certain types of behaviour, jokes round the coffee machine … All these things are still happening today, and companies are currently working to create a much more inclusive culture.

German board member (female): I can give you another example from the 2015 annual general meeting. A man goes up to the lectern, a shareholder, and says, 'Women lack leadership skills and have no place in management.' I'm sitting there thinking, 'Are we on Candid Camera?' But no. The audience claps. There we are, three of us female board members sitting there on the podium, we're there to render account. And there's applause in the room because women have no leadership skills.

French CFO (female): So, it's difficult and pernicious. I've seen behaviour and jokes and things sometimes that can really make it feel like a man's world. I've seen it all. Even jokes that are sexist. I don't think it's usually done on purpose. We tend to favour people who are like us. For example, men in dominant leadership positions tend to recruit men who come from the same university and have the same résumé, and they mentor younger men who resemble them. And it's still the case nowadays that men appoint men.

Motherhood as a career-limiting factor

The women, like the men, said that taking maternity leave would in most cases be a career killer. Mothers must choose between bowing to societal expectations and taking a career break, or defying those expectations. That's harder for German, American and Japanese women than it is for Chinese and Russian women or women from former East Germany, as they grew up with the norm of women working full-time. The alpha women note that other women often lack a clear career orientation and are less confident about their own effectiveness.

In a previous global study involving 110 senior female executives from five countries (Al-Sadik-Lowinski, 2020), eighty-five per cent of the women were mothers with one to four children. Less than twenty per cent of them took career breaks for the sake of their family. Only seventeen per cent of them had 'stop-and-go careers', in which women attempt to balance career and family, with the latter taking precedence. This career type did not occur at all among German and Japanese participants, suggesting that in contexts with low gender equality there's more pressure on women to adapt to male-oriented career rules and company systems if they want to advance to higher positions. At present, these rules still don't allow for extended career breaks, even for mothers. And even when companies do offer specific programmes for mothers, these often lead to a 'mummy track' that traps women in the middle ranks. Some of the female executives report how after returning from one year's maternity leave, they were effectively shut out. Most of the responses indicate that women were able to successfully pick back up if they remained invested in their job around the time of the birth or, as with many of the Chinese women, strategically used the time to switch companies and then took a longer break, though usually no more than a year.

> Swiss CFO (female): I took a year off after giving birth. That's not a legal entitlement in Switzerland, but it was offered by my company. When I came back, it was very strange. My boss had put a less qualified man in charge of the most important project, even though I was supposed to be taking it on. I was shut out. Eventually, I was fired. Simply dropped by a high talent. Looking back, it was a mistake to actually take a break for that year. I should have stuck with it. I was really gone for a whole year and that was a mistake. I should have stayed in touch.

> French HRD (female): I've seen situations where young women have come back from maternity leave and have been given inferior jobs because people thought that when they came back from maternity leave, they wouldn't have the energy or the desire to travel any more. But in some families, it's the man who stops working. I think that stereotypes still exist that make young women vulnerable to indirect discrimination.

> German board member (female): In Germany you don't have to look far. Women, no matter what they do, are never seen in a positive light. So, I'd like to back that up. The way I always describe it is: women who don't have children are randy women's libbers. Women who decide to work part-time, well, they probably have to because their husbands don't earn enough. Or because they want to find themselves. Women who work full-time and have children, well obviously they're the typical bad mother types and are only interested in themselves.

Lack of confidence and rejection of power

The female top managers agreed with the men that women often lack the confidence needed to make it to board level. One aspect that wasn't touched on in the interviews with the men was men's and women's different attitudes towards power. Chapter three will consider potential power strategies that women can adopt. Men may believe that women make far more use of their female advantages in competitive situations than is actually the case.

> German administrative board member (female): I'd say men tend to be afraid of losing power. To them, it's everything. It's linked to competition. I got this job at the top, I'm the CEO now. So there's nowhere else to go. And for men, losing that position of power is purely about competition, it's all about fear. Women aren't like that. Women are more afraid of gaining power. Because power is still characterised by domination, force, abuse of power.

> Russian CEO (female): Women are afraid of power. If they want it is absolutely possible, that is why I gave only five. In our company we are five women, all bosses are women. Every year ten to fifteen per cent more women.

German HRD (female): It's important to be self-confident. To be stronger. I'm talking about my company, not generally about Germany. I've observed women belittling themselves. Like, 'Oh no, I can't do this and I can't achieve that.'

Rivalry among women

One important topic in the French women's accounts, which is likely representative of other countries too, was rivalry and lack of solidarity between women. In particular, they described a generational conflict between older women in senior management and younger women who hoped for solidarity but were refused it. The older women had fought hard for their positions and believe the next generation should have to go through that same struggle too. That often involved unconditionally complying with standards set by men: for instance, working family-unfriendly hours in the evenings, which is very common in senior management in France. Younger women don't think they should have to do that to have a successful career. The older women can't accept the new generation of female managers rejecting these norms and refuse to offer solidarity. The 'queen bee syndrome' mentioned earlier might explain this behaviour: one possible coping strategy used by successful women who have had to fight hard every step of the way is to distance themselves from the disadvantaged group, in this case other women, so as to win acceptance in the higher-status group. In a male-dominated work environment, they do this by adopting male traits and values.

French administrative board member (female): But there were and still are places where women don't support each other and still see each other as competitors. So maybe that's still a problem. I personally have always been viewed as a woman who's helped a lot of other women. I've also always been surrounded by a lot of other women. The question is, what do we think when a new woman arrives on the executive team? Do we think, 'Great, another woman,' or do we think, 'Oh no, maybe she'll outshine me'? It depends how you look at it.

French general manager (female): I think women are not supportive and not unified. Me, recently I've come to the conclusion that the main reason why women will not make it is because there is still that biological instinct to fight against the other woman, which men don't have. Men, they might fight if they're in competition for something, and that's normal, but then if they're not, they're going to co-opt each other, they're going to help each other. Women, we say we do, and then if you're in different companies, different industries, for sure we do. When it comes to the same industry, the same group, I think women are our own worst enemies.

French CFO (female): That's a really interesting question. I have had a mentor; mentors are very important. Women aren't great mentors for other women though, generally speaking. I think that's a real problem. Women who give other women advice, there's a degree of competition and so on and so forth. If the woman's older than the mentee, then there's often envy, and that's not a great thing.

On many points, the female top managers were in agreement with the alpha men. They believe the underrepresentation of women in management is due to bias and women lacking confidence and a clear career orientation. Another key factor is motherhood.

Discrimination was reported as coming from both men and women, though mainly from the former. Compared with the male interviewees, the women reported more cases of hostility from, and exclusion by, men. In many cultures and companies, men and women are still caught in a battle of the sexes over the most important positions. A more collaborative approach, in which companies harness the strengths of both men and women to improve their performance, has not yet been universally established.

3 Conflicts between alpha men and alpha women

Companies around the globe that want to improve their performance need to build diverse leadership teams that involve men and women equally, and harness the potential of both. Before that can be achieved, however, it's necessary to defuse the tensions between the sexes. This chapter will look at some of the direct conflicts the alpha men have experienced with women in their day-to-day work. It will also explore sensitive issues such as men's worries about being shown up by their capable female colleagues, the #MeToo movement and the use of erotic capital to expedite career progression.

Alpha men on conflicts with alpha women

In the public debate, alpha men are often collectively blamed for the lack of women in senior management. They stand accused of discriminating against and excluding women. Women, on the other hand, see themselves as victims, who are forced to forge their identity in a management world still dominated by men. As a result, many female executives try to act like men and imitate typical male patterns of behaviour. Male executives often don't know how to deal with the changed roles, and react to conflicts with their female colleagues in the same ways they've been socialised react to conflicts with other men.

What is the impact of male executives' concern that women may diminish their power and autonomy, or even replace them? Do men worry that the changes taking place at their companies will see women supplant them from their primary role? A psychological analysis of relations between the genders reveals deeper motives for possible conflicts between men and women in the workplace. Hollstein (2004) even claims that the history of masculinity is the history of male anxiety about women. He postulates that policies to promote gender diversity and women's equality will continue to fail unless they address this deep-rooted psychological problem. If this theory is correct, it is important not to concentrate solely on the needs of women, who still represent a minority in senior management, but also to consider men's perspectives and their conflicts with women. Researchers including Swope (2012) have studied why some men find it challenging to work for a female superior. Swope delves deep into traditional ideas and roles handed down from history. He notes that 'men have both admired and feared women since ancient times and across cultures'. One example of this ambivalence is the 'awe and fear' provoked by women's power 'to give life'. In Greek mythology, men's fear of women's anger is expressed in the figure of the Furies, 'monstrous old women depicted with snakes twined through their hair'. Other examples of powerful women in myth include Scylla, a monster with six heads and twelve feet. According to Swope, men still feel a combination of fear and awe at women's power.

https://doi.org/10.1515/9783111172651-003

Dutch CEO: What we could discuss is this fear of men. 'Oh, I don't feel comfortable with women in the group. I feel attacked, surpassed, exposed, outsmarted.'

Many men attach value to performing their socially learned role. That holds true in management too. 'Femiphobia' is the scientific term for a fear of anything feminine. It causes many men to avoid feelings and behaviours that are not considered masculine. Psychological studies s have shown that many men are motivated by a desire to conceal their feminine side. In Kierski and Blazina (2010), men talked about their fear of losing status or suddenly finding themselves exposed and vulnerable. Three scenarios in particular were reported as making the male study participants feel destabilised: when women display superior ability or have a higher hierarchical status in a professional or social context; when women are outspoken or aggressive (both traditionally more masculine behaviours); and when women act like protective mothers and make the men feel like little boys. In other words, men feel uncomfortable working with women who exhibit superior ability, confidence, anger or maternal care.

Japanese CEO: Some men may feel pressured in this gender-dominated meeting environment. It depends on personality. For myself, it's completely fine. But I understand that some men feel uncomfortable in a meeting setting where only female attendees are present. I can understand some people may feel pressured or awkward in this kind of setting. It all depends on the person.

Japanese CFO: Yes, that's my fear. That roles will completely switch. In my case, my wife is a housewife. She worked until she got married to me, in her late twenties. Afterwards, she quit her company and focused on our family. Recently, she has done some part-time work, but not full-time. I can't imagine a situation where she was professionally more successful. Maybe, to be honest, I would get very jealous. That would mean that I hadn't been at all successful in my career. That would be something. Let's say, OK, my wife has a higher salary than me. She gets the promotions. Then she starts saying she needs help to manage at home, and asks me to quit my job. I would be seen as a loser. Yes, to be honest, that's my fear.

German CMO: I think gossip at the bar after work is different between men and women. When men complain about someone or express their opinion, they're much more direct. Women are more condescending. Back then, we had a lot of female directors for different brands. They were really full on: who can do what, who's close to the boss and so on. From what I saw, when men had a beer in the evening, they were very direct. Like: that was completely out of order, how stupid can you be, he really doesn't know what he's doing and so on. Women are more subtle, I often found. I once had an Australian who was a master of it. Along the lines of, 'Do you really think what he presented was up to speed or up to our standards?'

Men's responses to women managers who act like this vary from individual to individual. They can range from reflection, disengagement or unspoken rejection to covert or overt aggression. The very candid interview excerpt below articulates the unease felt by some of the alpha men.

Dutch CEO: I've seen it very many times. Projects where very successful women were actually intimidating their bosses. They were confronted with some of the weaker sides of their personality and leadership style. The truth is they often felt intimidated. That's the key thing. I also saw at some client organisations that men felt outsmarted. Another strong woman comes to mind who left the company a few months ago. She was very judgemental. In a way, I agreed with her, but her way of expressing those judgements created even more distance and discomfort. I think if you want to swim with the sharks, in a sense you sometimes need to be the shark and still be true to yourself. Some female leaders I'm acquainted with could be extremely judgemental about something, and then actually express it and make a point, and that created more distance.

Men have their own set of rules for resolving conflicts with other men. But if women, come into a professional environment and start showing men up with their superior ability, or display aggression towards them, men feel like they're being attacked outside the framework of those rules. For them, it feels different to encounter this behaviour from women rather than men. In a group of men, the rules of the game are clear and they expect certain, typically male patterns of behaviour. Once a woman starts acting the same way too, it becomes unacceptable, and they'll respond the same way they would to another man. The interviewees described how typically male behaviour, often described using the metaphor of 'sharks', is changing in the modern world of work, but fundamentally the same old rules for how men treat other men still apply. They expect different, more ethical behaviour from women, including in situations of situations of conflict. This goes back to the division of roles described earlier, in which women's typical role is to provide support and comfort for men in the family home, and not to get involved in external conflicts.

Russian CEO: She's a brilliant communicator. And she doesn't fight with men for power but, and this is only my opinion, provides a safe environment for them. She doesn't fight but saves her energy for her own role. Of course, I would say that if a woman comes to the boxing club, then nobody will treat her as a woman. Everybody will say, 'You want to box? Let's box.' That woman chooses not to box with these men, but to find her strengths and use those strengths to manage those alpha men. Do you see the difference? If you come to a boxing club, and you want to box with the men, then why would you expect that the men will treat you like a woman? They will treat you like a boxing partner. Doesn't matter whether you're a woman or a man.

Spanish CEO: I think that a man, in order to get a position, is willing to openly criticise his competitors, and he's often able to put some obstacles in their way to make it easier for himself to get the job. I think that women have a more ethical attitude. I think they're much less aggressive and violent. I don't expect those bad things from women. That's how men act. They kill each other from behind. I think women are much more moderate. The men are willing to kill to get a position. I don't expect that from women.

Men want loyalty from women

Based on socially learned roles in which they traditionally held a dominant position, men expect women to recognise their authority in public settings. Traditional roles are based on a subordination of women to men. Precisely because they value women's empathy and sensitivity, male leaders expect support and loyalty from women, especially in meetings and when other people are present. That includes women not showing them up or criticising previously agreed decisions in front of other people. The alpha men don't want women to suddenly start displaying competitive male attributes in business contexts. Rather, they would like female colleagues to clearly distance themselves from intra-male competition and men's rules for dealing with conflicts, which they described in the interviews with a mix of self-criticism and humour. In chapter two, we saw that modern men nowadays expect companionship and emotional support from women. For the interviewees, loyalty, reliability and trust are important qualities. Criticisms at large meetings should be made with diplomacy and tact, or even better discussed in smaller forums beforehand. If women publicly criticise male colleagues or superiors, it can cause great annoyance. The men's responses in the interviews show that they are afraid of being criticised by women at the wrong time and in the wrong place, even if they know that this criticism will often be well founded. They can more easily accept criticisms in a personal discussion than in front of a large group. Although men bring out the big guns against other men and will happily point out women's weaknesses before the whole team, they find it hard to cope when the situation is reversed. In mixed meetings, they want women to stay in their feminine roles and create a safe, secure environment for the men, and in return they will give their support to the women. If women act like men, openly criticising them or arguing against previously agreed decisions, they may unexpectedly find themselves being attacked, in line with male norms of conflict resolution.

> *Irish CEO: If I may, I'd like to mention an example that just happened with one of my female leaders in the last twenty-four hours. There are nine of us in our leadership team, eight of them reporting to me. We meet once per month to review the Covid situation. With a very clean agenda, for just one hour, we review the actions we need to take as a business. What we need to review, what we need to revise, what we need to respond to in the ever-changing environment of Covid. The team has been very effective throughout the crisis, very collaborative, but in one area it wasn't able to reach a decision. We have people working from home, and different departments are working from home at different levels. Now, we've decided as a group that it makes sense to be focused not on one policy, but on what is appropriate for the group. As Covid progresses, some of the teams who have been working from home a lot are increasingly becoming disconnected from the rest of the company. We discussed it in the group for thirty minutes, but at the end no one was willing to make a change. I said, 'I'm going to take a smaller group, only three of us, myself, the vice-president of HR and, ironically, the vice-president of quality.' Not because of her quality role, but because she led what we call the clock team, the Covid learning team. During the next meeting, the woman actually said after we presented our proposal, 'This is not the way I would have done it. I would have involved you all.' To me, not only was that undercutting the CEO's role in front of the rest of the team, but it was also taking away from the work that she had been involved with. If there was a time for her to say, 'I don't think it is appropriate to take this to a smaller group,' it would have been in the previous meeting when we made that decision, not afterwards.*

> *Australian executive: Guys don't take it personally. They can let things go very easily. One of the things that I learned from my past was that if I was in a fight with, say, my brother or my dad, we'd both have a drink and then we'd be done with it. It'd be forgotten and we would never talk about it again because both of us were sorry. It also didn't come back in the second fight or in the third or fourth fight, because that fight was in the past. It had nothing to do with the current or the next fight. But in meetings with women, they often bring things back up.*

Spanish CEO: I've observed that men tend to follow the leader more blindly than women. In other words, men are less critical than women are, so when I conduct a meeting with only men, things go faster. There is less discussion, the agreements are made a little bit more easily because there is less need for explanation, less need for discussion, less need to create some consensus. Women tend to express their opinion quite freely and with very good arguments because, as I said before, their analytic sense is more developed than men's. Then once you have made a decision, they accept it with a lot of discipline. As they have less ego than men, even if in the end the decision I have taken is bad, they won't say, 'I told you we should have gone to Paris instead of London.'

American CEO: There are different kinds of loyalty, I guess. I'd say loyalty with the heart, with passion, is generally speaking more common among female staff, maybe because they've spent more time getting to know the whole person. That person may feel that they have their back a little bit more. Male loyalty is, perhaps, more driven by tasks and cool stuff or the attraction of the leader. They're making things happen, they're going places. 'I'm going to be loyal to that person. Maybe I don't know them that well but I am one hundred per cent behind what they're trying to do and that's the source of my loyalty.' It's a different kind of loyalty, I'd say.

Dealing with #MeToo

When considering the tensions between men and women, it's impossible to avoid some of the sensitive, complex issues at play in the relations between the genders – including at the top levels of companies.

The #MeToo movement, which dates back to the mid-2000s, seeks to raise awareness of sexual assaults against women by men. The slogan became internationally known in connection with sexual harassment in the film industry. A global movement formed with the goal of preventing and prosecuting sexual harassment of women in the workplace. For the first time, women had a prominent media platform to speak about inappropriate behaviour in the workplace and push for action to be taken against it. Studies on how men view the movement have observed responses such as reticence, uncertainty and sometimes hostility. Since the start of the campaign, male executives have been less willing to serve as mentors to talented woman, as they are worried about being wrongfully accused of inappropriate behaviour. In one study on gender equality initiatives, seventy-four per cent of male senior managers who were interviewed described fear as a barrier to entering into mentoring relationships (Soklaridis et al., 2018). Other studies have found that men prefer not to have meetings alone with a woman they don't know well or who is junior to them. They fear false accusations that could damage or even end their career (Miller, 2017). These responses to #MeToo mean that women are less able to benefit from mentoring relationships with men in positions of power in their organisation – relationships that, according to the interviewees, are a highly effective way for women to advance in their careers.

This is creating what sociologists refer to as an 'anxiety culture' among both men and women. The anxieties in question can create barriers between the genders, even if they have no basis in reality. Consequently, alongside all the important positive aspects, the #MeToo movement has also undone some of the previous progress in mentoring.

Men feel aggrieved because they think women are getting unfair advantages, and respond by withdrawing their support. In this context, men perceive gender equality as disadvantaging them. As they see it, women are advancing at the expense of men.

American CEO: I believe the key is that men don't feel comfortable. They think that they can't talk openly, can't make jokes. The jokes have to be changed.

French CEO in Thailand: The old rules – where men really behave in the old style, where they're dominant and act without any second thought, no restrictions, no constantly regulating their behaviour – don't apply so much now. Because image is important today and they don't want to damage their image. We're under a lot more scrutiny now. Everyone is paying a lot of attention, because anyone can shoot a video on their mobile phone and put it on social media.

Now you see that people are constantly regulating their behaviour because of #MeToo, because you don't want to create a bad image of yourself. Sometimes it was just a stupid joke or a stupid kind of behaviour, which didn't reflect what you really think. A stupid, easy joke between friends. People don't do that any more. You control yourself more, because you know that a lack of self-control can have big consequences. It's true for everything now. You're permanently scrutinised. You can be filmed and that video can be shared with anyone. Some people really pay a lot of attention. Like football players, when they leave the pitch and when they talk to each other, they put their hands in front of their mouths so people watching them on the screen can't try to figure out what they're saying.

Now, it depends on the trend: you don't want to be a white male Protestant, because you don't want to be categorised as part of a population which was dominant and not deserving this position. Then you don't want to be seen as racist, and now you don't want to be seen as a macho, prehistoric male who hasn't understood the evolution of society.

It's not because it's women, it's because there are some trends and there are some ways to behave imposed by society. You need to know the codes and respect them. Especially if you want to manage people, because you have a diverse range of people to manage, and if you want to be accepted as their leader you shouldn't reject or be rejected by a proportion of this group. You want to build a consensus and that's the big risk. You want to build a consensus, you want to be nice to everyone and you spend your time managing your image.

The big risk we have today is that we spend more time managing our image or way of communicating. We think twice before using a single word, we pay attention to how we look on camera and so on, and this is very superficial. We forget the essence of our job, our responsibility, which is to take the right decision at the right moment to maximise efficiency and effectiveness, and this is the big risk. Today it's because of this diversity issue, yesterday it was about something different and tomorrow there will be another way of dividing the population into 'dominant' and 'victims'. You don't want to be the bad guy, so you swallow it and do that. You know, you don't touch, you don't kiss, you just work. Here it is easier. Women here in Thailand are very elegant, very elegant and beautiful as well, but not sexy. We have that in France, Spain, Italy also.

Here I can really behave like the person I am and I don't have to constantly think, 'Am I doing the right thing?' You just manage. Yes, it's much less complicated than in Europe.

Australian CEO: Honestly, I personally don't see that. What I see is that if you treat people the way they should be treated, which is respectfully and appropriately, then there's never actually a problem. I think that if you do something very inappropriate, there's a problem and you should be accountable for it. I've worked in the US from 1996 to now. We had a break overseas in Australia and in India, and I have never had a problem. I treat every woman the same as I would treat a member of my family, which is respectfully. I'm married, why would I be inappropriate? There are rules and there are expectations, but they're there for a reason, because it's inappropriate to do the wrong thing. I think it's great that we have rules to make sure that people who don't understand what's right and wrong are held accountable. If someone's worried about the rules, they're probably worried about their own behaviour. Instead of worrying about the rules, they should be thinking to themselves, 'Is there reason to question my behaviour?' As opposed to, 'Do people look at me and never question my behaviour?' I've had to run investigations where people have been inappropriate, and normally they're either inappropriate or they're pushing the boundaries of inappropriate, and their awareness of what's right and what's wrong is just not correct.

It takes two people to make a problem, so again, I don't understand or support that claim, I just don't. If I say to a guy, 'OK, somebody said something inappropriate, you did something inappropriate,' – if somebody feels they did something inappropriate, they were probably not reading the situation correctly or they were pushing the limit or something else. There are some people of both genders who always make accusations, because there are always people who just get things wrong and it's always going to be that way, but I think the rules are mostly good and help you. If you have strong values, the rules are easy: 'Do I want someone grabbing me or touching me or saying inappropriate things to me?' I don't. I would feel very uncomfortable. Why would I want to treat someone like that?

It's the same as ethnicity and religion and sexual preference and any other difference between people, and gender is just the most obvious because half our population is one gender and half our population is the other. If you respect the people around you and recognise that they may be different to you for whatever reason, I don't think you'll ever have a problem.

Feminine wiles – using erotic capital to rise through the ranks

One question that has been largely neglected in the literature is whether managers (male or female) rely not just on their qualifications but also their 'erotic capital' to work their way up the corporate ladder. It's a difficult topic, which is hard to disentangle from issues of sexual harassment and assault. Many researchers consider it taboo, which explains the dearth of literature on the topic. And yet it is an aspect of the tensions between alpha men and alpha women. Although both genders presumably have opportunities to use their erotic capital to advance their careers, it is primarily women who are accused of doing so.

The term 'erotic capital' was coined in 2010 by Catherine Hakim, a sociologist based at the London School of Economics, and caused a stir among feminists and newspaper columnists.

Hakim defines erotic capital as 'a combination of aesthetic, visual, physical, social, and sexual attractiveness to other members of your society, and especially to members of the opposite sex, in all social contexts'. It 'includes skills that can be learnt and developed, as well as advantages fixed at birth'. The philosopher Henri François Marion (1880) argued that someone who wants to be loved must actively work to bring it about. He ranked seduction and the art of love on a par with other ways of achieving prestige and recognition, such as the cultivation of knowledge. Hakim likewise regards erotic capital as a form of knowledge that we can cultivate. What makes Hakim's work provocative in the age of women's quota debates is that she takes a topic more normally associated with private, intimate contexts and relates it to professional life. Erotic capital is a fourth type of capital alongside the categories of economic, cultural and social capital distinguished by Bourdieu (1986). Erotic capital is made up of six elements: beauty, sexual attractiveness, social or flirtatious skills, liveliness, social presentation and sexuality itself. Many leading French and German feminists have responded positively to Hakim's theory. In their view, given that we are still so far from real gender equality, women have the right to use their 'feminine wiles' to fight for career opportunities. Notably, Hakim claims that, due to a 'permanent male sex deficit', women have more of this capital and work harder at it. US researchers have also turned the gender cliché on its head by emphasising not women's powerlessness but rather their sexual power. Schmitt et al. (2012) claim that women respond to this 'permanent male sex deficit' in line with 'evolutionarily predicted patterns'. In more common parlance, people speak of 'feminine wiles', which refers to certain physical and psychological qualities that a woman can utilise to achieve her goals. There are very few studies on how common it is for women to use erotic capital to advance in their careers, and how successful their attempts are. The issue is complex and attempts to address it are often met with resistance, since it must also be viewed in the context of the #MeToo victims' abuse by men in positions of power. Hakim notes that women's relationship to their erotic capital is shaped in part by their negative or positive experiences with men.

> French CEO: Whichever way you look at it, a male–female relationship has this underlying connotation. We can complain about it, or not like it, or even decide, like the US is doing, to try to introduce a number of rules, so that this issue would completely disappear from life. I think this is just hiding from reality, I'm not really a fan of all that. I guess, again, it's just a matter of understanding that this is part of life. That's how nature is. And if you get people who want to get into seduction mode, I've got to tell you that there are a bunch of men who use seduction on other men in business environments.

There have not been any quantitative studies that cover all six elements of erotic capital – the concept was, after all, only formulated relatively recently – but Hakim does make reference to studies that look at one or more of the individual elements. One might assume that appointments to managerial positions would be made on the basis of knowledge and expertise. But even for the sparsely populated upper levels of the management hierarchy, there are studies suggesting that appearance and social presentation may influence how these positions are filled. Interestingly, research on the 'beauty premium' suggests that it benefits men more than women. Good-looking men start with higher salaries and get more pay rises than good-looking women, though the latter do earn more than less attractive women. In management, social skills – one of the elements of erotic capital – are a key factor, as is personal presentation, that is, the ability to present oneself in a manner appropriate to a given occasion.

Men are aware that women possess more erotic capital, and worry that women may use this to gain an advantage over them or keep their rivals firmly in check. This contributes to tensions between men and women. Men are suspicious of how much use women make of this strategic advantage, and in what situations. Hakim suggests that many men would make greater use of erotic capital in business contexts if there were demand for it.

> *French CEO in Thailand: There's always the risk of seduction. It's a slippery path where you can easily generate problems that you had no intention of generating. It's a risk. It's more of a thing with women than with men, it's true, especially if the woman is good-looking and so on. There's a risk, but she can't exclude herself from these games.*
>
> *If you need to have your own internal connection to get support, make yourself better known in the group, build your reputation, have access to meetings and be on the list of people preselected in personnel reviews, you need to make sure people know you. If you go back home immediately after work and you only work nine to five, nobody will ever remember your face, nobody will ever know who you are and what you've done. That's true in life. If you're too shy and you never try to raise your profile, if you don't try to make people remember you with any kind of unique traits, they just won't remember you. In France, Spain and Italy, people are always flirting. It's part of the culture. If you mix everything up, you get confused sometimes, and so many women try to avoid any risk. They pay a lot of attention to how they dress on the street. Non-sexy, non-flashy colours. Very restricted. Probably they're right to do so in France, because relationships between men and women are a constant thing there. It's funny, because here in Thailand that doesn't happen, since we're completely different societies. Women are elegant but not sexy like in France. Seduction doesn't exist in this society. I don't need to think about it. I can be who I am.*

In the remainder of this chapter, findings from some of the few available surveys on this topic are presented. Based on a survey of 1,500 people, Theiss and Pohl (2009) report that over one in ten Austrian women aged sixteen to twenty-nine had at least once considered sleeping with a male superior for career reasons. They interpret this as evidence that women 'can use their traditional weapons to deal the *coup de grâce* to their male rivals'. With examples including Madame Pompadour, Ivana Trump and Carla Bruni and an analysis of the modern world of work, the authors describe the strategies they have observed women using on men during their rise to the top. Seventy-four per cent of all the Austrians who responded to the survey believe attractive women have it easier at work. Seventy-three per cent reported at least one case where they believe a female co-worker had deliberately used her femininity to advance her career. These findings are subjective perceptions; it is unclear whether they correspond to reality. One in ten respondents had considered the possibility of becoming intimate with a superior, and half would not regard it as an objectionable career strategy.

Penz and Sauer (2016) conducted interviews with professionally successful men and women on the topic of attractiveness and careers. They concluded that ambitious women are well aware that attractiveness is crucial to their success and so invest a lot of time and money in their appearance.

> *Russian CEO: It's not reality, just my imagination. If a beautiful woman comes to the negotiations, then all the men will just open their mouths and say 'Oh, yes. Great. Good to have you here.' At some companies, especially in sales, it works very well. Because she's such a beautiful woman, she's able to get much better contracts than men or ugly women. But generally speaking, I don't think it makes a difference whether someone is a woman or not. All that counts is whether they're professional or unprofessional.*

German head of region: I started my vocational training back in '89 before going to university. And you could see it plain as day. Those circles of old men who all dressed the same; those certain codes; the secretary in the waiting room who later became their mistress. I saw plenty of that.

The problem of vertical intimacy – that is, intimate relationships between managers and their subordinates or people in different pay brackets – also falls into this category. In the US, line managers, most but not all of whom are men, are expected to follow the rule 'no hanky-panky with the payroll'. Men who break that rule could easily suffer reputational damage, while female subordinates they have affairs with will be accused of calculatingly trying to gain a career advantage.

German executive: Which I personally find a shame. For me, men and women are completely equal. I really don't have a preference. I perhaps tend to connect better with women. Unfortunately, I've also known a lot of women who wanted this equality, but then still used their feminine wiles and found some idiotic men who liked it … I've encountered that very, very often in my career.

According to a representative survey by the market research company Ifak, 2.9 million of some thirty million people in employment have had an affair or relationship in the workplace (Ifak, 2018). Ninety-one per cent of German HR and finance managers have no problem with relationships between colleagues (WirtschaftsWoche, 2008). In another study (Xing, 2017), one in six respondents admitted to having had a workplace fling; among that number, one in four of the women had been intimate with a superior. Thirty-five per cent of respondents aged thirty or under had no problem with people sleeping with their boss to help them along in their career (Spiegel, 2013).

Ultimately, it remains unclear just how much influence erotic capital and flirtation or seduction in the workplace have on women's – and men's – career success. So the jury is still out on this sensitive topic.

German CMO: Let me give two examples. There was one woman, from the UK, who became a VP. She wanted to be tough, wanted to be truly equal. But when she gave a presentation to an all-male committee, she still dressed very sexy. See-through top and bra, tight-fitting skirt and so on. She could afford it too. Or she'd look at you with these big eyes. The other woman was just the same. She had it easy, since she was smart, she was the best by some distance, but she could insinuate to male bosses that she found them incredibly attractive, would do everything for them, really valued them. The way she sat down, the way she listened, came closer, always stared with big eyes. We had a boss back then who completely fell for it. I don't think people should be doing that, it's not appropriate in the office. Then she very quickly became a high potential and was promoted to the USA. And then she ran into a woman, who fired her because she wasn't up to speed. Then there's also that androgynous style women have, all in trouser suits, short red hair.

Japanese CEO: I'm not sure if that's the right word or not, I don't know. I don't mean beautiful or not beautiful. I mean this kind of charm that many people find appealing. Not all employees, whether men or women, are close friends of the CEO. They stand out at town meetings with their special insights and comments. Some men also have this same charm, but mostly it's women who have it. Maybe it's women's strength. They can win over the men in their teams much more easily. And anyway, I don't like meetings with only men.

Men's ambivalence about quotas

Quotas are based on the assumption that it makes business sense to have a higher proportion of underrepresented groups, such as women, in certain positions. This in turn assumes that the distribution of relevant abilities is gender-neutral. Women's quotas seek to increase the proportion of women in top management positions by requiring companies to meet certain targets. In general, a distinction is drawn between statutory quotas, where a country's legislators stipulate that a proportion of certain positions in industry must be held by women, and voluntary commitments by companies, which set their own targets for recruiting and promoting women. Policymakers in several countries, including Germany, prefer the latter approach because it is seen as more effective.

The goal of quotas is to increase the proportion of women managers so that parity between men and women in key leadership positions becomes a realistic long-term prospect. Supporters of women's quotas believe that having women in the top team improves company performance. This belief is supported by a wealth of research. Some economists disagree, however, arguing that there is no direct causal link between company performance and governance. Another possible explanation is that successful companies have a culture that is responsible for their better performance, and also happen to recruit more women.

> French CEO: *If they want to have the same access to the same responsibility then they need to accept accountability for the job, for the risk they've taken. They have to accept being judged, evaluated, assessed. And I think it muddies the water less. It's just, 'Are you good or not? Do you accept the KPIs as an evaluative criterion?' Then we have discussions about, 'Is it the pertinent KPI? Is it the right KPI to assess my job?' If, by contrast you have to give a job to a woman, no choice, then there's this feeling that they got the job because they're a woman, not because they're the best for the job. It muddies the water.*

Norway is Europe's trailblazer when it comes to gender quotas. Back in 2003, the country introduced a forty per cent quota for supervisory boards at state-owned and listed companies, with some very tough sanctions for companies that failed to meet them, up to and including the company being dissolved. Ten European countries (including Belgium, Germany, France, Italy, the Netherlands, Norway and Spain) currently have statutory quotas, though the precise form they take varies considerably. Another twenty-one European countries have no statutory quotas, though at least eleven of these do have non-binding recommendations that usually apply only to selected (typically listed) companies. This latter group includes Sweden and the UK. In 2014, Japan's then prime minister Shinzo Abe introduced his 'womenomics' strategy, with a voluntary target of thirty per cent of managers being female by the year 2020. The country is still a long way off reaching that goal. Karl et al. (2020) ranked European countries by the ambitiousness of their statutory quotas. Austria, the Netherlands and Germany scored very low, particularly with regard to the companies included in their statutory quotas. The Norwegian quota system came top, with 4.1 out of five points, while the German quota system came bottom, with only 1.85 points. In 2015, Germany introduced a binding quota of thirty per cent for supervisory boards at listed and fully co-determined companies. A woman's quota was introduced for the boards of DAX companies in 2021. The proportion of female board members has risen since then to fourteen per cent – albeit only in DAX companies, which are relatively few in number.

In 2022, EU member states agreed to a quota of forty per cent women for all listed companies from 2026 onwards.

> *German CMO: Recently, I've often seen women being preferred over men to fill quotas. I heard from a good friend who had come back from Russia that there was a good job at the head office. There were three applicants, and of course the woman was taken. It looked better. Because then some bosses feel better about having met the quota.*

There have been various studies on the impact of women's quotas on company performance, which have found positive, neutral and negative effects. In a 2004 study by Catalyst of 353 Fortune 500 companies, the companies with the highest proportion of women on their boards performed better on average for the indicators return on equity and total return to shareholders. A study of German companies (Laible, 2013) found a small but significant negative correlation between the proportion of women in top management and the performance measures turnover, turnover per head and value added. A study of US firms (Adams and Ferreira, 2008) found that the variable gender diversity has a negative effect on company performance but a positive one on dependent variables such as attendance and monitoring, and concluded that women's quotas could worsen performance, at least at well-managed companies. Nine out of twenty-six studies included in a meta-analysis by Reinwald et al. (2015) found that having a higher proportion of women had a positive effect on relevant performance indicators, while three found a negative impact. The authors concluded that this is not due to a simple causal relation, and that the effect depends on various factors. A positive correlation occurs if there is a high proportion of women in the workforce, a business focus on private customers and/or a strategic focus on innovation intensity. A negative correlation was observed at companies with a strong 'adhocracy' culture (online organisational culture).

Critics of institutionalised women's quotas complain that although the current discussion is supposed to be about fairness and equality, it focuses only on the proportion of women in a very small number of senior positions at businesses. If the debate were solely concerned with the social issue of equality, it would be necessary to consider other, less attractive professions, such as waste collection, roadbuilding, sewer cleaning and hazardous goods disposal. Hollstein (2011) regards the discussion about quotas as dishonest, calling it 'nothing more than a wrangling for power between the sexes'. He argues that 'the debate about women's quotas overlooks that women are no longer poor victims. The true scandal is that society systematically ignores the disadvantage of men.' This argument echoes the worries expressed by many male executives, as seen earlier, that they will be forced out by the changes currently underway. The ambivalent research findings on the impact of women's quotas are reflected in the alpha men's attitudes. Some support quotas, others reject them because they fear companies could be pressured to fill positions with unsuitable candidates. This is a particular challenge in STEM sectors and heavy industry. Some men believe quotas or voluntary targets could disadvantage men.

Men and women are locked in a struggle over the allocation of well-paid senior positions. Women are making inroads into company boardrooms, while men feel like their opportunities are being limited. As a result, quotas have become another source of tension between the genders.

> American CEO: My youngest child is just leaving college in the US. He has a business management degree with a specialism in HR. He's a very open-minded young man. He's been raised by two equals in terms of his mother and father. My wife's a scientist. He sees that mutual respect in our relationship. He sees family decisions being taken which have at times been for the benefit of my wife's career and at times for the benefit of my career, and we decide that together. What he's saying just now is, 'Dad, this isn't the right time for a white boy to be looking for a job.'
> He's actually experiencing it from a very open-minded perspective. He's not expecting a favour. He's saying that what most companies are looking for either overtly or not is a diverse, female candidate. He's finding himself in the minority now, which is interesting. To answer your question, I still think that on average men have it easier, but it's changing rapidly. Small pockets of groups, for example, graduates coming out of college, are seeing that it's more difficult today if you're a white man than it is if you're a Black woman. I know that's not the norm across all of society and I would still say that life is much easier as a white boy than it is as a Black girl. We need to do these things to redress the balance. We must get to a new balance point.

Men are caught between fear of being shown up and a desire for recognition

Many of the interviewees fear being shown up by capable women and losing face as a result. They crave recognition from alpha women, rather than aggression. At the same time, the alpha men believe that women, including women in management, deal with conflicts better than their male colleagues, and welcome their pacifying influence. They recommend that women should not adopt a male way of acting, but should concentrate on their strengths, especially their social skills.

The men interviewed for this study feel they've been unfairly lumped together with sexual abusers by the #MeToo movement, despite the fact that, as fathers of daughters, they are supportive of women. They also claim that harmless behaviour that men engage in when they're 'alone with the boys' is now being viewed out of context and equated with actual cases of sexual assault against women by powerful men. All the men who participated in this study unanimously condemned such behaviour, but feel they can no longer freely relax around other men. The men also talked about the taboo topic of whether women use their erotic capital to ascend the career ladder. The relatively few comments on this topic ranged from nuanced positivity and admiration to rejection of the claim that women take advantage of their erotic capital.

Only one interviewee mentioned the possibility that men could use erotic capital too. The men were ambivalent about women's quotas, and tended to view them negatively. Alpha men want women who wish to rise up the ranks to drop the victim role and follow the same rules of career progression and performance evaluation as men. Their desire to help women is in tension with their worry about being forced out of their positions and their feeling of being subjected to unfair competition, in which they could lose their privileges to female candidates who may be less qualified.

Alpha women on conflicts with alpha men

In the interviews with C-level women managers, it was striking that although they are not happy about the inequalities in management, they do not use them to excuse their own decisions or failures. They aren't trapped in a victim role, prevented from advancing by dominant men. These successful women know exactly what they want. They take situations as they are and develop their own strategies for dealing with men in positions of power. After a difficult learning curve, many of the women now feel they can take any challenges they encounter in their stride. They know the strengths that set them apart from their male colleagues and use them to help executive teams synergistically achieve the best results. This includes recognising men's weaknesses without getting into unnecessary conflicts. Many of the women realise that their past attempts to imitate male behaviour were counterproductive. They now instead seek to create a counterpole in male-dominated meetings, by embracing and building on their feminine strengths.

> *French administrative board member (female): In the past, there was a culture where positions of power were all held by men. Women must learn to find their own place within the corridors of power, and learn to work with men who follow different rules of competition.*

In retrospect, the women regard the times when they got into open confrontations with alpha men, in which they often came off worse, as mistakes. Conflicts between men and women in management tend to follow certain patterns rooted in gender roles. It may be helpful for women to learn about these patterns and better understand the effect that their aggressive behaviour can have on men, so that they can deploy strategies that are more conducive to their goals. Only some of the female top managers described using their ability to pacify situations as a possible strategy, which suggests that many women still believe they need to imitate predominantly male characteristics. The alpha women also discussed past situations in which they were excluded by men. These situations were often preceded by incidents where they publicly confronted men over their lack of competence. By confronting the men in this way, they sent the signal that they couldn't really be trusted and weren't easy to manage. The alpha men, worried about being toppled from their throne, often retaliated forcefully and ultimately fired the women. The women described how they had to learn over the course of their careers how to deal with powerful men and difficult situations with male colleagues.

German board member (female): I think I was a nuisance to him, because he knew I wasn't completely at his beck and call. He now knew I had better solutions. I'd made that clear in meetings. Unfortunately, I was too sure of myself. And he had to get rid of me, probably because he was worried I'd find out something about him or whatever.

German CHO (female): I'd say I prefer compromise, but in the end I'll always fight. I need to walk away feeling like I'm the winner. Like my husband says, no matter what we do, I always have this need to get better and better and be the best.

Russian CEO (female): If it's in my hands, I try to avoid the fight and find a way to avoid the conflict. The best way is talking to the other side. I was always good at negotiating. In my experience, conflicts usually happen because people don't understand what the other person meant. Not because they have to put a gun to your head. No, it's usually just a deep misunderstanding.

French director (female): There were eight men there and I was introducing the new advertising campaign. The team had worked really hard on it. And one of the guys suddenly decided to start talking about a particular problem. At first, I was irritated. The guy was telling me I'd done something I hadn't. And in the end, he told me I was a liar. In front of everyone, just like that, he said: You did this, you said that. I said, 'No I didn't!' I didn't know how to react. What I should have said was, 'This is not what we're discussing at the moment, we can talk about it later.'

German board member (female): I was preparing presentations and seminars that we were going to deliver to all the country heads. And while I was doing that I was invited to go to the CEO right away for a quick chat. I told my boss I had to pop out briefly, I had another meeting. And he just said, 'OK, see you in a bit.' But he already knew I was about to be fired. I went there and thought we were going to talk about Covid and how we'd been getting through the whole pandemic up until now. Whether I had any ideas for improvements and so on. Or maybe he simply wanted to a quick chat with me. The whole conversation lasted ten minutes, and he simply said, 'Your boss can't work with you any more.' And that was it. In that moment, of course, I didn't really know what to say. True, I'd always quarrelled, things weren't easy between me and my boss. I knew that. But that was only directly with him. And I knew it wasn't down to me, it was down to that alpha male. Because he's someone who controls everything from the top all by himself. And if someone else had a different opinion? Even though he said, 'What do you want, let me know, my door is always open,' he didn't mean it. He's an absolute patriarch. It's a leadership style I really can't abide.
I made my views clear, but I never yelled at him or anything like that. I presented my opinions very forcefully. Because I feel I'm past a certain age, and now have so much experience, that I'm no longer prepared to buckle to other people's opinions. And so one thing led to another. And although it came as a big surprise to be turfed out the door after so many years, looking back it wasn't surprising after all, because I think I played a big part myself and provoked what happened. I often felt like I wasn't being listened to. And probably I had a lot bottled up, so I kept voicing my opinions more and more candidly. I can't work for people I don't respect, people I don't feel I can learn from. Especially at senior level. It's not compatible with my values, because I'm not a – the only word I can think of is one I don't want to say – because I'm not [laughs] an arse-kisser. And so I wasn't a good fit for that company, because of course I can't completely transform a company. And I can't completely change the top boss or the owner. So you always have to really ask yourself: what's my circle of influence, what can I actually change?

Showing loyalty to alpha men to get things done

One notable quality of the successful women is that they are able to build men's trust by working loyally and with integrity in their departments, in return for which they are entrusted with senior positions. Especially in Asia and Russia, male leaders trust women far more than men when it comes to compliance, integrity and loyalty. One strength of the women interviewed for this study is their ability to forge strategic alliances with men in positions of power. That includes showing understanding for men's role in meetings and in front of other people. Rather than challenging this role, the women use it for their own ends.

In situations where men and women are directly competing, woman often end up on the losing side. A number of the female top managers who were interviewed, especially those from France but also some of the German women, described situations where they had clashed with men in order to push for their own goals. The French women said they were unafraid of conflict and tackled it head on, though they also explained how their way of resolving conflicts has matured. In France, compromise as a conflict resolution strategy is frowned upon; what matters above all is winning. The French women are fighters who aren't afraid to speak bluntly. They are willing to stand their corner and slug it out.

The women realise that it's better to build strong, robust relationships with male leaders from an early stage, so they can gain allies to fight their corner. They have learned they shouldn't surprise men by attacking them head on, even if the nature of the disagreement is about business rather than anything personal. That includes ensuring they have powerful supporters for new or unpopular ideas ahead of important meetings and deferring the topic to a later date if not. In response to the men's desire for loyalty, the women involve their superiors at an early stage before controversial topics make it on to the agenda at big meetings. The women make sure the alpha men see them as loyal. They show loyalty to men in influential positions so that they can secure their support on divisive topics, and don't publicly criticise men if they make mistakes or missteps.

German CFO (female): One issue for many women in my network is their CEO. A story you always hear is that they leave the company, because their relationship with their direct superior simply wasn't working. OK, it might be that nobody admits to being kicked out because they didn't hit their targets. At [company XY], it was a little different: she was removed because she expressed herself the wrong way on the topic of racism. But apart from that, almost everyone says it was because they didn't have an alliance in place.

German COO (female): In other words, I was basically indirectly telling them, 'That plant you set up isn't any good, it isn't doing well and it won't do well in the future.' I still stand by that today. But there was I ignorantly mocking it. And I mean, some of the other senior managers had already seen the presentation and the proposal as well. And either they just didn't think about it, or – but I don't think they intentionally set a trap for me. I don't think that's what happened at all. But it was unpleasant. And then people were thinking, 'She just can't see it.' But that's not true at all. I could. I just misinterpreted what I needed to do at that moment. That was my actual contribution to the blunder.

From a commercial point of view, my solution was the right one. It was just that I presented it poorly. I didn't even get to the end of the presentation, they were interrupting me and carpeting me in a really unpleasant way. And afterwards it was so awkward. I just didn't feel very comfortable in the Champions League. You know, when someone cuts you short in front of an audience and portrays you as incompetent, then you lose faith in yourself and it turns into a vicious circle.

French CEO (female): I go at things head on, I go straight in, I'm like a pit bull. I'm fearless and there's no filter between what I think and what I say ... but maybe I have a tendency to go in too fast and not take enough time to listen and find compromises.

French CFO (female): When I need to do battle over something, I get depressed, and any time I've had to fight, it's always been against men and not women. But that's because men want more territory. For them, the company and their territory are part of the same thing. I never attempt to expand my own territory, but if you try to expand into mine, I really don't like it. And then I'll defend it, and I'm prepared to do anything ... anything ... I will always fight to maintain my territory.

Chinese CEO (female): Men, I believe, are more afraid to lose face, so you have to be more careful because they're men. But for women, for some regional managers, my observation is they're tough. They're aggressive. Otherwise they wouldn't be in that position. They're very competitive. Very, very competitive. They don't realise they're very competitive. They're not afraid to lose face because they are so competitive and so aggressive. They fight back and they want to win. They want to win always. If one is a woman and there's a man in the same position, normally the woman is three times stronger than the man. That's the comment from my boss ten years ago. When I look at the women managing in my team now, I will remind them they are very competitive and their peers may not be so comfortable dealing with that.

Chinese GM (female): This came with age. At the beginning of the joint venture I was young, and I fought until the bitter end and achieved it all. Now I am better, more willing to compromise. Little things I will let go, peanuts. But with important things I fight until the end. I fought all the way up to the CEO, I will go everywhere. They say I am assertive.

Strategic use of erotic capital?

At various points in the interviews, the alpha women mentioned using some of the six elements of erotic capital as defined by Hakim (2010). In particular, they made reference to their appearance, the effect of their femininity and the social aspects of nurturing relationships with men. The German women talked far less than the French and Russian women about the effect of their appearance. However, many of them reported that over the course of their careers they had consciously focused on their appearance and sought advice on the right choice of clothes and hairstyle. Attractiveness, the women agreed, can be a career advantage, but only if it is paired with competence and knowledge of how to co-opt men in the pursuit of professional goals without getting into 'certain problems', that is, situations where women are forced to turn down sexual advances from men. When using erotic capital, there is a fine line to walk to make sure you don't end up in unwanted situations.

German CFO (female): You have to think it through carefully, if you want to build close relationships with men in positions of power. It's a fine line and if you don't take care you'll end up in bed.

German COO (female): Well, let's put it this way. You have to learn to live with what God's given you. If you're attractive, you have advantages and disadvantages. If you're attractive, you have the advantage of hearing colleagues say they like inviting you round. It's a feast for the eyes when she's in the room. Of course, you have to be able to handle that. To make sure that people don't overlook the fact that you're productive as well and bring something to the table. I think that's especially difficult when you're younger. That's when being attractive becomes a nuisance. On the other hand, it can open doors for you. I think it's just a question of how you handle it. Whether you're able to use it to your advantage in some way or other. And if you are attractive, congratulations. That's great. You'll have the men interested in you of course. You just have to make sure you redirect it in the right way, that it's not misplaced interest. Don't flirt too much. Because it can quickly get dangerous. You don't want to be in a situation where you have to slam the door in someone's face and say, 'Keep your hands to yourself!' But I'm sure in some situations it can open doors for you.

The Russian and French women are looking for a female identity as top managers, whereas the German women take a more pragmatic approach. They have no issue with cultivating what might be termed a rather androgynous business style, and they vary their style according to circumstance. They use their appearance to their advantage, to enable them to stand out from the colourless mass of male executives, though they make sure not to send the 'wrong signals' to men. Rather than making the company a showcase for their femininity, they adopt a business style. The same is true of Chinese and Japanese women. The former believe that being too good-looking is more of a disadvantage on the career ladder; it creates distance and leads people to misjudge them or dismiss them as 'unprofessional'. Their socialisation and the legacy of the Cultural Revolution, in which men and women were treated as equal, give them a diametrically opposite perspective to their Russian and French counterparts.

Chinese GM (female): I saw some not very good-looking women leaders at very senior level ... very smart, very sharp and also very political.

Russian CEO (female): I use the power of women from this side. I often make use of this general attitude to women in business. I can become stupid. It's a very good option, to play your own game, 'I'm a woman, I don't understand these figures,' and to observe the reaction. When you're in negotiations, you play the role of this stupid woman. Your opponent loses his attention. You can get faster and bigger results than you decided before or your opponents expected. Because when our men do negotiations with beautiful women, they don't pay attention to the topic of the negotiations. I don't consider myself beautiful, but I know that I have friends, women who are very clever and who are really beautiful. When men speak to beautiful women, they naturally think they're not clever. They can't combine cleverness with beauty, it's a different range. A woman can use this power.

French director (female): I have always been very keen not to gain weight. It's very important to me to keep in shape. I've always been very feminine. I wear lip gloss every day. I make sure I look chic. I don't want to look like Cinderella when I'm at work, you know. When I was on Wall Street, I wore pants every day. I wore suits and a shirt. I always take great care. I'm meant to be the face of the company. I like to have the right shoes in the right colour with the right bag. In the summer, I have always painted my toenails. It's really important to me. I don't like looking masculine. My daughter has picked that up from me. So yes, in France, women in certain sorts of jobs should, as we say, 'tirée à 4 épingles' ('be dressed up to the nines'). If I go and see clients and I'm not excellently dressed, then I'm not excellent generally and then I think, damn, what have I gone and done? I think the image we project is really important. And at the same time, we are representing French society, where taste, fashion and chic still exist. That's always been important to me. And I think that's what counts for my daughter too, she's very feminine and uses jewellery to her advantage, and I think that she projects that kind of image too. And I had a very elegant grandmother. My mother was older and didn't dress up as much as my two grandmothers. It was my grandmother's image that was my inspiration. I would recommend to young women who are out and about in public and who play a representative role in society to be astute about these things. Especially in France, where fashion and taste are so important.

French board member (female): Codes, well yes, I think there was a time when women in France – but not just in France – used male codes in order to be successful. They thought that to be successful you had to act like a man and be like a man. And so, they dressed like men, in grey and black or whatever. And there were behaviours that they associated with masculine behaviour, being tough, in other words ... They tried to adopt male codes and attitudes. I don't know, maybe that was the only way, back then. But I believe you should be yourself. So, I always dress in bright colours and I wear something sparkly ... Besides, I never had a problem because of being a woman. I'm very womanly, it's not an act. But I don't like using charm at all. I'm a woman in every sense of the word and I work on the basis that it's good to be a woman. And I've never tried to be like a man in how I behave. So, you see, the problem with the codes is that the first time you meet someone, you're evaluated, everything's evaluated: your stature, your general appearance, how you look, how you shake hands. It's only later that the real you comes out.

French communication director (female): What is still a problem in France is the status of men, many of them don't want that to change. They don't want society to change. Some men think women are taking away men's rightful place in the world. When we see what happens in politics when a woman comes into the National Assembly and talks about the sorts of things that really happen in a country like this, it's scary. I think an important cultural thing in France is the relationship between men and women. I mean on an intimate level. It makes men see women like prey. Men chase women as if they were prey.

Studies on Russian women (Chirikova and Krichevskaia, 2002; Metcalfe and Linstead, 2003; Metcalfe and Afanassieva, 2005) report that they strive to assume a female leadership identity. A very feminine style of dress, make-up and feminine behaviours are regarded as integral to female professionalism. These debates are in keeping with contemporary studies on gender and management which focus on aesthetics, health management and gender fluidity. Gvozdeva and Gerchikov (2002) found that in order to gain access to employment opportunities, education and professional development programmes, Russian women have to actively consider the question of femininity and sexuality. 'The expectation that women be beautiful is a Russian phenomenon. In Russian society, beautiful women are venerated and idolised,' writes Daria Boll-Palievskaya (2009) in her book *Russian Women*. The same applies to French women. In both Russia and France, there is ongoing debate as to how best to achieve a female managerial style in which professionalism and femininity are combined. This is also evident in differences in media coverage: women are judged in the French press not only on the basis of their performance, but above all on their appearance and their clothing. French women can also signal their superiority to men through a more sophisticated way of using language. By accentuating both their femininity and their intellect, they are able to carve out a distinctive place for themselves that sets them apart from men.

Russian CMO (female): There were a lot of people who obviously think that I've slept with literally every single CEO of every company I've worked at. This is the kind of prejudice that can happen here. Everyone that knows me personally, they obviously know that none of that is true. But the thing is that you can see the prejudice here. I think in Russia it's, I should say, a little more obvious than in the West.

Russian COO (female): Women in Russia love to dress very much, they're often overdressed. When they have money they invest in brands and jewellery. Women in power all dress up well. In hierarchical companies, you should demonstrate your position or your wealth. Of course, you can wear sneakers, but Prada or LV. Rolex and Zara are possible as well. There has to be something to show that 'she's OK,' she's not a student. If you're a pretty woman, men will admire you. Everyone likes beautiful people.

German CEO (female): You have a definite advantage when you go somewhere. If I'm going to a conference, I put on a red jacket. That way, if you're sitting in the audience and you want to say something, you always get chosen. If you're just a man in a dark suit, you don't stand out and you don't get asked. But the women, people remember.

German GM (female): I think you have to find a good balance between staying feminine and looking business-like. Short skirts and plunging necklines are counterproductive, to put it bluntly. Which isn't to say that it can't be an advantage in some situations, but in moderation, of course. For example, when I'm going to be having a really important conversation, I'll always put on a skirt, because I'll score extra points for being womanly.

German HRD (female): And if you're too good-looking, you might have other problems. You might get competition from other women. Well, that's what I assume would happen. It's not a statement of fact.

Top women managers have learned that quotas are needed

The women critically discussed policies such as quotas for supervisory boards or certain listed companies that have been introduced in France, Germany and other places. They agree with the men that in principle senior positions should be filled on the basis of merit. French and German women would rather make it to the top based on their own achievements, rather than because of quotas. Many doubt whether women can really earn acceptance from male executives and sceptical female colleagues through quotas. Women who made it without needing quotas often reject them as a means to an end. However, since the quotas in France and Germany have been successful, most of the female top managers have come to support them as a temporary measure.

French board member (female): I was against quotas for many years. I was sure we must achieve success without them. But then we learned that without them nothing will change. Or it will take too long. That's why I am now pro-quota until we have reached a certain number, when it becomes the norm that women are on the board as well. Of course, most men have problems with quotas. That's just natural.

German CHRO (female): Or else people say, 'Oh, she's the quota woman.' C is on the board now, I don't feel like I'm a quota woman, but I don't think I'd want to be one. I'm here because I do an excellent job. I think it's a pity that a quota system had to be introduced. We won't solve the actual problem that way. And it changes men's sensibility and awareness, and women's too. So that's why. I don't always want to be only saying negative things about men. I also think that a lot of women are just too, well ... they never come out of their shells. And targets for the number of women you had to have would definitely help us.

French CFO (female): Because I think in France, we're fortunate to have a very strong legal arsenal when it comes to equality. We already have laws that are very strong and then it's just a question of enforcing them. There are laws and there are procedures for imposing sanctions. We were one of the first countries to implement a law saying that forty per cent of boards of directors have to be women, the Copé–Zimmermann law. So we're ahead of the game there too.

4 Old boys' networks and business meetings: men's natural playgrounds

In the debate about why women are underrepresented in top management, one factor that is often mentioned is old boys' networks: networks of influential men that systematically exclude women. There is a wealth of research on the links between membership of strong networks and career success. In this chapter, we hear first from the alpha men and then from the alpha women about the relevance of networks to their careers. The alpha men describe their networks as arising naturally out of friendships with other men. Some of the German men mentioned internal male cliques at companies that systematically exclude women.

The alpha men want women to become more visible and speak up more in meetings while at the same time pacifying men's aggressive behaviour. That requires them to concentrate on their strengths, and to be less reticent and reserved.

Male bonding is based on simultaneously competing and cooperating

The term old boys' network or old boys' club refers to 'an informal system in which wealthy men with the same social and educational background help each other' (Merriam-Webster, 2022). Originally, its scope was restricted to alumni of British elite private boys' schools, but now is used more broadly for any kind of closed system that provides its members with exclusive opportunities (Palmer, 2000; Lalanne and Seabright, 2022). It can thus refer to former members of a particular university or school regardless of gender, similar to an alumni association. Internationally, there are slight variations in how the term is used. Australia also has old girls' clubs, while in Finland there are 'good brother networks' made up of influential men who help each other out. In Switzerland, the UK, Hong Kong and India, old boys' networks comprise male alumni of elite private schools. In the USA, the term mainly refers to close-knit professional networks of influential men, though sometimes also to alumni of elite universities (McClain, 2018). Over time, student clubs become professional men's networks that strengthen the group bonds forged at university. Following the principle of sticking with what you know, members turn to other 'old boys' when looking for a job. In their interviews, the male senior managers talked about both external men's networks and ones internal to a particular company. German interviewees were especially likely to mention the latter.

> *German executive: You're in the fireplace and the fire is kept stoked. Not necessarily by your own individual performance, but by a boys' network. I once interviewed for a position at [company X], where the interviewer said something interesting: 'Dr S., you'll need to be X-ianised first.' That's the issue in a nutshell. That fireplace, the X fireplace, has a professional side, the actual job, and*

https://doi.org/10.1515/9783111172651-004

then, alongside it the – in inverted commas – 'social' side, which is more than just social. It's very much linked to the job, and it makes people's careers. That's just how it is at [company X].

Spanish CEO: I think it's true that we men have this social attraction or orientation. We like to spend time together, we like having parties together, having a nice dinner together, doing exercise together, because we're like big boys or big teenagers. That remains true throughout a man's life, whatever his age. That feeling of being surrounded by friends and companions, and being among men and drinking and joking together. I do these kinds of activities from time to time, but not with colleagues from my company. I very rarely go to have a friendly dinner or a party with colleagues from [company S]. Certainly not with my subordinates, but also very rarely with my boss or my peers. I do that much more with my peers from other companies.
I think it's about having fun and it's about building a close-knit network, which is certainly helpful. Not really for your career but for the business itself. And if you do good business, that's going to have a positive impact on your career. I think that the primary goal is to have fun, because we like doing that, and then to create some connections that could result in some good opportunities for the business.

Old boys' networks may operate within a single company, or may span multiple companies and sectors. Various researchers have characterised networking as a micropolitical power tactic that members of an organisation deploy to strategically and systematically shape and use the network of relationships around them to further their own interests (Reiners, 2008; Rastetter and Cornils, 2012). These networking activities are best explained in terms of social and interest-driven rationality, rather than economic rationality (Ortmann and Sydow, 2003). Neubauer and Rosemann (2006) define micropolitics as 'the arsenal of "small", everyday techniques used to build and deploy power, expand one's agency and elude control by others', and organisations as arenas in which stakeholders undertake interventions and negotiations guided by their interests. Max Weber (1978) defines power as 'the probability that one actor within a social relationship will be in a position to carry out his own will despite resistance'. Personal power, as opposed to hierarchical power, derives from micropolitical tactics such as networking. Every leader is enmeshed in a dynamic network of internal and external relationships, in which each member is working to gain power. Power tactics are used to cultivate and harness power within this mesh of relationships. 'Micropolitical competence' is the ability to adopt suitable micropolitical strategies yourself and to identify those being used by other people (Cornils and Rastetter, 2012). Networking and cultivating robust stakeholder relationships are career advancement strategies. A closely related tactic is the building of alliances. Senior managers generally have to deal with many stakeholders, including colleagues, employees, superiors, service providers and business partners. Each of these stakeholders has their own interests, and the right tactics to use for a given stakeholder will depend on the situation at hand.

German executive: There are plenty of companies that have this culture of cliques. But there are also companies where it's totally normal for women to be involved too. They have social events with a very different dynamic, where there's more focus on the social side than you get at traditional men's barbecues, with the 'let's talk about cars, football and women' kind of thing. It always depends on the company, of course. But I think it's incredibly difficult for a woman to fit in at traditional male-dominated events, and I don't necessarily think they'd enjoy it either.

The basic elements of hierarchical systems are exclusion and group bonding (Türk, 1995). Special mechanisms of exclusion create exclusive opportunities available only to members of a given network. Women in management are often excluded from or unable to access networks that could support them in their careers. This phenomenon can be attributed to a combination of gender, group bonding and 'social closure'. The latter term derives from Weber (1978) and refers to the monopolisation of privilege, power and resources. Group bonding and social closure are key functions of men's networks (Jüngling and Rastetter, 2009). Classic examples of group bonding among men can be found in the all-male communities that exist in the military, in churches and in men's clubs and fraternities (Doppler, 2007).

> *Japanese CEO: It's true. In Japan we have men's clubs. Golf clubs are a typical example. I myself play golf twice every month. I'm a member of a golf club and I have friends there, including some senior executives of course. We're always talking about business or politics or the papers, but there are no women on the golf course to be honest. We forge connections, relationships, and then they might be relevant beyond the golf course, in a business situation. I just pick up the phone and call them and ask what I need to know for the business. To be honest, I prefer having dinner or drinking just with my friends. 'My friends' means men. When I go for drinks or have dinner, I try to expand my business or personal relationships and get insights into the other company or inside information. It's an opportunity to expand my personal relations beyond my company and have some connections with other companies. These male societies are typical in Japan, perhaps in the US or Europe too.*
> *The question is how women can have those kinds of societies too. I have no answer, but I have seen a lot of new female executives. Maybe women should try to do the same things, like a women's club, to get a network. Then maybe at some point, men will recognise that perhaps it would be better for our business to gain access to women's networks. It's not so easy for the women, as many have children. I play golf and my wife stays with the kids. She complains about it. That's why I go only twice a month.*

Through team games, boys and men learn from an early age to simultaneously cooperate and compete with other boys and men. Bourdieu (2001) calls these the 'serious games of competition' that men play among themselves. Male habitus is 'constructed and perfected' in all-male spaces where these competitive games are played out. Such spaces can be found in fields as varied as business, politics and science, as well as in clubs, societies and friendship groups. Women play a not insignificant role as spectators, in whose gaze men can see the most positive image of themselves reflected back. Men relate to other men half as partners, half as rivals. Competition doesn't divide men from each other. Rather, the pairing of competition and solidarity is essential to male bonding (Meuser, 2008). Student fraternities, where men experience both competitive pressure and camaraderie, are a good example of this apparent contradiction. Another is drinking games, where men simultaneously drink *with* and *against* each other. In German fraternities, there is a practice known as *Mensur* fencing, where men bond by attempting to inflict injuries on each other.

The construction of masculinity follows a logic of distinguishing oneself, firstly, from the dominance of other men and, secondly, from women. Bourdieu (2001) refers to this as the *libido dominandi:* the desire to dominate. The first male friendship circle, the clique, emphasises a demarcation from, and often a devaluation of, women. Male networks are also characterised by the 'strength of weak ties': men benefit from other men, even if they don't necessarily like or agree with each other. Men's competitive mindsets incline them to think of relationships in impersonal, instrumental terms.

Men's networks are based on practices of male bonding. One key motivation for men's networks in companies is to stabilise male identity. Masculinity continues to be defined by leadership despite the shift towards more gender diversity in management. In the interviews, it was primarily the European and Japanese men who spoke about the exclusion of women from internal networks. The men who work in Russia and other Asian countries painted a more positive picture and talked about networks that are open to women.

In the Chinese context, networking has a special significance against the backdrop of *guanxi* principles, which are firmly embedded in society and so are of far greater importance for careers than networking as understood purely in Western terms. *Guanxi* is defined as a system which is used to exchange favours or a way of achieving private goals (Bond and Hwang, 1986). These favours are equal exchanges that do not infringe upon any rules or regulations, and as such are not corrupt in the narrow sense of the term. The Chinese are very conscious of the role of *guanxi* in constructing relationships, consolidating interpersonal bonds and building personal dependence. *Guanxi* 'exercises power over one's career and has significant impact on the accomplishment of personal goals' (Leung, 2002). Although men and women both ascribe the same strong influence to *guanxi*, they see it as having different benefits for their careers. According to studies, men are in a stronger position to develop *guanxi* relationships. *Guanxi* is associated with 'face', the public self-image that a person strives to present. The reason why women make less use of *guanxi* in their careers is mainly attributed to the fact that traditionally a woman's reputation can suffer in Chinese society if she forms overly strong bonds with men in order to advance in her career.

Chinese GM: Networking? You mean guanxi or relationships with foreigners? Without guanxi nothing gets done in China. Women do it, just like men. Perhaps it's easier for men, like in the north. But here in Shanghai women are strong at networking. They do their business the same as men, sometimes better. Perhaps sometimes women need to draw a line, but they know exactly what they want when they deal with male businesspeople.

German CEO: I can understand it. I can understand it very well, in fact, and I've seen it too. But I've never acted that way. I always found it tiresome. I know these boys' clubs exist and they've always rubbed me up the wrong way, because I'm not at all the kind of guy who does that sort of thing. Aside from the fact I don't like barbecues and don't eat meat. It sounds stereotypical, but it's the reality in many companies and cultures.

Dutch CEO: When I was in that car, I asked myself, 'What would happen if there were a woman in the back? How would that go?' I had no answer but, of course, you always need to clearly set your boundaries. That earns you respect. 'This is my line.' And you always protect it, defend it and never go over it. I think if you're in the right company, everybody will respect it, and the moment people don't respect it, for me that's a signal you need to go. You need to be assertive. I think they went to bed on average at three or four o'clock in the morning. One time I joined them, and two times, I just did my own thing, which is, of course, respected and that's OK. A foreigner in China told me that the Chinese team went out for dinner and he didn't join. Then in the morning, they said, 'All the decisions were made during dinner.' He wasn't there.

Women need to find a way to be at that table, to be part of that discussion. If you say, 'Hey, having dinner isn't for me. I'm not going to do it,' then you won't be part of that discussion. So the question is, how can you be part of that discussion and still be yourself, and protect your own boundaries? If you completely avoid it and you aren't part of that discussion, you'll be left out.

A number of researchers have investigated the effect of networks on career prospects and advancement opportunities. Some (e.g. Kanter, 1977), have studied the influence of 'shadow structures' within companies and shown how women and minority groups are excluded from informal information and social activities, limiting their access to promotion opportunities.

This argument is consistent with the benefits ascribed to old boys' networks, whose members are typically powerful men who gain access to influence and status through the networks. Membership of these networks also provides informal access to career-related information and more promotion opportunities (Hogan et al., 2005; Oakley, 2000). Conversely, exclusion from these networks makes it harder or impossible to access important information, to progress at a company and to obtain good positions at other companies.

French CEO in Thailand: I play golf and I like barbecues and I do business like that. Recently, I organised a football tournament all across Thailand. Sixteen cities in one year. We had a lot of fun. People came with their families, wives, children. We played football, we had a barbecue and we drank beers together. And we created a very special atmosphere, a relaxed family atmosphere. It's a way for the CEOs to mingle with ordinary workers at small companies. Within the company, we don't have that sort of thing. Especially in France, I'm surprised we don't have fraternities like at American universities, but there is a special relationship in France between people who graduated from the same school. That does happen. No, I don't think you can prepare your career by spending most of your time on internal relations.

Of course, if you have connections, it helps, but most of the time, the best way of being remembered by people who can influence your career is by speaking loud and clear during meetings where there's an audience. This is where they are really observing and sometimes identifying talents. Which is also crazy, because you take the microphone, you speak for three minutes and you're trying to be brilliant, and everybody remembers you and they put you on the list of potential talents or fast-track talents, just because you made a good impression on stage for three minutes. Sometimes it's scary. If you only work nine to five, nobody will remember your face and what you are capable of. That's reality. If you're shy and you can't make others remember you, your uniqueness, then they won't remember, simple as that. That's how it is in France. If you're an engineer from a certain école, you'll pick an engineer from your university for the job. Whether they're a man or a woman. Doesn't matter. What matters is the école network, not the person's gender. Should women join in with that? I think they should, absolutely.

German CFO: I've always found these boys' clubs tiresome. I mean, I couldn't have withdrawn from them one hundred per cent. Percentage-wise, I took part in about five per cent. So out of a hundred meet-ups I went to five, more or less. Maybe as much as ten per cent. Why do people go? Quite simply to build a close-knit network. You're with the line manager there, with your head of department. It's about showing your face, helping your career along, scheming and plotting. In the UK, it was the done thing to belong to a club, sometimes a gentlemen's club that was only open to men. Where men could be with other men. It was almost like a separate caste. There was something very con-servative, very conspiratorial about it. Before that, you had student fraternities. A lingering relic of the past that people like to hold on to. In Germany, it's a barbecue round someone's house, without any women. But there is still hierarchy. The bosses, the classic alpha males, stay in their role, get to produce a certain image of themselves, and the topics of discussion fairly quickly become very, very one-dimensional. And there are plenty of people who feel very, very at ease in that environment. For many of them, it's definitely a kind of escape. Along the lines of, 'What am I supposed to do at home? I've got my wife there with the two young kids. So before I put the kids to bed or whatever, I'd rather be with my friends, or go play golf on Saturdays.' And yes, there's an awful lot of truth in that.

Dutch CEO: Actually, I do the same. I'm not a drinker, as you know, but I have two or three whiskeys, because it's important for my client. He likes to have the strategy discussion in the car when he's driving, usually somewhere far away.

We went to Croatia, and then we were just driving in the car with the young boss. There was no agenda, no plan, nothing whatsoever. Then, in the evening, we went drinking. I had to go with the flow, but I still had my own agenda in my mind, and I brought it with me and looked at whether I could just tweak it. I had two or three drinks in the evening because I knew if I didn't drink at all, that would feel awkward, so I had two or three, and I still brought my own agenda, kept in mind what I wanted to achieve, what I wanted to get out of it, and acted accordingly.

When asked about the role played by old boys' networks in their own careers, the alpha men distinguished between business networks outside their company and inter-nal relationships. Most of them maintain external networks with people from other companies. The primary motivation, especially for expat CEOs, is to do sports and other hobbies together. Making useful business contacts is a welcome side effect. Some of the CEOs who work in China reported that women will automatically be in-cluded too if they share the same hobby.

Several expat CEOs explained that they don't organise any internal networking ac-tivities at their local subsidiary that exclude certain groups, due to the position of re-sponsibility they hold at the subsidiary and the value of treating employees equally. In China, this is standard business practice, and social events in the evenings involve both men and women. The focus of the alpha men's networking activities has instead shifted to outside the company. Since they've already reached the top, the most valuable inter-nal connections are not to be found locally, but back at the head office.

French CEO in China: You're right. I also did a lot of team sports when I was younger, so yes, I get that it's a male bonding story. I love doing music as well. I always had groups of male friends and we went out and did stuff. But that's not exclusive to men. My wife also has a group of female friends and they go out. It's time just for me. I think it's good for personal development. Male bonding, for me, is about friendship. It's not just that you're two men together and then you start drinking. That's what you would find in China, I think. You have dinners and the guys expect you to get drunk just because you're in a business relationship, and with you are two men. And also women, by the way. It's not my kind of thing at all. I can have a good drink with good friends. I can't have a good drink with people I don't know, or with people from work. They're not necessarily people I'd like to have a drink with.

A few of the men, who describe themselves as introverts, aren't fans of the barbecues and evening drinks that are typical men's social gatherings in English-speaking countries. They belong to the minority of male executives who avoid both all-male and mixed social events, because it's not in their nature to socialise in groups, and reported that this behaviour had sometimes prompted criticism or judgemental attitudes. For their career progression, they had relied on mechanisms such as sponsorship rather than networking. Despite this, they still believe that, as men, they had an easier time pursuing their careers than women would have done.

American CEO: I think it's offensive to think that all men function the same way, just like it would be offensive for a man to think that all women function the same way. At a personal level, I don't play golf, I don't drink. I'm very introverted. I love the company of my wife, as a friend and a colleague and a partner, more than anyone else. When I'm interviewed and I get that strange question about who I'd most like to have dinner with, my answer is simple: my wife. Because I can be the most comfortable with her. I can be myself. I think what you've described is a rather narrow-minded view of perhaps what some men are like, but perhaps also some women are like. I think it depends what you define as a boys' club. Do men have it easier? Historically, yes. Absolutely. I think in any society or culture, the dominant group will be more likely to promote people who are like them rather than those that are different. I think that's natural, whether it's a tribe of Aborigines in Australia or a group of Scottish youths drinking in a park on a Saturday night, who are fearful of what is different. I don't think it's surprising that it can be perceived as a boys' club. I think there are layers we all go through to get to the very top. I mean that, for CEOs and C-suite executives, I'm actually not convinced that those boys' clubs are actually of value. I think to get to the middle, they're very valuable, but I think you have to actually perform to get to the top. I wouldn't say they're normal. I think describing something as a network and describing it as a boys' club are two very different things. I think that if you look at a network just as a drinking club or golfing club, that's a very naive way to look at the value of networking.
I don't think there's any advanced management psychologist who says networking is a bad idea. If a woman were to interpret that as a boys' club, I think reframing the words in another way would suddenly make it sound positive. I think networks are obviously very important when used correctly. To give a strange example, I don't use social media other than LinkedIn. I've no interest in Facebook or Snapchat or any of them. LinkedIn I use because of the professional network. I'm very happy to connect. Let's say we use our relationship as an example. You've reached out, someone I know has made a connection for me. You're professional. You have a specific interaction in mind. It sounds like you're a good person to network with, regardless of whether that person is male, female, sixty-five years old or twenty-one years old.
I might be the wrong person for some of these questions. I personally don't feel comfortable in golf clubs, in drinking clubs, in barbecues. I'm a working-class guy. It feels like many other managers see me as not being in their club. It's difficult for me to think that way.
There's no doubt in my mind that men have and continue to have an easier route for most things that they choose to do. But that's changing.

Australian CEO: I come home to see my family and spend time with them. I don't play golf, I don't go to the bar. I definitely don't have a boys' club. I definitely have friends who are guys, but I also have friends who are women. My reason for going home is to be with my family, my wife and my daughters and my son. I think that historically – I say historically, even now it's present in some places –

it's definitely been the case that guys go drinking after work, they hang out. Traditionally, women have been more of the home carers. I think that it's only been in the last generation that that's started to change, but it hasn't changed as much as it needs to, it's still a little bit skewed. Interestingly, one of my sisters, her husband is the stay-at-home parent and she's the senior executive. I have another sister who runs her own company, actually two sisters who run their own company, so I think the environment that I have been exposed to in my family is a little bit different.

There is also discussion in the literature of 'new old boys' networks'. These are networks that emerged out of online communities. It was initially hoped they might be more diverse than the old boys' networks, but researchers have found that although they appeared younger and trendier from the outside, at their core they were very similar to the old networks. Griffin (2000) argues that this is because most senior decision-makers in the internet industry are men. Women have always been in short supply in technology-related fields, and the 'new old boys' networks' create barriers for the few women who do try to pursue careers in this sector.

American CEO: In Silicon Valley-based STEM start-up companies, I would say it's lower than ten per cent. That's a very new type of boys' club, because it's not about drinking and golf. It's about computing and code and sitting in front of the computer for twenty-four hours per day. The club grows because more boys seem to want to do that.

When the men were asked how women could get into relevant company networks, there were divergent views and some moments of thoughtful reflection. The men are aware that male social gatherings or extended trips away can present women with a dilemma. This is often described as women having to walk a 'fine line'. The men know examples of women who managed to 'hold their own' at drinks evenings by copying stereotypical male behaviours, but noted that doing so in a business environment put them at risk of being socially ostracised.

Japanese CEO: It's true. In Japan, golf is a leisure activity, but also a way of developing business relationships. Sometimes, it's an excuse to go out with someone just for fun. So I think there are a mixture of reasons people do it. From women's point of view, that's very strange. Japan also has barbecues, but I think drinks are more common. Having dinner after work, a social dinner or dinner with a customer, used to be a very standard practice but that's becoming a thing of the past.
Now, I think some top business leaders never play golf with anyone, they don't like to go for drinks. They prefer to have a meeting, a breakfast meeting before work or a lunch meeting, I think that's probably the compromise way to do that. Things are shifting in that direction, but still a certain number of men believe the old-fashioned way is probably effective. I'm paying very careful attention to that fact, because about half of the employees are female. Of my twelve direct reports, five are women, seven are male. So, I need to pay careful attention. Some women just don't like to go out in the evening, because they have to take care of the kids, need to pick them up from nursery. Another interesting new view that's different from the past is that employees are asking if they'll get overtime for these sorts of activities. A generational shift. Another recent example: one of the government ministers described how she climbed up the ladder. She never refused to go for drinks. I think that caused a lot of controversy. Some took the view, 'Maybe that's what women need to do.' But others said, 'What? That's an old-fashioned view.' In the past, women politicians who were willing to socialise after five o'clock might have got a better position, but nowadays there's a mixed reaction. Maybe

some companies still do that, others don't. Probably half of companies are already modernised. The rest still need to do it. Unfortunately, women may need to choose companies properly. Company cultures are very different. For women, it's important to choose somewhere with the right fit.

Russian CEO: I think that's already outdated. Maybe in the past, it was like that, I'm not sure, but nowadays I don't see such a big difference in career paths between men and women. Me personally, for example, I don't drink beer, I don't drink alcohol and I don't eat barbecues. I don't play golf, but I do a lot of sport. First, I do martial arts. Yes, there are mostly men and a lot of white-collar people who go there to release stress. That's where we have our men's club. Second, I also do swimming and running, which doesn't involve any communication with women.
When I was doing business with my Chinese partners, we would always spend time in restaurants or nightlife venues, visiting saunas and having our discussions there. If a female boss came from Russia or other countries to China, then my partner would host them. After we met for our negotiations, she would accompany them to visit a sauna or spa, or do some women's things. All negotiations would happen inside the boardroom, inside the negotiation room, and that's where the contract would be signed. The only difference was that afterwards the women wouldn't be in the men's group but would do something else.

German CMO: I agree with some of that, but not all. Where I can definitely agree is that men stay longer in the office so they don't see their kids. That's definitely not the case for me, but it's something I've seen a lot. Only a few really got involved, did grocery shopping and so on. I knew a few men who really liked having the kids come for a good night kiss, but apart from that they didn't have to do anything. I still saw that behaviour in Australia in 1997: having barbecues and drinking and going to the club and so on. But it's become a lot less common, I think. Because we men are taking on more responsibility, helping out at home. I think that what the Americans or British describe as 'butch', these cliques of men, is changing.

Men recommend more women's networks and solidarity among women

The men considered various ways that women could strengthen their networking. As well as suggesting that women learn the art of socialising with men, another recommendation at the top of the list was that women should start their own networks. The men believe there is still not enough critical mass in many countries. Another weakness they have observed in some women is their lack of solidarity with other highly successful women, which prevents them from getting effective support. They've seen women undermining other women due to bias and negative judgements of their ability. The men who have done a lot of work on diversity issues attribute this to the fact that women have still not learned how to simultaneously compete and cooperate, due to the way they've been socialised. The men step in to help if they become aware of conflicts between women. They recommend that female colleagues should provide unconditional mutual support, both in women's networks and at meetings where several women are present.

German CFO: Whether a parallel event is set up and they simply do things the same way, except just by and for women, or they deliberately do something different by launching a mixed, diverse event ... If you're in a line organisation, that would of course require women who can actually make it hap-

pen and act as spokespeople. Women currently on the board, for instance. Like C at Deutsche Telekom or P at PWC. And I think it's important that this diversity is actually put into practice.

American CEO: I think women create competition at times that can be much crueller than that between men. Men are like a blunt instrument. We're like a hammer. It's very clear when a man is beating up another man and I don't mean physically, I mean verbally, intellectually. Women are much more like a scalpel. Many men assume that women will help each other because they're still in a minority. When I speak with women from my team, I often hear that another woman puts them down instead of supporting them. I think that's a human trait. Instead of saying, 'Oh, it's fantastic that Bettina's been promoted to VP of quality. That's a great step,' there begins a subtle erosion of Bettina's competence in the eyes of men. Negative comments come from women. Of course, not all women like all other women, not all men like all men. But there's a sense that we think, wow, two women in the lion's den, you'd think they would protect rather than sacrifice each other.

German head of region: Things might be fairer in Germany. Depends where you ask. In the East, it's knives out. To the death. Women even factor that in and launch pre-emptive attacks. And in Russia it was pretty brutal, what I saw of how women treated each other. My boss simply had to be the strongest wolf in the pack, because everyone else wanted her job and made it very clear. She's now head of the Ukrainian office. There's something Stalinist about those pre-emptive attacks. It's similar here; Germany has a very specific culture. I haven't seen it elsewhere in Europe. France is perhaps different because of the elite cliques. That's something different. Some women in America were very aggressive too, and would badmouth each other. Because in America it was all about the competition to become VP.

Alpha women can pacify men's aggression in meetings

Meetings in companies are like arenas. They're important sites of social interaction, where key information is conveyed about the organisation's culture, goals and standards of behaviour. Participants quickly learn what role they and their teams have in the company. They also learn what status is accorded to gender diversity. The social interactions that take place at meetings are affected by the proportion of men and women. A team's gender composition has a significant impact on its performance, conduct, values and social influences.

> *British CEO: The qualities they bring include courtesy; women are in a certain sense more emotionally mature. When men get together, they sometimes drift into boys' stories, which at a certain age, really, is just ridiculous. I think women bring more maturity.*

McGrath (1964) drew particular attention to the importance of pre-existing interactions and relationships between meeting participants. He studied how these dynamics play out during meetings and what effect they have on the outcomes. Other researchers (e.g. Baines, 2010; Berger et al., 2015) have made three main findings with regards to meetings. Firstly, derogatory attitudes towards women and their professional role are common, for instance in the form of jokes at women's expense. Women are also systematically treated like assistants or secretaries. Secondly, men are more likely to form alliances in meetings with other men, with a key role being played by old connections that were originally forged outside the meeting and are then consolidated during it. This makes it harder to build new relationships with women. Thirdly, as a consequence of the first two points, women distance themselves from their femininity by adapting their behaviour and attitudes. For instance, they might flaunt their knowledge and expertise, or they might play down critical situations in meetings when negative attitudes are expressed towards women. These studies confirm the importance of gender constructs in organisational contexts, especially meetings, and their negative effects on female participants.

> *Irish CEO: What do men do to undermine women a little in meetings? They speak too much, they interrupt, they humiliate them in certain ways. They slightly and ever so subtly change the topic, moving the discussion away from the correct and important points the women have made. You hear men say, 'Yes, but you've never been out in the field, or I bet you've never visited any of our clients.' Well, so what? The woman could say, 'And you've never been to the factory. You've never been in charge of quality.' Instead of countering the objection, I think women let themselves be intimidated. They could say, 'He's right. I haven't visited clients. I don't know them as well as he does. But equally, he hasn't been to our factories. He doesn't know about production.' Women rarely do that.*

> *German CFO: But what's incredibly important, especially for a CEO, is to create an atmosphere where women feel comfortable in these meetings. And I have to say, I've never been in a meeting that was designed to make women feel comfortable. Only one time was it different. If these meetings sometimes make even my skin crawl, then I don't even want to know what a woman would think.*

> *Irish CEO: Men are disagreeable. Men like to have fights. Men like to win. Men like to create conflict even when it's not necessary. Women in the main take a slightly bigger picture. They're less interested in conflict. They're more interested in the group winning. Now, if I draw a profile, if I were to draw a Pareto, men and women would overlap, but if I said to add the most agreeable and the very highest extreme of agreeable, I'd bet it'd mainly be women. At the very low extreme of disagreeable, I'd bet it's mainly men. That doesn't mean that all women are more agreeable than all men.*

> *Russian CEO: When women are in a meeting, the atmosphere will change immediately. Mature? More friendly, one could say. But in order to have this atmosphere, the women must be themselves, and not start playing the aggressive games that men play among themselves.*

Leave men's cherished networks and social events alone, and create new, powerful women's networks instead

The alpha men defend old boys' networks and the benefits that result from them where the networks in question are ones external to their company. Not all of them believe that internal men's networks were important for their advancement. Expat CEOs in particular regard their local internal networks as less important than their external networks. They believe sponsors and relationships with stakeholders at the parent company are more relevant to their careers. The interviewees were critical of male-dominated networks within companies that deliberately exclude women, with examples coming from Europe and Japan. In the alpha men's view, women who want to be successful should get involved in certain networking activities, though the question

of how they could fit in as women ultimately went unanswered. There was a dissonance among the interviewees. On the one hand, they very much enjoy their all-
male social gatherings, but at the same time they know that women have been disadvantaged by being excluded from clubs and networks. The alpha men believe one particular challenge for women is to hold their own with men at alcohol-fuelled events,
without overstepping the 'fine line'. They gave various examples of how women can
avoid this problem when networking with men.

The alpha men also believe that women could achieve the same benefits with their
own women's networks, though they acknowledged the constraint that these would
have less influence and a smaller pool to draw on.

A lack of mutual support and solidarity between women undermines talented
women, making it harder for them to progress in their careers and hold on to leadership positions.

In meetings, women have a pacifying effect on men. Their core strengths, such as
empathy and communication, can help make meetings more efficient, but only if
women don't adopt aggressive masculine behaviours.

Alpha women and their networks

Cultivating professional networks is very important for women's careers too. Having
the right networks gives women access to information and strategic advice that can
help them in their careers. It also gives them access to mentors and sponsors, who
can raise their profile on key committees.

Some research, however, suggests that women's professional networks are less effective than men's in terms of career benefits. According to the 'wrong networks' view,
women and other minority groups often belong to networks that don't provide them
with enough relevant information about the labour market or their company (Fernandez and Fernandez-Mateo, 2006), meaning they often won't hear about job openings.
This would suggest that women should cultivate diverse networks so they have better
access to valuable information about jobs (McDonald, 2011).

Unless women understand the workings of male networks, which are characterised by mutual support, male bonding activities, reliability and solidarity, they may
struggle to overcome exclusion from internal networks and become accepted as network members. Men understand the rules of behaviour better in all-male social settings. Solidarity creates social cohesion and mutual recognition, which helps to stabilise
male identity. The higher women rise, the more likely they are to find themselves in the
minority, which means they will need special micropolitical strategies (Rastetter and
Cornils, 2012).

*French CEO (female): Women just don't have enough time here. They're always running after their
children or their families. They skip things when they have children. So, then they get punished for
that, they're at a disadvantage. I carry on despite the children. Women are OK at networking, not*

great, but OK. Women don't get much out of networking. When people are looking for board members, they hire their friends, good friends, and they have lots of those. Or else they go to a headhunter and he has lots of friends too. They don't even look at your CV. In France, the process isn't a very rational one. It's still about who you know, friends and the like. They're not going to go looking for new board members in some random women's network. Know what I mean?

Previous research has identified gender-specific differences in the size and quality of professional networks. According to these studies, women make fewer contacts overall and tend to have less powerful and influential network partners. This places them at a structural disadvantage.

A study of female leaders in German companies (Greguletz et al., 2019) found that as well as extrinsic structural barriers that exclude women from powerful networks, a role is also played by intrinsic barriers, such as women's hesitation to instrumentalise social ties. This analysis attributes structural exclusion to work–family conflict and 'social homophily'. Men and women have different intrinsic motivations for networking.

Nine per cent of female German executives surveyed by Henn (2012) reported that they didn't have a network or had deliberately chosen not to have one. Twenty-three per cent said they don't make use of women's networks or are bad at networking.

With regard to women's reluctance to engage in networking and become actively involved in powerful networks, researchers such as Rastetter (2021) have identified two relevant factors. Firstly, a relationship-oriented morality, which refers to women's disinclination to seek one-sided personal advantage from network relationships. Secondly, a tendency for women to be overly modest and underestimate themselves in professional contexts. The research findings show that women are hesitant to extract more benefit from networks than they feel they can contribute in return. Men take a utilitarian approach to their networks, while women take a more social one.

German HRD (female): This unnatural sort of networking, based on the idea that today I'm networking and that's why I'm going to this event or that and I've got this or that strategy and now I need to get to know such and such a person, that's not my thing at all. I go by gut feeling. But networking in the sense of attending events and lectures and finding people who I really like talking to and who really have something to offer, without always having my career in the back of my mind, and staying in touch with people, that I really love. I'd like to be able to say that Generation CEO has really helped me, but it's getting bigger and bigger and more and more anonymous. I'm a person who likes to connect with people and I don't like to see my network as some sort of institution. Either we click and I like meeting up with a person and we talk about more than just how we might be able to help each other, but I also like people to go jogging with or something, or just people to meet up privately with. It has to come naturally, it has to just flow. Instead of thinking, 'Wow, this woman is such and such and so I'll get out my business card.' That wouldn't be me at all and I don't like it when other people do it, either.

Strategic networking by women can overcome traditional gender barriers and allow them to access men's networks. One possible strategy is to make use of mentors who can open doors for women. Female leaders can network most effectively with men by striking a careful balance between closeness and distance. By gaining access to traditionally male networks, women can challenge stereotypical gender roles. Thus, networking doesn't automatically reproduce gender inequalities, but can reduce them.

According to Rastetter and Cornils (2012), alongside networking women need to clearly communicate their career ambitions, and must avoid being too strongly tied to a single mentor. The larger and more diverse their network, the more opportunities women will have to signal their career plans and, if conditions are unfavourable at their own company, to find new positions elsewhere. In all networking activities, especially those involving close relationships with male colleagues, superiors and business partners, women must be mindful of maintaining appropriate boundaries.

> French GM (female): Women haven't always understood the importance of networking and networks. You [i. e. the interviewer] should ask women if they are in networks or networks. And insist on this point, because women don't understand the importance of forming groups. We also have to insist that women stand together to help each other, just like men. Sometimes women compete with each other, and that's a shame. So these are issues that should be addressed with women so that they understand the interest of having a network based on mutual aid, rather than competing with each other. I do a lot of things. I organise events with women who I invite to my home. There are years when I have three dinners with twenty people at home in the summer. I'm very involved in associations.

There are great benefits for women who prioritise investing time in their networks. Many of the women interviewed for this study have well-established networks. The main time they use these networks is if they are considering changing jobs. In France, networking is essential to a career in management. Women who come to France from abroad will soon find themselves being advised that in order to establish themselves professionally they will need someone to introduce them to 'the right networks'.

Access to specific networks and power circles is thus extremely important for a career in France. But in all the countries included in this study, women's career success is linked to a willingness to invest time in this area – time that is already scarce. It is also contingent on the skilful use of networks and the contacts resulting from them. From the point of view of French women, networking events organised purely for this purpose are less effective than the established networks of the French elite universities, large corporations, private circles and other business connections. The mixing of private networks with professional interests is something that French women have observed to a greater extent among men, who apply this strategy very successfully.

The German alpha women explained that, until now, women have tended to view networking purely as a way to expand their contacts and exchange information and advice, rather than as a tool for furthering their career goals. Women like to share their experiences, learn from each other and talk about the challenges they face.

> German HRD (female): It's extremely important, because men have been doing it for decades. And when jobs become available, they just call each other. There are a lot of jobs where people are hired privately because they just know each other. Deal. And women can do the same. It all starts like I said. But we need to do it much more often, it's extremely important. It's equally as important as one's performance.

German women remain ambivalent about whether and to what extent they ought to use their network to achieve their career goals. This indicates that most are still learning how to use their networks instrumentally to benefit their careers, as well as how to give back.

They haven't yet learned the idea of give and take in relation to their careers. There's no set of established rules for the use of professional women's networks and what you should put into them. There's also a fear of disappointment, in case a woman network member breaks the rules in a game she hasn't yet learned how to play and takes out more than she puts in. Moreover, the fear of being considered a token or 'quota' woman and fear of promoting a 'quota woman' limits German women's ability to create truly strong networks.

> *Japanese president (female): In my early company I started from a junior level. I was automatically enrolled into those networking systems. Later, in my next company there were diversity KPIs. I actually experienced a lot of difficulty being at the centre of discussions, because men have their own networks to discuss and decide things, and they didn't want me to be involved. In Japan, because I was the most senior woman, I started a network for senior women at my old company to encourage everybody to start working together, and that's something I still have to do now as president of the organisation because there's no existing network and I'm the most senior woman.*

The Japanese women described many occasions on which they promoted themselves. They actively volunteered within their companies to participate in one-off projects, such as initiatives for the advancement of women, in which they acted as role models. Due to their unusual positions, the women quickly became well known within their professional environments and were nominated for high-profile external positions.

Another question for Asian women is how they can gain access to the male-dominated foreign networks in the multinational corporations they work for and position themselves skilfully within them. The women interviewed for the present study analysed the dynamics in their parent company, sometimes assisted by a coach, and identified strategies to expand and consolidate their relationships with foreign men in key positions.

For Chinese women, just as for Chinese men, their parents' *guanxi* networks often helped them to secure their first jobs. Around eighty per cent of Chinese women who participated in an earlier study (Al-Sadik-Lowinski, 2018) mentioned their extended family's *guanxi* connections when asked how they got their first job at a state-owned company or government institution. It wasn't possible in that study to precisely ascertain how big a role *guanxi* networks played in these women's careers. Since they were operating in a culturally mixed environment and the people who decide on appointments to senior management roles were usually foreigners, it can be assumed that although *guanxi* networks played a role, these women also had to learn intercultural networking strategies. Some of the Chinese women's networks were situated within their companies, but others cut across different companies or into their personal lives. All of the women interviewed for this study had invested time in developing diverse, complex networks.

Alpha women 'among the boys'

The women described the different ways men and women behave in meetings. These differences become more pronounced if men comprise a large majority. If only a few women are present, men will keep acting the same way they do when they're 'alone with the boys', as described above by the alpha men, and women may encounter some of the unpleasant situations mentioned previously. The female top managers try to stay calm in these situations, and many exploit the advantage they have as women.

> German HR director (female): And the topics get thrown about like a football. Their body language sometimes makes me chuckle. What's very striking is that they use much coarser language than when women talk to each other. They say things like 'fuck' or 'we need to get rid of that weirdo!' I've almost never heard women talking about people like that. Things are much more business-like with them. And of course, if I have meetings just with women, we talk about different things than we do at ones dominated by men. I feel I talk differently from men. And their choice of language sometimes makes me twitch a little, because I just don't think it's appropriate at C-level. Maybe I'm a bit old-fashioned. Sometimes, they'll sit with their legs spread wide. Everyone knows the pecking order, who sits where. You know exactly who's sitting at the front, up at the top. And everyone has their designated place. You absolutely mustn't sit anywhere else. I've experienced less of that at women's meetings. And even when it's a standing meeting, it's all a bit more demonstrative. The way they stand, their hands in their pockets. They show with all the means at their disposal, 'I'm the alpha male and I know everything. I'm talking now.' I can see them doing it right now.

5 Alpha men on successful women's personality traits and leadership styles

In this chapter, the male senior managers describe the qualities and abilities they have observed in highly successful women, in particular, self-confidence, ambition and career orientation. They recommend that women communicate their career goals more clearly. The men believe women are, generally speaking, less decisive, slower to act and less willing to take necessary risks. They also discussed the need for women to find genuine allies and build strong stakeholder relationships in order to strengthen their positions in their companies. The men clearly described the demands that women in in particular must meet in terms of combining family and career, though they do not have any instant-fix solutions. The analysis concludes by looking at the female leadership strengths that the alpha men admire in alpha women.

Self-confidence empowers women to be successful

Successful leaders, whether male or female, need a lot of confidence. That includes knowing your own strengths and trusting in your own abilities. The alpha men believe women tend to be less confident than men, and there is evidence in the literature to support this view. Shrauger and Schohn (1995) define self-confidence as a person's appraisal of their skills or competence and ability to deal successfully with different situations. It results from a belief in their own capabilities and a high level of self-esteem, both as a person and as a leader, and is expressed in a self-assured demeanour. Leaders are generally characterised as self-confident. Employees want leaders to have faith in their actions and decisions, so that they can guide their teams to wards better solutions. Self-confidence is also linked to leaders' effectiveness. Leaders with high self-confidence can motivate staff to follow their vision, while those with low self-confidence instead have to use compulsion or lack vision altogether (Gamson, 1968).

> French CEO: It could be a lack of confidence in herself. 'No, I'm not going to do it. I'm not going to make it.' Or sometimes the complex of not being as good as other people. They always think they aren't as good as other people around them, which most of the time isn't true. If you don't have self-confidence, you can't lead others. You need to trust in yourself if you want other people to trust you. What I tell all women I know and appreciate who ask me for advice is, 'Trust yourself. Number one, trust yourself, you have this complex that you're not supposed to have this job.'

Women struggle a lot more with their confidence in the workplace than men (O'Neill and Hopkins, 2013). In *The Confidence Code*, Katty Kay and Claire Shipman (2014) report that only fifty per cent of women describe themselves as highly confident, compared with seventy per cent of men. Consequently, women feel less ready than men for promotions or new career opportunities, and have slower career progression. Men are also more likely to help their careers along by publicly taking credit for their achieve-

https://doi.org/10.1515/9783111172651-005

ments. Research suggests this can be traced back to behaviours developed in early childhood.

> American CEO: Men always think they're the best and that they truly deserve their position. They don't waste time thinking about it. Women have this complex of not being legitimate, which is why I always say to them, 'Stop thinking about it, it's a waste of time. People aren't stupid. If they picked you, it's because you deserve the job. End of story. And anyway, at the end of the year you'll be able to see from the results how good you are.'

Various studies have shown that women in leadership positions are less confident in their performance than men (Gill and Orgad, 2015). These findings suggest that women in senior positions often feel out of place, but that should not be taken to imply that women aren't effective leaders. Zenger and Folkman (2012) actually found that women are considered more effective leaders than men. In another study (Flynn et al., 2011), around fifty per cent of women reported feelings of self-doubt about their performance compared with thirty-one per cent of men. A lack of self-confidence was correlated with less willingness to apply for jobs and promotions. Stereotypes and bias, such as the assumption that women react more emotionally in the workplace, affect the self-confidence of women managers. Bias also impacts on how women are perceived by others.

> French CEO: There are two reasons why women don't get promotions. Firstly, because they're rejected. But secondly, because they think they'll be turned down, so they don't even apply. My sister is a mum with four kids. She always outshone me at school. She graduated from a top school in France aged just seventeen, two years younger than average. She had a glittering career. She became a CFO in China at the age of thirty-two, and I simply said, 'Wow, you're a wonder woman.' Then one kid, two kids, three kids, four kids. After that she was only responsible for taxes, and then there was a shift. It felt like things were drifting off course. She stayed at home to look after her fourth baby and didn't go back. I could see the self-censorship in her head. We had a talk, and I said to her, 'I think you've been beaten down by your environment, but perhaps you've beaten yourself down too.' That might be a little unfair, but I said to her, 'Think about the next thirty years and what you could do in a company.' A year later, she took another executive position. I think we have the responsibility to fight against women's self-censorship and champion women. That's how I see it.

Women leaders must be liked in order to be perceived as competent and self-confident, while men can be perceived as competent and self-confident even if they're not liked (Guillén et al., 2018). Leadership positions require 'agentic' qualities such as dominance, self-confidence, tenacity, rationality, individuality and certainty, which are stereotypically associated with men (Eklund et al., 2017). Women with 'communal' characteristics feel disadvantaged by this. This affects their self-confidence, since their colleagues and subordinates like them but don't view them as capable leaders. Women with agentic characteristics, on the other hand, are seen as capable leaders, but are generally unpopular with their colleagues and subordinates. This creates a barrier for women in the workplace, since they are never seen as both capable and likeable – it's either the one or the other.

French CEO: In my view, it's not about male or female, it's about the person's personality. The fact that you put yourself forward, raise your hand, isn't related to the fact that you're male or female. My older daughter, she's more into the fashion business. There's no issue there, because they have around seventy per cent women in that industry. She's already in a senior position and it looks like she'll be moving up very rapidly, no question about it. What I tell my daughters is to be confident in what they have. To observe and to understand the people around them, because the difficulty sometimes – and again, it's not specific to men or women – is that it takes you a bit of time to understand what all these characteristics are and how you can use them to help yourself develop in a company. Those are the main discussions I have with them. I ask them, 'Do you believe in yourself?' I just tell them – because I'm at an age today where I can tell them, and I believe they can trust my judgement – I tell them, yes, I believe you have this capacity. Believe in it.

Flynn et al. (2011) identified four behaviours displayed by leaders with less self-confidence. The first is being 'overly modest'. Men are 'more willing to take public credit for their successes' while women 'believe their accomplishments should speak for themselves'. As a result, women's accomplishments are more likely to be overlooked by their superiors, colleagues, subordinates and clients. Secondly, women are often passed over for promotion because they don't apply in the first place. Many women see it as a risky step to apply for higher positions, and for various reasons don't ask for promotions. The third behaviour is 'blending in'. Many women avoid attention, and go to great lengths to blend in at board meetings. As a result, they miss important opportunities to 'sell their ideas' and stand out from their colleagues. The fourth characteristic behaviour is 'remaining silent', something that in Western cultures (unlike in Asia, for instance) is associated with low self-confidence. Women often don't speak up during important discussions in meetings. Depending on context, however, this is essential for career development.

In their article 'Nice Girls Don't Ask', Babcock et al. (2003) present further explanations for why many female leaders display less self-confidence than their male counterparts, and so don't ask for what they want and deserve. Taken together, the results of these studies indicate that men are more likely than women to talk about what they want. This may be because women are taught as children to put other people's needs ahead of their own rather than pursuing their own ambitions.

Australian executive: Men are probably not fully qualified, but feel confident that they could learn it and do the job in the future. Men will say, 'You know what? It's a stretch. I'm going to go for it.' Only ten per cent of women will do the same, according to a study that we did in Australia. The tendency for women is to say, 'I'm not sure I'm ready for that.' Which isn't true. They're both at the same level. They're both capable. They both bring skills and capabilities and value to that role. How do we build that confidence to articulate that they can get there, versus being good at articulating, 'I am here'? It seems they all had the same experience. It's interesting because when I coach women within the organisation, they're like, 'Well, do you think? I'm not sure?' And I'm like, 'Actually, I think that you would be amazing. If I compare you to your peers, I see people applying for this role that you're performing better at. Your leadership is as strong, if not stronger, and your potential is probably higher.' Obviously, I have a role to help build that confidence, but how do you also have leaders at all levels of the organisation? You have to speak boldly and be willing to push that personal agenda and take that little bit of a risk.

Japanese CFO: Men are probably more dominant. It's not a fact, but my observation is that women have less self-confidence to speak up. I think they have good ideas but they lack confidence to speak and tend to stay silent. But if somebody asks them, they'll voice their opinion.

The male executives interviewed for this study have observed that highly successful women have a lot of self-confidence, combined with a calm temperament. These qualities are the key to their success and help them to defy stereotypical expectations.

Ambition and decisiveness as drivers of career success

An analysis by Hays (2016) suggests that, for various reasons, women usually set their career goals lower than men, limiting their ambitions to mid-level management roles. Fewer women expect they will have reached general manager/CEO level by the end of their career. This tallies with how many of the men interviewed for the present study described talented, qualified women, who in the men's view often lack clear career ambitions or fail to clearly communicate their ambitions.

Japanese CEO: Some women just don't want to be promoted. But in order to rise you need to want it. I respect it when a woman chooses another life.

American CEO: More than anything else, I think hunger drives people.

Ambition can be defined as the desire to apply your talent to make changes. The equivalent German term, *Ehrgeiz*, which literally translates as 'greed for honour/glory', has negative connotations. It suggests a self-interested desire to achieve personal goals such as success, recognition, influence, control, knowledge or power. In the English-speaking world, ambition doesn't have these negative connotations, or at least not to the same degree. It is a more positive term, referring to a 'desire to achieve a particular end' (Merriam-Webster, 2022). Ambition is a prerequisite for a high-flying career (Assig, 2012).

Ambition is a classic case of double standards being applied to men and women. In male entrepreneurs and businessmen, it's a quality that is celebrated, while in women in the same position it is seen as something negative. Voters don't trust female politicians who are too 'ambitious', and powerful women are seen as 'unlikeable'. Sociocultural influences, which vary depending on context, cause women to curb their ambitions and set their goals too low.

Spanish CEO: I think that's maybe one reason. I'm not certain, but it's a kind of intuition. I think that men compete more aggressively. When you have to fight to get a position, a promotion, a man is more aggressive. He's ready to go further than a woman, who is able to take some distance from the situation. She's not ready to do whatever is needed to get the position. You know what I mean? The men are ready to kill to get the position, whereas the majority of women are not that aggressive in their pursuit of their personal goals. I think that a man, in order to get a position, is willing to openly criticise his competitors, and he's often able to put some obstacles in their way to make it easier for himself to get the job. I think that women have a more ethical attitude. I think they're much less aggressive and violent. They're much more moderate. It's obvious that they're going to try, saying, 'OK, I'm the best candidate,' but they won't do morally questionable things. I would say, Whereas the men, I think they're much more prepared to do so.

Another study (Kray et al., 2017) investigates how fixed beliefs about gender and gender roles in Western cultures affect our perceptions of each other, and argues that men and women in certain societies adopt predefined, gender-specific roles that are continually legitimised by social expectations. These expectations are often shaped by psychological stereotypes about who is suited to particular roles. Leaders are regarded as aggressive and dominant, qualities normally associated with men. Seeing women in male occupations can, depending on a person's socialisation, lead to cognitive dissonance and weaken beliefs in fixed gender roles. One possible way out of this dilemma would be a 'dual power' approach, which recognises the value of both traditionally male and traditionally female leadership qualities.

> *Dutch CEO: One word that pops into my head is determination. I love that people are determined and they want to make things happen. My wife Eva, for example, is very determined to make it work and you feel that in everything she does. Some female leaders in our company are also really determined to make it work, and there's a lot of passion there. We have one female leader who's around forty, is head of our research division and loves the research. She loves supporting clients. In everything she does, you feel that determination. That's why she was promoted.*
> *She's also a person who goes out for a drink, and then also literally at three o'clock goes to the hockey match or whatever. She's very open about her goals. That's just how I want leaders to be. If women aren't very clear about where they want to go, how are things going to change?*

The traditional expectation in many parts of the world is that women will primarily focus on serving others and furthering their ambitions. The extent to which gender roles are seen as fixed and immutable varies according to sociocultural context. In Japan, a gendered division of roles is still very much in evidence. In many Communist-influenced countries, by contrast, traditional roles have become more fluid after several generations of women in full-time employment, including in typically male occupations such as engineering and roadbuilding. People's self-perceptions are always influenced by social stereotypes, which is why many women find it difficult to admit to their ambitions. A person's willingness to embrace their ambitions also depends on the prospects of achieving success and recognition. This is problematic for women, as they often get less recognition for their accomplishments. Another factor that limits women's ambitions is their fear of failure.

The men's remarks on this point reveal some sociocultural differences. Men from Communist-influenced countries were more critical of women with unclear ambitions than men from societies that emphasise women's role as mothers.

> *Russian CEO: I would say it doesn't matter whether you're a woman or a man, what really matters is your personality. If a person has a goal and wants to change something, then they'll take the path corresponding to that plan, so they can get to that outcome. Some women have been brainwashed to think they have to sit at home and raise their kids. They find convenient excuses like, 'Oh, the world is*

terrible, with those men who go out for beers and form their cliques.' Or, 'It was glass ceilings that stopped me from succeeding.' I see lots of female CEOs in Russia and China who are very successful and wealthy. They say, 'Beer and barbecues? Who's stopping me from joining in?' Or, 'I succeeded because I worked hard and didn't just get drunk like the guys.' We're not in countries like Afghanistan where women have no rights. If we're talking about Europe, or Russia, then it's all down to individual attitude.

Australian CEO: She needs to speak up louder and push her career agenda and take some risks. She must make clear in the company what her targets are and what her skills are. And she must say clearly what support she needs.

French CEO: You have your own vision, your own project, and then you follow that project. Maybe women could have different ambitions in life, outside of work. You might have the ambition of having a well-controlled life or a good friendship or other things. I think in this respect, women are more diverse than men, although with the new generation it's changing a lot. With the new generation, things are much more even.
When I came out of school, I was clear that my objective was to develop a career. There wasn't even a question about it. I think today, with younger generations, it's very different. Younger men and women are more similar now. At my age, for me as a man it wasn't the same, the only path for me was to develop a career in a company. Again, I think women have always had a little bit more of an open mind about life and all the things you can do. The younger generations are more like that.

Women who understand the system at their company and look for allies

There are three factors that distinguish successful top managers. Firstly, they identify, analyse and make use of the power dynamics at their company and position themselves accordingly. Secondly, they study the logic of career progression in their company and make sure they understand it. Many women still believe that they will earn promotions by doing their job well, and don't pay enough attention to the rules that determine how senior positions get filled. For instance, they may not realise they won't be able to progress at their current company unless they're willing to relocate, and may need to switch to a different company if they want to advance in their career. Regularly reviewing their goals and comparing them with the system in their current company can help women to better understand the career opportunities and requirements at that company. Thirdly, successful leaders build up a close-knit network of internal and external allies who will support and defend them in difficult situations. Since women are still a minority in senior management, these factors are very important for them to progress further up the ladder. All three should ideally be developed early on in their careers, alongside other management skills. It would seem that many women focus more on developing and strengthening their professional skills, and neglect these crucial factors.

Dutch CEO: They weren't part of the network, had no ties to the management team. Normally, it was a personal decision. It wasn't that they had to leave the company. More that they simply didn't play *the game. In a certain sense, that's about adaptability and understanding the system, having a feel for it and being able to find a role for themselves within it. They need to find a balance with it, and of course they need to link themselves into that network. A few women do come to mind. They were heading up project management and were completely absorbed in the planning and so on. At the end of the day, it's about people, and that determines eighty per cent of your success. What matters is how you treat people. Can you inspire them? Can you motivate them? If you forget that, there's no place for you on the board.*

Chinese CEO in Hong Kong: I'm thinking about some examples of successful women. They did a good job of connecting with their peers and other departments, and really creating a strong relationship, a lot of trust, a lot of collaboration, both with men and women. Perhaps it's easier for them to create a relationship with a woman here. My head of HR, for example, was a woman in both cases, but I think she worked really hard on her relationships with her male counterparts. This particular individual had created a bit of an island that didn't serve her well. Again, I feel that's happened with men as well, but I think it goes back to the point I made earlier about the importance of really trying to create those strong peer-to-peer relationships with both men and women around the work we're doing, so you can get the support, so they can have your back when you need it. And you will.

From intentional invisibility to intentional visibility

The alpha men have observed that successful women set their own career goals and clearly communicate them to the relevant people – such as the alpha men themselves. Just like men, these women make sure to keep a high profile in meetings and other important arenas, so that they're well positioned when it comes time for promotions. This brings us to the topic of self-presentation, which Miner (1978) defines as the ability to 'stand out from the group'. In social interactions, individuals can strategically control their self-presentation, by both verbal and non-verbal means, to influence how others see them and create the most positive possible impression. There is evidence that both an exceptional capacity for self-presentation and a complete lack of it can be positively received in professional contexts and have benefits for a person's career (Williams and Bendelow, 1997). Leaders without this capacity are seen as more honest, while leaders who have a flair for self-presentation and highlight their accomplishments receive more support from colleagues. The capacity for self-presentation is important right from the earliest career stages. Managers with exceptional self-presentation are regarded as highly effective leaders by other people. However, doubts may arise about their competence.

Research on female leaders shows that some women deliberately remain behind the scenes so they can avoid backlash and conflict, and 'maintain a professional status quo' (Ballakrishnen et al., 2019). This intentional invisibility allows women to 'balance professional and personal demands while projecting an authentic sense of self' and 'quietly pursue feminist goals and aspirations at work without falling behind on the feminine demands of their modern partnerships'.

Other studies have similarly found that even women who have expressed career ambitions prefer to remain invisible (King et al., 2017). But this strategy may come at a cost, given the importance of visibility for career advancement (Correll and Mackenzie, 2016; Ibarra et al., 2013).

The women who choose to remain in the background recognise that this can limit their opportunities for advancement, but pursue this strategy regardless in order to 'avoid conflict, project an authentic self, and gain a sense of stability'. The alpha men believe that career advancement requires a certain degree of visibility on key committees, even if they don't see the 'game of self-presentation' as an unqualified positive. They wish more women would clearly communicate their career goals and have a stronger executive presence.

> Dutch CEO: Female leaders are sometimes not explicit enough about what they want. I said a long time ago, 'Hey, I want to be CEO because I want to be in a position where I can be of most value to the company.' I expressed what I wanted. If you don't express it, then maybe you won't be on people's radar and they won't know you want it, and then they won't consider you. Male leaders really go for it. 'Hey, I want to be in that position. If I don't get promoted, I'll leave the company.' And so on. The women always believe that 'if I do the hard work somebody will notice and I'll get the credit', and that's worse. You also need to be your own brand ambassador and show it. That's what I did. Sometimes female leaders are too modest.

> French CEO: When I was young, I already had some ideas of what I wanted to do. I remember very clearly that one day, I wanted to go to the US. Don't ask me why, but I wanted to go to the US. I remember I was working at a French company at the time. I went to see a guy I knew, who was relatively high in the organisation. We had a fairly good relationship, but he was two or three levels above me. I went to see him, and I said, 'Yes, I want to go to the US. Can you send me there?' He wasn't even in my direct line of hierarchy. I was in another organisation. I knew he had an organisation in the US. I went to see him, and said again, 'I want to go to the US.' That's a bold move in a way. It was probably one thing that helped me, because when I came back from the US to Europe I was immediately in a senior management position, which was a big kick-off for my career. If you want it, you might get it. The other thing I remember clearly was a time when I was working for a family-owned business. Obviously, the one thing with a family-owned business is that every morning in the elevator you might meet the owner. That's a slightly different story: it's not exactly your boss, he's the owner. That's a little different. I remember one day he invited me for lunch to talk to me about a new organisation, where I would have a job I didn't like. I told him right away, 'No, I won't do that,' and I can tell you, nobody said 'No' to this guy. Then he asked me to stay for a bit longer, but I moved on. I quit. I said, 'No.' I had no clue what I would do afterwards, I had no idea what my future would be, but for me, my personal values are more important. Respect and recognition are more important than anything else. Each time I find myself in a situation where I feel I'm not being respected, or that I'm being mistreated, then I decide very quickly. I think that helps me as well. After that, I moved to my latest company, and that move turned out to be a good one, because I'm still here today.

Perseverance and a tolerance for frustration in the face of setbacks

One factor that researchers consider important to career progression, especially in management, is a person's emotional stability. This is understood as the ability to rapidly move on from setbacks and to respond to stress in professional contexts in a calm, measured way (Hossiep and Paschen, 2003). Neuroticism refers to the exact opposite: emotional lability. This denotes people who are less able to control their emotions and desires, something that is an essential component of emotional stability (Costa and McCrae, 1992). People with low emotional stability tend to see their professional situation in a negative light, and are more prone to stress and burnout. High emotional stability, by contrast, helps people to tolerate stress and is associated with more robust health. The top managers interviewed for this study believe that successful women have the ability to deal with setbacks and to resolutely pursue their goals despite any obstacles that arise.

> German CEO: A number of different women come to mind. A female colleague of mine who I've been very close to for years and who I'd say I discovered or, rather, woke from a deep slumber, did actually make it right to the top. She's now on the board of a UK company. What made the difference was that she had a certain tenacity to stick with things and a very, very high frustration tolerance. In the sense that, well, you do it again and again, and you grin and bear it if you fail and have to do it again. And that requires tenacity, persistence, resilience. I think that's something special, which other people don't have. Sure, professional qualifications, you would have to say, are the basic foundation. You need to keep your skills and knowledge up to date. But I'd say that just goes with the territory. What really separates the wheat from the chaff is the resolve to tolerate setbacks without being discouraged, and instead to keep tenaciously plugging on, to say, 'I'll show you.' That's an essential trait, to be sure.

> German CFO: One essential quality if you want to progress in your career is tenacity. That means, roughly speaking, keeping your eyes on the goal and always remembering that you'll need an extremely high tolerance for frustration, a great deal of tenacity and resilience, to achieve that goal. And that it won't be simple. Even for a man it's not simple. You mustn't underestimate that. It's incredibly lonely at the top, on the board, and for a woman it probably feels even lonelier.

Men think women should be more decisive and take more risks

All the alpha men said that men and women differ in the way they weigh up risks and make decisions. They gave examples from a range of cultural contexts.

Leaders have to take decisions on a daily basis and these decisions involve risk. Research, however, has found that women tend to make less favourable risk decisions than men. Like leadership, risk-taking has long been viewed as a hallmark of hegemonic masculinity. Socially, women are stereotyped as 'highly risk-averse'. Arnett (1992) theorises that a person's risk-taking depends on two factors: endogenous tendencies, such as a desire for attention, and cultural restrictions on risk-taking, such as laws, norms and educational practices. Cultural influences can reduce but do not wholly eliminate a 'sensation seeker's' tendency to take risks. Arnett cites studies indicating that men's greater propensity for risk-taking is consistent across different cultures.

> British CEO: I think this agreeableness, when it's at a critical balance, is helpful for a team to try to come to a consensus, to try to evaluate more of the scenarios that a situation could result in. For a man, sometimes that's like, 'Oh, my God, we've slowed everything down.'

French CEO in Thailand: Successful women have energy, more energy than other women, and natural leadership: when they speak, people listen to them. You don't learn that in school. You either have natural authority and leadership or you don't. These women know how to manage people, they accept the need to take risks, they're not permanently protecting themselves. They accept they have to take some risks and consequently accept responsibility for the results. They're responsible and accountable, which aren't easy qualities to find, especially here in Thailand. Many people are good, smart, very clever, but don't like to take risks. They're always happy to stay in their comfort zone and would never put themselves in jeopardy.

They would prefer to sit down and let somebody else take responsibility or take initiative. That's how you make the selection. You need energy, you need leadership, natural leadership. Then you need to be organised and have minimum technical skills, of course. Also, you need to have a sense of responsibility. You need to be happy to take responsibility, which means risk, because you can't do business with no risk.

Wilson and Daly (1985) similarly note that differences between men and women are not observable in all cultural contexts, but that in contexts where there is greater divergence between the sexes men tend to take more risks. They argue that a 'taste for competitive risk taking' is an 'aspect of masculine psychology' that evolved in primate societies in response to competition. According to their theory, competition forces dominant individuals to take risks to attain positions of power. The greater the reward gap between winners and losers, the more incentive there is to take risks. This implies that men will only have a greater propensity to take risks than women in competitive situations where there is a large reward gap; in other contexts, the difference between men and women would presumably be less.

Risk-taking may be viewed as 'unfeminine' and contrary to established norms. Maxfield et al. (2010) surveyed 661 female American managers and found that women take risks too. Risk-taking is motivated by factors such as power, self-efficacy and networks. Nonetheless, the stereotype that women are risk-averse persists, in part due to the low visibility of women's risk-taking. According to the authors, this invisibility is a product of society and women themselves. They surmise that the reason American society does not notice women taking risks is that they are not culturally expected to. Women tend to be more modest about their risky decisions and often use the collective 'we' when talking about their own accomplishments, which shifts some of the responsibility for those decisions to other people (Tannen, 1993).

Spanish CEO: I think that one fundamental selection criterion is the ability to make decisions quickly and execute them efficiently. It's true that – and I don't know if it's due to genetics, or if it's the nature of women, or if it's the education of generation after generation of women – it's true that for many years it was difficult to find women who were ready to make quick and fast decisions on their own. Maybe it was due to the need for consensus, maybe it was the need to get everybody to agree on something, but it's true that it was very often missing among women, the ability to make fast and agile decisions in a region like mine, where the environment evolves very quickly.

When I chose the four women who today are managing directors or CEOs in my region, that was one fundamental factor. Apart from all the traditional positive points that female executives have, they also have this ability to make fast decisions and to convert decisions into actions pretty quickly. I like this action orientation very much, and for me it was an important factor for choosing those women rather than others. My world is my world, so I don't know if it's representative of the whole reality.

Probably not, but when it comes to decision-making ability and action orientation, I think these qual-
ities are more common in men than in women. I think men might make decisions faster because they
need less explanation. I think that, generally speaking, women are more analytical and they need to
have reasons for each decision. Whereas men – I mean, they're not stupid, and they also need a ra-
tional decision, but they're more inclined towards a fast decision-making process without getting all
the details and without getting all the reasons.

Deborah Tannen's (1993) sociolinguistic work explores differences in men's and wom-
en's decision-making. According to her theory, men understand the world as a hierarchical social order in which each individual is placed either higher or lower than others. Conversations are negotiations in which they need to win or maintain the upper
hand. For men, what's at stake in conversations is their status and independence.
This affects their decision-making: decisions are often simply taken, without them necessarily seeking consensus first. By contrast, women understand the world as a network of interpersonal ties. Conversations are negotiations of emotional closeness, in
which people give affirmation and support and try to achieve consensus. The ultimate
goal is intimacy and the avoidance of isolation, in pursuit of which differences are
minimised and consensus is sought. Decisions are therefore discussed before being
made.

Spanish CEO: Frankly speaking, I believe that a diverse organisation is by definition stronger than a
monolithic organisation. For sure, you also need to create the conditions for you to run the business
at the right speed and on the right path. What I'm going to tell you is very personal, but I think that
a leader is much more than somebody who is there counting the votes or the opinions on one subject.
My role is not to say, 'OK, who wants to go on vacation to London and who wants to go to Paris?'
Then three people want to go to Paris and four want to go to London. I disagree with this democratic
view of the role of the leader. In any case, it doesn't work in countries like China, in countries like
Japan, in countries like Korea and so on. I think that a leader is somebody who gets input from the
team and creates the conditions for the team to provide him with the best inputs individually and
collectively; and then, having listened to everyone and having taken in that input, makes a decision,
no matter if eighty per cent are in favour or against. For sure, it's better to have everybody in favour.
I like to say to my teams who are working with me that there are two different phases. The first is
the discussion phase, and the second is the decision phase. During the discussion phase, we're all
equals, and my role is to create the conditions for everybody to express his or her opinion freely
and without any constraint. I really like people who are independent and who express their opinion
without considering what I want to hear. After that, the decision is made and everybody has to make
the decision their own decision. I hate, for example, people who say, 'OK, I want to go to Paris on
vacation.' Then I say, 'No, we're going to go to London.' And then before we board the flight to Lon-
don, that guy says, 'You see, it's raining in London. I told you that we should go to Paris.' That's over.
The decision has been made. We all have to collectively and individually abide by that decision.

Japanese CEO: There's still the argument in my generation that women are always avoiding the final
decisions, always listening. They are good listeners, good at hearing various options. But in the end,
we have to make a final decision in a short time. Quickly. Women are always wondering about de-
tails. Women are better at getting opinions, comments and suggestions. Thanks to this communica-
tion ability, we're strongly motivated to freely express new ideas. This changing environment may be
the right thing one day even though one day earlier it wasn't, because the atmosphere has changed.
Like in the situation of investing money in a bank. There are a lot of choices and then we have to pick
one or two. That's the situation we're facing now in our business, because nobody knows the right

answer. We have to think about what will be happening five years later. Very difficult questions. As I mentioned, men are comfortable working with a military chain of command. They're always talking about efficiency, speed or whatever. What's important is that there is no right answer. We move this way, but the situation changes, and then we quickly have to adjust.

Dutch CEO: In general women should be bolder and braver about taking a decision. They should believe in it. I think in general that in order to be heard, you sometimes need to make slightly black and white statements. That's what I often see with male leaders. They have a quick conclusion, it's very black and white and they stick to it, saying, 'Well, I don't care. It just needs to be done.' I don't see many women doing that. It's not my style either, but then sometimes to be heard, you need to do it and just make a decision.
Just go for it, no matter what other people say about it. Don't change course because of what they say. That's actually what I learned in Holland in the last three years: sometimes it's best to make a decision and then stop listening and just go for it. Which is not my style, but I learned that no matter what people say, just go for it. Sometimes a CEO just needs to say what needs to be done. During Covid, that brought me pretty good results.

American CEO: Everything is now going to take ten times longer. What does a man do? Even I do this as a man with mainly female role models. I sit and think, 'Oh my God, I feel like I know the answer we're going to get to. Or we just have to spend the next two hours allowing everyone to see what I thought allowed us to reach the answer.' I think this is where diversity is valuable. You do want to have that some of the time. I use the example: you're on the Titanic. You see the iceberg. You don't pull the crew together to ask them their opinions on what we should do.
On the other hand, if you're just leaving the port of Southampton on the Titanic and twenty-five of the guests are asking if they could have a different type of music at dinner, that we should discuss. Now, I don't mean to demean the two styles, I just think there are times that call for quick decisions. The decision may not be correct, but we need a decision. It's worse to not make a decision. That's where I see some women fail. I won't pretend to know why, but you see them not being decisive at times when that's what is needed.

British CEO: Successful female leaders and some successful male leaders are reflective decision-makers. They don't think about the little details, though they're still thorough. Patient, but not slow.

Women should stay on track and in touch even as new mothers

The desire to combine family and career is a hotly discussed topic in many countries. In recent years, there have been growing calls from women's groups for companies to make it easier for women to strike that balance. That is necessary, they argue, to increase the proportion of women in senior management. The male top managers interviewed for this study believe that it's more challenging for mothers to juggle family and career than it is for fathers. However, views about the balance each parent should strike between work and family life are changing among the younger generation. Further research is needed on this shift away from mothers' and fathers' traditional roles, and how it impacts on women's ability to pursue careers in senior management. The alpha men are aware of this trend, but based on their current perspective in the international business world, they believe that women should invest as much time in their careers as the alpha men themselves do, as men and fathers. They gave examples of women who have managed to do so by switching roles in their families with their partners, who support them fully. However, both men and women who have already made it into senior management positions doubt that a perfect work–life balance is compatible with a high-flying career.

> *Dutch CEO: Yes, I get angry when women vanish from the stage for maternity leave. Because I like the idea of flexibility. It was the same with my wife when the children were born: she went back to work two weeks later. You take your time, you sleep, but you don't just disappear. Two or three weeks completely off, OK, but not four or five months. Of course it's legal, but I think it's not good if you're a manager – male or female. It affects how I view that person. It's still different with women, I accept it more, but not with fathers who disappear. Personally, I like it when people are connected when they're around. That doesn't mean they work eight or ten hours a day, but at least they're there. Maybe my point of view comes from China, because people were always close at hand there. If women have high positions and want to become and stay mothers, I prefer it if they're available. Provided, of course, that everything went well during the birth.*

> *German head of region: I think there's a correlation between how much you want something and how much work you put into it. You need to be smart, of course. But I have some really great women here, who do a fantastic job, but they say, 'I still want to have a married life and a family.' And that's important to them. But I think that women who want to get to the next level up are more disciplined. For instance, I know one woman from East Germany, she's now head of Europe or something like that, who somehow managed it. Her husband looked after the kids, and she tried to keep the husband happy so that he didn't run off. But when everyone was in bed at nine, she turned the laptop back on and worked till midnight, and then only slept five hours. She's tough. There are also lots of women who stay put in middle management and don't take this extreme step. They'd be perfectly qualified, perhaps even better qualified, but for them family is more important.*

What men see as women's strengths: communication skills and relationship-building

The alpha men were unanimous about the areas where women generally have an edge over men: women are more empathetic and better communicators.

Academic research has shown many differences in men's and women's communication styles. Generally speaking, women are expected to use their communication skills to improve social ties and relationships, while men use language to reinforce their social dominance (Leaper and Ayres, 2007; Mulac et al., 2001). The biggest difference between men's and women's communication styles is how they view the purpose of conversations. Men see conversations as a way to establish themselves and maintain status and dominance in relationships. Women, by contrast, see the main purpose of conversations as being to develop and nurture their relationship with the other person.

> *Russian CEO: Successful women are able to manage very talented people the right way. They find the right way of communicating and fine-tune it. Women can translate the language of the company's IT workers for clients. They're brilliant communicators. They don't fight with men for power, but, and this is only my opinion, provide a safe environment for them.*

> *Spanish CEO: I think that this kind of aggressive male attitude is gradually becoming much more moderate because of education, but also because of the governance systems that most companies*

are putting in place. For ten, fifteen years, those balancing elements weren't there and women weren't protected at all. These kinds of attitudes were not only not punished but even considered normal. Now they're forbidden in many cases. I think that the sharks are going to become, bit by bit, less dangerous, and then their environment or their teeth are going to be less [chuckles] dangerous. In this new environment, typical female attitudes when competing for a job are going to have better prospects of success.

I don't think the solution is to try to be as aggressive or as violent as some men can be, but to try to intensify this evolution to making the sharks less shark-like, and maybe to convert them into dolphins or something like that.

In *Men Are from Mars, Women Are from Venus* (Gray, 1992), John Gray describes what he sees as the main differences in men's and women's communication styles: men are focused on goals and define their self-image by their ability to achieve results, while women focus on relationships and define their purpose in terms of feelings and the quality of their relationships. Many men respond to stressful situations by withdrawing, while women seek contact and want to talk about their stress. Men want to feel needed, venerated and admired. Women, by contrast, want to feel respected, appreciated and cherished. Men and women also differ in how they interact with other people in situations such as meetings: women are more social, while men value their independence.

Women tend to interrupt less than men. Researchers have speculated this may be due to their lower perceived status (Thorne and Henley, 1975), which is also a reason why women often weaken their assertions. Another possible explanation is lower self-confidence and fear of making mistakes, something that has also been linked to women's perceived inferiority to men. Basow and Rubenfeld (2003) note that women 'use more expressive, tentative, and polite language' than men, while men are more assertive and seek to 'enhance social dominance'. Many of these gender differences can lead to women being perceived as weaker and subordinate in management meetings.

A meta-analysis on gender and influence strategies found that male leaders use more direct, assertive influence strategies than women. Women exert influence on female employees by offering advice or by attempting to inspire or flatter them, whereas with male employees they use barter tactics (Carli, 1999). Consequently, female managers find it easier to build close bonds with other women who have similar communication styles, than they do with male colleagues who do not.

Women are better listeners and empathetic leaders with integrative power

Due to their interaction-focused communication style, women tend to be better listeners. The alpha men described numerous cases where they'd seen women displaying this strength to impressive effect. The ability to genuinely listen is something they admire in many women. In their experience, women are also often more empathetic and sensitive to their employees' needs than men, which allows them to build more robust relationships with their employees and to protect them when necessary. All these qualities are rooted in women's strong integrative power. The alpha men see this as one of women's particular strengths over men, and one that makes a valuable contribution to their work together in companies.

British CEO: The first female manager I had was back in the early 1990s. It was a very different time. I give even more credit to that person for their resilience given the challenges at the time. One thing I did note as quite a junior manager – I was a supervisor at the time and she was the department manager – was that she listened. She came across as actually listening to people's input. One of the male managers in the same factory would listen, but he didn't look like he was listening. He looked like he was just waiting to say what he wanted to say. Whereas this woman, her body language, her responses, her questions, her probing, you knew she was listening. That was something I would say was different at the time from most men in managerial positions.

Japanese CEO: I think women have stronger communication skills. One woman at our company is a great communicator. Both in terms of language and interpersonal skills. She can manoeuvre very well among people from different cultures and adapt to different interests. She'll always get things done efficiently. She has great communication skills. I think she can easily learn what's going on deep inside people's minds. That's a skill set women are sometimes very good at. She doesn't necessarily have great technical skills, like in accounting or tax, but she does create a great atmosphere. Women create a great atmosphere.

French CEO: They're very good at strategy, both of these women. They're very eager to progress and they take advice as a gift. I'm amazed when they say, 'Wow, OK, I'll try that,' and then they put it in place. They're both also really willing to say, 'Well, no, I disagree.' If they disagree, we don't do it. Maybe a bit more than with men.

Japanese CEO: We see lots of ambitious women who are more independent and capable of working in a global business world. They speak much better English, which nowadays is a passport to doing business around the world. That'd be very difficult without speaking English. In general, Japanese women are more likely than Japanese men to speak English and other languages. They're more motivated to be better than men. Do you understand? That's my very personal view. Communication is very important to lead a company or organisation. My sense is that women have better communication skills than men. Men sometimes run things in military style, you know? It's about orders, not creativity – you're given a task and then you complete it. It's a simple, traditional organisational style. Now that's changing with the social atmosphere. Nowadays, we need to get lots of advice, opinions and feedback on the right approach. But there isn't a right answer. In those sorts of situations, I think women are more flexible than men. They're willing to listen to other people's opinions.

German head of region: I don't know whether it's a female thing or down to individual personality, but in Beijing I met her for thirty seconds on the way to the toilet. We briefly talked about the Russia project, and for those thirty seconds she really made me feel like I was the only person in the world. Another example was a Russian woman, hard as nails. But she was always there for you. That kind of protectiveness is perhaps also a female thing. There's a story I loved about this time she found her secretary sobbing in the office because her mother-in-law, who she lived with, had given her a real dressing down again. Faster than you can blink, the manager drove over to the mother-in-law and made sure she knew what an amazing daughter-in-law she had. She then gave the secretary a loan so that she could afford her own place.

Dutch CEO: A lot of successful women are aware of their strength. They don't want to play a game. That's not really them. I think that's really important. They don't try to be strong if they're not. Really staying true to who you are: I think that's crucial. I think that's what I see. They also have a strong sense of what the key trends are, what's happening in society, where we can be of value. They're in close contact with our partners, with clients, and there's a lot of communication there, a lot of sensitivity. They're outspoken about what they want to achieve. What's my goal? They don't tell people what to do but they energise people around that vision. I like that they are sensitive and have empathy. That they listen. Of course, you need to be independent and have your own way, but that connectedness for me is crucial in this network-based society. If I look at where we are in time, then we need to be more innovative, more creative, more connected. There's a lot more networking. Also, if I look at how we work, that sensitivity and that being connected, it's a more female leadership style that's in high demand. It's a strength a lot of female leaders really bring to the table. If you're a female leader and those are your qualities, stay close to them and make them even bigger. Make use of your strengths, make use of your advantages. If you expect you won't be part of the group and that's why you avoid it, then you'll never be part of it. Be bold, go for it, but always in a way that fits you.

Women's leadership style is transformative rather than hierarchical

Women are less hierarchical than men. The alpha men see that as an advantage, as it allows women to take diverse perspectives on board. By contrast with some of their male colleagues, who they find egocentric and authoritarian, the alpha men value the respectful and appreciative way that female top managers treat their colleagues, which creates an environment conducive to good ideas. They believe this transformative leadership style can help to find the best solutions to problems.

Spanish CEO: Men are different. They're a bit more basic in discussions. They agree with the boss. The input of men is not as rational and not as well prepared. Because they have big egos, their sense of discipline is less developed. In my experience, women express their position, and then aren't so concerned whether they lose or win. They're OK. Their ego doesn't suffer. Whereas the ego of men suffers a lot. If one man is fighting in a meeting for something and he loses, his ego is much more impacted.

British CEO: In those days, I often felt looked down on by Oxbridge graduates. I didn't go to Oxford or Cambridge, so I was looked down on by managers who did. I didn't feel looked down on by that female manager. That may be a female strength, but it could just be a nationality issue because she was American. At that time in Britain, class and class structures were very obvious.

French CEO in Thailand: What sometimes makes women different is they're better listeners than men, especially in Europe. They're more analytical, and more easily create consensus and conditions for good collaboration. Sometimes better than men who try to impose their view based less on consensus and more on strong leadership and authority. The women I've had experience with, they were good at remaining calm, creating a favourable environment for discussion and ideas, and were strong enough to summarise, to synthesise and to take the best out of the brainstorming. Whereas the guys would be very good at imposing their own views on the rest of the group because of their education, and they could influence people's behaviour. Even in France I could see that.

German head of region: Eventually, we'll have a world where we swim about like schools of fish, able to quickly change direction without anyone needing to give the order. And I think we men still have a very hierarchical mindset. A certain coldness. I think men feel much more comfortable in the old military commander's role. The worst for me was Austria. They're still living in the 1950s there. Often you'll get men who weren't the most popular at school, like this one nasty little guy who did a doctorate and then suddenly people were fawning on him. Including women. 'But of course, Herr Doktor, can I get you another coffee?' But if you got rid of the doctor title and the suit, people like that would be totally unexceptional. Maybe men have different symbols of power. I think the waiting rooms, the suits, the ties, keep people at a distance and give men a certain authority. And then there was this woman on the board. No suit, but she was there. She had presence. She could be tough. But then she had no luck with the launch, and afterwards was fired. But I'm firmly of the view that we no longer need these symbols of power.

Women should 'stay women' and make use of their integrative power

In the interviews, the alpha men frequently expressed disapproval of women who 'masculinise' themselves by copying traditionally masculine behaviours that the men themselves don't regard as wholly positive, such as one-upmanship in meetings or hyper-aggressiveness. Some women, they claimed, have a 'women vs men' mentality. They regard these women's strategy of staging confrontations with men in meetings or one-to-ones as unwise and counterproductive. It sparks a lot of resistance and makes men who actually want to be supportive into women's rivals. The men experience dissonance due to their conflicting perceptions. Traditionally, women are not expected to engage in the kind of fierce competition that is common between men. In the men's view, women possess integrative power, exceptional empathy and a talent for building strong relationships. This mix of qualities, combined with their communication skills, also makes women good at promoting intercultural understanding in culturally diverse teams. Research has found that Asian women at multinational companies have a particular aptitude for 'moving between cultures' and a global mindset that benefits their team's productivity (Al-Sadik-Lowinski, 2018). Women have a positive influence on groups of men, as they are able to channel men's aggression and competitiveness in a more constructive direction. But in the alpha men's view, in order to exert this influence women must 'stay women' and 'not mutate into men'.

German head of region: Because women often think very quickly, and I find they have more of a human touch. Perhaps that sensitivity is simply part of female nature. Though as I said, that's only true when a woman isn't forced to prove herself and ends up becoming masculine. I think it's a mistake to do that. I've met so many women in that mould, I could give you ten examples. Trouser suit, white shirt, short, dyed-red hair. They tried to act like men, instead of being themselves.

Russian CEO: In the Russian Federation's Ministry of Commerce there were also women in high-level government positions. To give one example: what I observed, firstly, was that she was smart. She was a brilliant professional in her field. She was able to communicate with women and men on the same level. She was able to adjust her manner to the mindset or personality of the person sitting in front of her. If there was a supportive minister from regional government, she would act like a lady, smile at him and act really nice, saying, 'Oh, he's the man, he's such and such.' Or whatever. Because she wanted to achieve the result. She was playing the game, not because of her ego, but because she knew how to manage that person, because she wanted to achieve her goal. She adapted her style according to the person in front of her. If there was a person with a democratic style of leadership, she would act on the same level and address how to deal with or solve the problem. She wasn't trying to prove herself or make the point that 'oh, because I'm this and that you should change'. No, she changed her behaviour depending on her goals.

German head of region: I think that if women were really women for once and men were more considerate, things would be better. We're getting there, but far too slowly. To reach that goal, women need to stay women and not become copies of us in leadership positions.

Men recognise the importance of typically feminine strengths for harmonious, diverse leadership

Managers continue to be evaluated by reference to masculine norms, behaviours and personality traits. We should recall here the 'think manager, think male' phenomenon described by Schein et al. (1996). The alpha men are caught in a state of dissonance between, on the one hand, their admiration for women's strengths and, on the other, the prevailing stereotypes about what a leader should look like. These stereotypes, which emphasise distinctively masculine behaviours, are in tension with the men's desire to see more feminine qualities in top management. The tension between these different strengths can sometimes cause further dissonance. The men interviewed for the study were aware of this complexity. They believe this dissonance will diminish over time, and that an ideal mix of male and female leadership qualities will become the norm in senior management.

The alpha men regard a high level of confidence combined with ambition and clearly communicated career goals as the key factors for women who want to succeed. But in their experience, many women don't meet these criteria.

The men believe men are generally more decisive and willing to take risks than women. In their view, only a few women possess the combination of fast and resolute decision-making that is vital for leaders. Those women who do deserve to make it to the top, and the alpha men are happy to sponsor them. In other words, they reward women whose style of decision-making resembles their own. This contrasts to most of the other areas that have been discussed, where the alpha men believe women should concentrate on their own distinct strengths, and then bring those strengths to bear when they work with men.

The alpha men wish women would make more use of their talent for listening, their nurturing, protective quality and their greater sensitivity. By doing so, they can exert a positive influence. 'Stay women' and 'don't fight with men for power' were common pieces of advice from the men in the interviews. As discussed in chapter three, which looked at conflicts between alpha men and alpha women, the characteristics that the men want women to display are ones rooted in their traditional roles. The men value women's integrative power, sensitivity, empathy and ability to reach consensus. Women are better able than men to 'move between cultures', which allows them to strengthen cross-cultural understanding in international companies.

In the alpha men's view, one good strategy for women to adopt towards men is to focus on developing their own core strengths, rather than trying to copy typically masculine behaviours that the men themselves are often critical of.

A promising route to harmonious relations between the sexes in top management is to productively combine male and female strengths. The dissonance between expectations of traditionally male leadership and typically female strengths can only be overcome if a new, diverse model of leadership becomes the norm for all stakeholders. There are two preliminary stages before this new, third stage can be reached. In the first stage, leaders simply observe the differences between men's and women's leadership styles, and try to understand the underlying causes. In the second stage, they use their knowledge they gained in the first stage and focus on their own strengths. Finally, in the third stage, male and female leadership skills harmonise into something new: a diverse model of leadership. In this final stage, differences between the genders are no longer seen as a source of division, but as something that can help create stronger, more efficient, better integrated teams.

Female top managers on leadership skills and abilities needed for career advancement

The female top managers agreed with the men on many of the points set out above. They too reported that many women lack self-confidence. Just like the men, they recommend that women who want to reach senior positions need to have more faith in themselves and their abilities.

> Russian CEO (female): I think it's the same task for men and for women, but men sometimes have an advantage. The people around them believe they can do it. But women sometimes think other people question their ability: 'Can she do it or not?'

The alpha women often have high self-confidence or have developed it over the course of their careers. A study of over 110 female senior managers from various countries (Al-Sadik-Lowinski, 2020), which coded respondents' self-descriptions based on the Business-Focused Inventory of Personality (BIP) developed by Hossiep and Paschen (2003), found that most responses from women from the leading industrial nations selected for the present study could be assigned to the category of 'achievement motivation'. Achievement motivation refers to a willingness to measure oneself against a high benchmark, to constantly measure one's own achievements, to compare oneself with others and, if necessary, to improve one's own performance. The women in the study group described themselves as ambitious. They set themselves high personal goals and benchmarks, and are very focused on success.

> Chinese GM (female): I should say I'm a very ambitious person. I want to be somebody because at [company name] I worked with many smart people. I want to be my own boss. That's always what I think. I want to be my own boss at the end of the day.

The Chinese women interviewed for this study found it very easy to describe their own strengths, skills and abilities. They spoke at length and without hesitation. None of the women appeared reserved, modest or shy. It was not unusual for them to use super-latives in their responses. The Russian and French women also spoke very directly about their strengths.

> Chinese HRD (female): I am the best HRD in China.

The Japanese women described their professional foundations and keen ambitions very vividly. Their confidence in their professional ability is the source of their strength; they're not dependent on what other people think. They have shaken off their countries' stereotypical expectations about women's roles. Their enthusiasm is unaffected by hierarchical thinking and how other people see them, and it's this factor which is their driving force and strength.

> Japanese CEO (female): I think the most important decision I made in my life was that when I had my first child, I decided to pursue my professional career without compromise. I asked for support from everybody around me, including my husband, my mother, my boss and my co-workers. That was the biggest decision I ever made. After that, actually joining a Japanese company or changing job. Look-ing back, that's not as difficult or as important as having the determination to be professional and wanting to climb the corporate ladder. That motivation and choice needs to come from women them-selves. I would like to be the head of the organisation. That's why I chose this job as a president. I realised very clearly that I wanted to be the head sometime.

The dilemma faced by many women around the world, who believe they need to choose between career and family, doesn't apply to these high-flying women managers. They became aware of their ambitions early on and are distinguished by their strong professional focus. That doesn't mean it wasn't challenging for them to combine family and career. Each of them developed their own individual solutions to manage these challenges.

Alpha women on their decision-making ability

The alpha men want women to be more decisive, with many of them seeing this as women's main weakness. The female top managers who were interviewed described themselves as decisive, but also reflected that women often try to build consensus by compromising. These particular women meet the standards of decisiveness set by their male counterparts, and agree with the men's assessment of its importance.

> German CFO (female): I would almost be tempted to classify women's leadership style as more com-promise-based. Though I personally don't think that's right. I believe it really depends on the issues. And it's incredibly important that as a top manager, a C-level executive, you're able to make deci-sions. That's an essential trait to have. Of course, there are also times when you need to work to-wards compromise. But having just one style won't cut it.

German GM (female): I'm very team-oriented. I'm not a big fan of hierarchies, even though I think we need them to be able to make decisions, but in my daily work it's important to me for us to work as a team. I also know when I need to make decisions. And I put a lot of trust in people. But when I notice that things are getting critical, I get very involved, which surprises people who are used to having a lot of freedom.

Russian CEO (female): I think that I'm very nice but I'm very tough. I understand business from both sides, from the front office and back office, and very often people from the front office can explain anything to their colleagues from the back office. That's why I can allow myself to be tougher, because I understand all the business processes in sales. Also, I am very, very good in terms of serious technical education. I believe that the main quality of a good CEO is to make decisions and take responsibility, and I know that I can do it. I can also inspire the team, and that's another main quality of CEOs.

Chinese COO (female): Before a problem arises, I think we should discuss it. Perhaps my manager has her solution and I have mine. We should put them all together on the table and discuss them in order to find the better solution. I don't like hierarchy. I think everyone is equal. Some people are more competent than others, with more experience or something like that. But everyone should put down his or her own opinion, then we can decide together.

The women's analysis of their weaknesses: lack of vision

Whereas the men bemoaned many women's inability to make quick decisions, in the women's self-analysis the main factor they singled out as a typical female weakness was their lack of vision. They believe this is an area where male senior managers are stronger, and that women need to work to close the gap. The women described themselves as practical in their approach rather than visionary. In contrast, one strength that their careers clearly demonstrate is an aptitude for, and a curiosity about, innovation. Although the Russian women, just like most of the women interviewed for this global study, tended to doubt their own capacity for vision, they were the only group in this cross-country comparison where the majority described it as their core strength. They developed this capacity to aid their career advancement, and continue to make effective use of it. Alongside their capacity for vision, Russian women are distinguished by their ability to communicate clearly, to formulate corporate goals and to develop well-defined ideas and strategies. In the other countries, women who described vision as one of their strengths were in a small minority.

Japanese CEO (female): I probably would say that, in general, I lack it. Some people are really good at being more visionary. I tend to be practical. I'm always inspired and impressed by people who are visionary and focused on the long term.

Russian CEO (female): I can clearly articulate the goal and explain it to other people. I've had great, great bosses who were mostly men. They were sometimes talented. I'm not a very popular person. No, I couldn't say that I love to be in public. I know some people who just have fun being in public and they get energy from people. I'm not that kind of person. But anyway for me it was much easier to cooperate with people and to explain what to do. I'm very open-minded, very well educated. I do my research on everything that's new. That's why I changed to digital when it just started. I don't want to be stuck in last place, in the past. I hate when people talk about 'Do you remember how things used to be better?'

Japanese president (female): Innovation isn't really an important thing, but vision is. People need to have a bigger picture, envisioning what your next five or ten years are supposed to be like. Not only on your career path but the other things you do in your daily job.

Russian CEO (female): I think in the course of my work I have the ideas. I have a vision and a very clear understanding of where we are going. It's not negotiable. I would always ask people to come up with ideas they have. And ask questions. I think in terms of the vision – and that goes back to the transparency and visibility of what is happening. So we do it together. We actually prepare a lot of things together. We throw a few ideas around and discuss them.

Russian CMO (female): In order to be informed about innovations and new technologies not only in our industry, but in management in general, I often invite external experts. So as not to be focused on my own vision, but to get several different visions to combine and get a better picture of the future. But it's not my natural quality.

Chinese GM (female): My ability is to know where the business is going, to anticipate it, to link my actions to the same direction ... to smell the changes that are coming.

Strong communication and leadership in difficult times

The women describe themselves as strong communicators, and think they make better use of this strength in their leadership than their male colleagues. This is in line with what the men themselves said in their interviews. One key consequence of this is higher employee satisfaction. Another strength is that women are better at supporting their staff's professional development, and unlike men they do so regardless of whether they stand to benefit. Women tend to support all employees equally. Men, on the other hand, tend only to foster the advancement of one or two of their closest confidants. The support of employees in general features prominently in the accounts, and is closely linked to motivation. Women see the issue of how to support employees, even during periods of restructuring or cost-cutting as a crucial part of their job.

Another area where women have an advantage over men, according to the female interviewees, is their approach to challenges. In their view, women are better at dealing with difficult situations, in part because they've had lots of practice overcoming challenges in their own careers. They believe that they can accomplish more than men in difficult situations, because men tend to be emotionally weaker in such circumstances. According to the women, they're also better listeners than their male colleagues and so make fewer mistakes.

Japanese CDO (female): I try and explain that this is how the decision is made. It doesn't matter to them, so I really think about other ways to motivate and engage them. I make sure that they have something that they look forward to that makes them excited to come to work every day. It could be a promotion opportunity; even though my organisation is shrinking, I can get creative to find a promotion opportunity. I'm proud that even though my organisation is shrinking and I'm getting promoted to the next level, we still don't have fewer opportunities than the other business units, because we export talents to other business units. I encourage them. Our product may be old, but we have a new innovative approach, so you're getting trained to be the sales force of the future. I try and find these other things, so that they feel that they're growing and developing, so that they don't give up. Those are the things I do.

German CHRD (female): I'm in a position where I'm wanting to grow my subordinate in order to replace me one day. In that sense, I think my motivation right now is to get the next generation up to speed and quickly [laughs]. That's something that I'm working on. Am I competitive to take another job? I think so, because of the fundamental skills.

Chinese GM (female): As a woman I'm good at communicating and persuading. I'm not good at logical talk, but I can convince people with good examples. The disadvantage is that they don't take women seriously (compared to German men). In the board meetings, for example, when I had ideas, at the beginning they didn't take it seriously. That's crazy, as many innovative ideas are difficult to accept at first. I had to prepare better. But here in China I'm always accepted right from the beginning.

German board member (female): I try to work with people who have different strengths. Knowing yourself, knowing your weaknesses. Rather than trying to get strong in the areas where I'm weak, I try to find somebody who is good in those areas. In the past, I was much more sales-driven and not necessarily inclusive. Now, I try to be more inclusive and discussion-based, or group-based, in my approach to decision-making and project delivery.

6 Alpha men's strategies for increasing gender diversity in senior management

A variety of approaches to increasing the global proportion of women in leadership positions have been discussed both in research and in industry. Most of these approaches are complementary. They can be divided into three main categories. Firstly, approaches that seek to support talented women in fields where it is generally challenging for them to pursue senior management careers due to the dominance of masculine leadership norms. Secondly, approaches that attempt to bring about structural and cultural changes at companies. Thirdly, long-term policies intended to enable more women to participate equally in professional life and to influence processes of social change.

When asked about their motivations for getting more alpha women into the top levels of companies, and possible strategies for achieving this, the men gave a host of different answers. They also suggested how their proposals for increasing the number of female executives could be presented in a way that made them more appealing to men. And they see themselves as having a role to play; many of their suggestions involved the alpha men themselves sponsoring qualified women.

Creating a gender-inclusive culture at international companies

The alpha men identified several core strategies to tackle the challenge of getting more women onto company boards and building diverse leadership teams. Suggestions already mentioned in the previous chapters include senior executives sponsoring talented women; filling the talent pipeline with strong female candidates; creating more role models; and establishing broader diversity programmes at companies. Many of the interviewed CEOs already have targets for the proportion of women at senior level, against which they measure their performance. For a majority of the men, one reason they support gender equality is that they are fathers of ambitious daughters. They also believe they can be more successful if they work with women. That means they have an intrinsic motivation to support women, and they see diverse leadership as a key priority. Many policies to promote gender inclusivity have already been implemented at the interviewees' companies.

But how can gender diversity be increased at companies in countries where CEOs, employees and society at large are yet to be convinced of the value of gender equality, and where stereotypes and bias remain the everyday norm? The alpha men shared their experiences of this topic.

The key challenge is to create a company culture where a belief in the benefits of diverse leadership teams is firmly embedded among executives and the majority of the workforce. The CEO has an important part to play here. If they don't really believe in the value of diversity, it will be harder to implement a gender-inclusive culture. However, the interviewees think it isn't enough for the people at the top to be committed to the

https://doi.org/10.1515/9783111172651-006

principle of diverse leadership teams. Rather, diversity needs to be embraced at every level of the company as one of its core values. All employees need to understand the benefits diversity brings, and ideally should wholeheartedly support efforts to make it an integral part of the company culture. At a gender-inclusive company, women will no longer be a minority in the boardroom, but will have a permanent place there – as representatives of half of humanity. In the ideal-case scenario, female senior executives would have a role model character to begin with, but after that diverse leadership teams would quickly become the norm. The gender-inclusive organisation would have a good mix of male and female managers at all levels, and all employees would recognise that diverse leadership represents the best way forward for the company.

The reality at many companies, especially in countries that still have a low proportion of women in senior management, looks rather different. People are socialised to reject mixed-gender leadership. Many men, and also quite a few women, have biases, discriminate consciously or unconsciously against women leaders or are afraid of losing their position.

> Dutch CEO: They won't play along any more. Stupid remarks, nasty jokes, discrimination. If they encounter that, talented women and young people will simply leave. In future, that will bring companies that refuse to change to their knees. We already have too few qualified applicants. People who can perform well in an international arena are in ever shorter supply.

The first step towards becoming a gender-inclusive organisation is to create a company culture that values diverse leadership. This culture will need to be jointly developed by the executive team and the company's employees.

A diverse company culture makes it possible for a wide range of different groups to participate equally. The alpha men identified several criteria that must be met to permanently establish a diverse culture. The most important is that the CEO and executive team must believe in diversity. Diversity also needs to be firmly embedded in the company as a guiding principle. Opinions diverged on whether this process should happen quietly, internally and more or less automatically, or whether it should be loudly proclaimed to the world. The very slow societal shift towards cultural diversity that is happening in countries such as Germany needs to take place at an accelerated rate within companies. This can be achieved by the CEO working with employees to establish a culture in which diversity is an integral value. Only then will qualified women have equal access to top positions and the necessary support from those around them. The men described a mix of top-down and bottom-up approaches to embedding diversity in a company.

> Chinese CEO: I would say that the most important thing is that male leaders need to be more open-minded and understand that diversity is important. Because right now we're living in a globalised world. If you just want to live within your comfort zone, you may not be able to deal with the complexity of this new world. Really, if you want to be successful in your business, you need to be more open-minded. If you haven't done enough to achieve diversity in your company and have more women in your team, you need to change in order to adapt to this new environment.

Chinese CEO in Hong Kong: I don't want to overstate it. As if ignoring the gender issue would be a fatal failure for a leader. I think that would be exaggerated. But if a male leader doesn't understand women's contribution to their business, they've definitely missed the boat. If that's the case, their chance of failing is definitely higher than those who understand the importance of diversity.

German COO: This diffusion of diversity needs to come from the bottom up. I don't think it achieves much to mandate it for the board up at the top, unless a certain mindset prevails further below. A female CEO needs to be able to find allies in the company, her own select group that she can rely on. It's extremely difficult for a woman to hang in there at the top, unless the organisation is ready for it. One example where it worked well was at [German company T], and that can be credited to the two CEOs. They're companions on the same journey, who did all those things together at the start and are still close today. The people in this group aren't young any more, they're now nearly sixty, but back then they were in their thirties, they thought very differently and were far, far more liberal. And they're still very liberal in their attitudes, so that someone like C [female CEO] can stay put, no problem. She comes to mind now as a female executive who endured for a long time and positioned herself accordingly. That gave her the opportunity to build her own power base, thanks to her network and the support of the CEO. But then if you take a company like X or E, there you have an old boys' club. Or a company like L. All the automakers.

Dutch CEO: We want to have an inclusive workplace where people can perform at their best no matter their sex, sexual preference or whatever. I think what coronavirus has brought us is a lot of flexibility. The downside is that work hours can lead people to overwork as well, but we want to be flexible and we're a company that cares a lot about the personal things that are going on in your life. If I look at millennials and young people, who are looking for a sense of purpose, they all want to have that balance. I think this behaviour will die out in a very short time.

Table 6.1: Ten steps to establish a gender-inclusive company culture

1.	Persuade the CEO and executive team of the benefits of diverse leadership
2.	Inform all employees about discrimination and bias, ways to avoid them and the benefits of a diverse company culture
3.	Create a gender-inclusive mission statement for the organisation, making sure to involve all executives and employees
4.	Set temporary KPI targets to increase the proportion of women in senior management and other specified areas
Processes and measures to embed a gender-inclusive company culture	
5.	Introduce measures such as equal pay and flexitime
6.	Establish a diverse recruitment strategy and gender-neutral selection process
7.	Introduce HR development strategies and new career models that take the specific needs of women and mothers into account
8.	Implement gender-neutral performance evaluations and promotion processes, taking account of the 'paradox of meritocracy'
9.	Establish a gender-inclusive meeting culture at the company
10.	Introduce measures to support women, such as information events, coaching for sponsors and mentors and specialised coaching for women

This ten-point plan for establishing a gender-inclusive company culture includes various measures to support qualified women and can be incorporated into, and so help strengthen, a broader diversity programme. The different points build on each other and can help companies to establish and implement a diverse culture. There are a number of studies that provide more detailed accounts of effective HR measures (e.g. Knight, 2017; Regnet, 2017; Vassilopoulou et al., 2021). However, the focus of the next section will be on the key ideas and insights on this topic that the alpha men shared during the interviews.

Alpha men can be won over by improved results

When asked what is the best way to win over male colleagues who are not yet convinced of the benefits of greater gender diversity at their company and have not previously taken any action on the issue, the alpha men agreed that the most effective argument will usually be to point out that companies with mixed-sex teams perform better – and that CEOs stand to gain personally too. Alpha men want to win. That's one reason they rose to the top of their company. And they have a personal financial stake in how well that company performs, so it's in their interest to find ways to improve results. In their answers, the interviewees discussed what could potentially be good, persuasive arguments.

> Spanish CEO: I think that there are two basic arguments. One argument is more about ethics. We want to have a fair world. We need a world in which gender diversity is a reality. It's just a matter of fairness, of not condemning half of humanity to a secondary role just because of the sex they were born into. That first line of argument is about ethics. Then there's the fact that it's proven that diverse organisations are more effective, do a better job, have better growth and profitability. Maybe you don't believe in ethics, you don't believe in this idea of equality, but you can at least be convinced by the fact that if you take a diverse approach, your results are going to be better than if you don't.

Several international studies have found that mixed-sex teams have a positive effect on companies' performance. A survey of over twenty thousand listed companies in ninety-one countries conducted by the Peterson Institute for International Economics (Noland et al., 2016) found that the proportion of women in leadership positions is positively correlated with a company's profitability. Other previously cited studies also suggest that having a higher proportion of women on boards results in higher profits, higher return on sales and improved company performance. Pioneering companies around the world have already recognised these benefits and taken structural measures to support talented women. The right mix of men and women in top management yields measurable benefits for companies, as they can productively combine the strengths and experiences of both male and female leaders. That allows companies to meet their targets and improve their results – while alpha men benefit directly in the form of increased earnings.

Male CEOs who surround themselves with women and appoint female successors benefit in other ways too. These men recognise that women are the world's biggest opportunity segment. Women already have enormous economic power as consumers, and control a large proportion of consumer spending around the world. In most sectors, including the automotive, tourism and housing markets, it is women who make the main purchasing decisions. A company that includes talented women in its management teams as a matter of course signals to its employees and customers that it treats women equally, which gives it a progressive image and also improves sales and results. Another effect is that female role models attract more women to the company. Finally, treating qualified women equally guarantees that managerial positions at all levels of the company hierarchy will be filled by the best people, which will in turn be reflected in better results. The alpha men are interested in strategies that can yield all these different benefits.

American CEO: At the end of the day, it comes back to winning and losing for a man. I don't think we will fundamentally change that for thousands of years, because I think it's an evolutionary thing, but I would try to. How does it help the male CEO achieve better results? Men love winning. I know that's a stupid thing to say. Because you would think everyone does, but men really love winning. I'm not sure that women love winning as much as men. I think it's important for the CEO to actually believe that a diverse group will win more. Sometimes that's hard to frame. If I use my example, the discussion about working from home vs working from the office and the team's reaction, I'm sure most men would say, 'I know the answer,' without involving everybody. Involving everybody is just going to take time and will get you the same answer anyway. Actually, it's about results. It's not about the balancing of working from home and working from the office, it's about the business's results. Convince them that the results will be better if you have more female leaders, who have a different perspective. I think most companies are now coming to this conclusion. Whether it's overt or behind the scenes, most decisions around the globe are made or influenced heavily by women. Most decisions. That's beginning to be appreciated by more and more companies. If they're not listening to the decision-makers, isn't that a problem? I think it is.

Dutch CEO: For any change, there needs to be a sense of urgency. What's a sense of urgency? It has to do with results. It has to do with women actually leaving those companies. If really talented people don't want to work there, and nor do successful men because they want to work at a diverse company. For example, if I worked at a successful company, I would leave if I didn't feel at home there. If I saw women being humiliated, being asked 'Can you bring me a coffee?', and that person then only talking to a male director. I was reading a story about what a CEO said to a senior director, 'Hey, can you bring me a cup of coffee?' Imagine. You'd want to leave that company. You wouldn't want to stay there. Things will only improve if men embrace that idea and have an open mind.

Men find broad diversity strategies more appealing than ones exclusively focused on women

What relevance does a broad diversity strategy, which includes all minority groups, have for the goal of building a gender-inclusive organisation? The alpha men believe such a strategy can help companies to achieve that goal, while also being more appealing to their male colleagues than strategies that focus exclusively on women.

American CEO: I'm at thirty-three per cent. I don't have a target. The head office has targets, but I'm already beating the global target of twenty, twenty-five per cent. I'm not criticising my company. I think we're overall a very balanced company. It's always a little slow. It's slow to truly embrace what diversity is. If you ask a French executive today, 'What is diversity?' they would say it's about men and women. The reality is they're not yet embracing different cultures, races, sexual orientation, disability and so on. True diversity occurs when you don't think about it.

Cultural diversity refers to 'the representation, in one social system, of people with distinctly different group affiliations of cultural significance' (Cox, 1994); these group affiliations can include gender, background, age, disability and sexual orientation. Company diversity policies aim to positively integrate people of all identities. That can only succeed if diversity is embedded as one of the company's core values. The traditional approach to multiculturalism in complex organisations was to expect members of a minority culture to adapt to the cultural norms of the majority group. Over the past two decades, an alternative approach has emerged that recognises the value of cultural differences and seeks to integrate them within companies. This development has been driven by various factors. For instance, a growing awareness of companies' and society's moral and ethical responsibilities towards members of minority groups has prompted a search for new, better paradigms that will create more socially just conditions for those minorities. International companies' desire to gain a global competitive edge has also created more pressure to recognise and act on the value of diversity (Amaram, 2007).

Australian executive: The big thing is, do those senior leaders who are male really understand what diversity is? It's not a numbers game of male vs female. Diversity is about different ways of approaching situations, and thinking and experience and knowledge, and understanding how you bring the most diverse group together to get the best result. I don't think you should be a senior leader if you don't believe that a diverse team is going to give you the best result. Is there further education and training and understanding of the true value of diversity for a successful team? If you don't have diversity in a team, and it can be in terms of age, of experience, of gender, of ethnicity, it can be in terms of anything, if you can't see the value of surrounding yourself with people who are different, who bring different ideas and different perspectives and different approaches to work, I think that you probably have a level of arrogance and ignorance. Everything you do must be perfect because you surround yourself with people like you and, honestly, that horrifies me. If I had to sit in a conference room with five people who had the same style as me and thought the same as me, what would we do? We'd talk about how good we are and it would just feed my ego. It would be horrible. It'd be like looking in the mirror all day, and that would be like, 'Oh, my God, this is terrible.'

The issue of gender equality in management can be viewed solely through the lens of gender diversity, or from the broader 'cultural diversity' perspective described above. The alpha men described the benefits of the latter approach, which expands the scope to consider not just women's interests but those of other groups too. They believe that addressing these wider issues will also automatically reduce problems of gender representation in management. A corporate culture that accepts all employees in their full diversity and treats them equally would benefit all groups, including women.

By committing to a broad diversity approach, companies can make themselves fit for the future. There are many benefits: they will be seen as more progressive; they can demonstrate their social responsibility and ethics; they will create a more inclusive environment; and they will be able to offer more forward-looking services and solutions. The men interviewed for the present study were clear that colleagues who embrace diversity will be winners over the longer term.

German CFO: And to do that you also need to stop thinking of diversity one-dimensionally solely in terms of gender. If you actually want to make a success of gender diversity, actually want to make it a reality, I think it's helpful to expand into other dimensions of diversity. And again I have to say that the UK and Australia, from my personal experience, are far, far further ahead than Austria and Germany, because ethnic minorities have a very different status there and so there's automatically more tolerance, more liberalism, more diversity.

You can of course view it negatively and say that women are being equated with these marginalised groups. That's absolutely not my intention. It can be good to look at individual strands of diversity, good to stand up and say, 'Let's look at gender diversity.' But I think, at the end of the day, when we talk about ways of strengthening diversity, there are approaches like statutory quotas. There's the approach of committing to HR development across the board, with a quota that applies further down, not just at the top. HR development needs to factor in women in a way that isn't merely static, along the lines of, 'One in five board members now needs to be a woman.' That's another way of strengthening diversity. A third is to construe the topic of diversity more broadly, going beyond gender diversity. A holistic approach will ultimately lead to successful results. We need to recognise the interdependencies. What won't be successful any more in future is intolerance: white men aged sixty plus taking big decisions about the generation of the thirty-five-year-olds. And I think this is probably the best line of argument to take. Further strengthening diversity by opening it up to include more than just gender. Having a quota that includes ethnic minorities or ethnic diversity, or people of foreign heritage. So that everyone has equal opportunities for advancement.

German CMO: Equality. And I mean real equality, where people think these differences don't matter at all. I think the LGBTQ discussion, which brings in whole other groups, is also having a big influence. We're no longer talking just about men or women, but also people in between. And I think that'll benefit this debate about women, because all of a sudden we're thinking far less just in binary terms, but also in terms of something intermediate, and learning to accept it.

French CEO: First, to be honest, I'm slightly opposed to this gender-diversity-only objective, because it's becoming a barrier. I'll give you a few examples. In my team, there's a Black guy, named F. He's an MD and after one year together he told me, 'I'm not taking a picture of myself for the catalogue.' I asked him why. He told me, 'Because I don't want to hurt the company. Trust me, I know. If I show a picture of myself as a Black guy as the MD of the central region of France, we'll lose customers.' I told F, 'OK. I'm sitting here and I'm now speaking to two different people. There's F the person and there's F the MD. F the person knows what it is to enter a shop and not to be offered a loan when white people are. You're Black, you need the loan because you don't have the money. That's something he told me one time. I know there are fifty years of this in your experience, which might justify what you're saying. Wow, I can feel the suffering that's behind it. But now I need to talk to the MD. As an MD, are you accepting the racist bias in your company, which you're imposing yourself?' That's the point I'd like to share with you. If we only manage to focus on gender, we're missing a big part of the equation. Another example is that I had an appointee in December, G, as the MD for our mountain region, the Alps, and in front of him people told me why he wasn't a serious candidate. He's forty-six. I was kind of speechless. I explained to them how he's brought numbers up in several regions in the past.

A gender-inclusive company culture with quotas – or without?

As discussed in chapter three, opinions are divided – both among the men interviewed for this study and in society at large – on the question of quotas or fixed KPIs for the proportion of women in top management roles. Until recently, many men and women believed that the goal of getting more women into senior management could be achieved without mandatory targets. In the interviews, the alpha men presented a somewhat divided picture. Most of them worry that quotas or voluntary commitments could 'force' companies to fill roles with women even if there are no qualified female candidates. The majority of interviewees believe that internal targets are a good way to promote broad diversity. However, the men would prefer it if all their male CEO colleagues were persuaded of the benefits of diversity, so that the necessary changes would be set in motion automatically. We can see here the dissonance that many men, and some women, feel. They want to support women, but not with quotas or measurable targets. Some of the alpha men fear that externally imposed statutory quotas will undermine the principle of meritocracy and force them to promote underqualified women to meet the numbers. In their view, diversity targets need to be paired with quality and performance criteria that apply equally to everyone in the company, including both men and women. Ideally, they should be set by the companies' own (diversity-supporting) executive teams, and should take account of conditions in the industry.

Women who have already made it into senior management have other concerns. They worry about being discredited as 'token' or 'quota women', and their professional qualifications and leadership abilities being called into doubt. However, many women who were previously opposed to quotas and targets have changed their minds due to the lack of progress. Some of the alpha men interviewed for this study also support quotas as part of the solution.

> Japanese CEO: I think quotas, like a requirement to reach a certain percentage or threshold, are the most efficient, fastest way. That applies not just to gender, but maybe also to sexual orientation, ethnicity or whatever. I think gender isn't the only topic we need to pay attention to. We also need to pay attention to all other forms of discrimination. I think gender discrimination could fade away if other forms of discrimination are eliminated too.

> American CEO: I tell HR that I only want to see bios of female candidates, in order to achieve my KPI. But in our industry it is difficult to find qualified female candidates. So we set specific targets for our recruiters.

The principle 'you cannot manage what you do not measure' also applies to appointments of women to top management positions. Experience shows that in environments where there have not previously been many women in leadership roles at companies, it will likely take forever for the situation to improve. The effectiveness of specific women's quotas for senior positions is well evidenced (Pande and Ford, 2011). Two key points can be noted regarding the effectiveness of quotas or voluntary commitments. Firstly, success requires the company's decision-makers to believe in the principle of diversity. Secondly, targets need to be translated into clear actions and transparently documented.

A number of researchers (e.g. Regnet, 2017) consider setting targets for recruitment consultants to be an important part of the solution.

> *German CFO: The expressions 'quota' and 'quota woman' have negative connotations, of course. I don't have a better term in mind, but I do think the choice of word simply isn't very helpful. But the fundamental idea of legislators introducing regulations that reveal the extent of the problem and force companies to open things up – they obviously won't do it by themselves, so they need to be told to – that's definitely sometimes helpful. We want to have social change, and society won't change by itself. If that's the case, then legislators need to intervene. I think that's the right thing to do. I know that plenty of women simply say, 'I don't need that, I don't want that. I can do it myself based on my own accomplishments.' But there are far too many cases where their accomplishments aren't enough. And there are organisational barriers. You could say, 'Well then, you'll have to look for another employer.' But we both know that's easier said than done. Going from left to right for a change, taking on a new role, positioning yourself in the new company and so on. None of that is easy. I think on the one hand you have quotas and on the other you have these power structures and old boys' networks. Taking us right back to the start. Companies need to grow out of it, and they will.*

> *German head of region: I think we have to change our traditional ways of thinking about roles. There used to be kings and sultans who had to control everything from above to prevent a revolution. In the digital age, what's key is having flat hierarchies, fewer symbols of power, less of our traditional ways of thinking about roles, more humanity. There are two extremes. One is that we artificially include any women whatsoever. The other is women who force their way in at any cost. We urgently need to change the rules of the game.*

A report by the AllBright Foundation (Ankersen and Berg, 2018) estimates that at the current rate of progress, it will take Germany another twenty-six years to reach gender parity in top management. That suggests, rather soberingly, that the voluntary commitments of the last fifteen years have made little difference (Regnet, 2017). Meanwhile, Japan fell far short of the target of thirty per cent women in senior management that was announced in 2013 by then prime minister Shinzo Abe due to the slow progress up to that point (Johnson, 2021). Successful examples of voluntary commitments and government quotas are offered by the UK and France, respectively. At the largest 100 companies on the London Stock Exchange, the proportion of women on boards rose from twelve to twenty-six per cent in the period of four years (Davies, 2015). This enormous change resulted from a voluntary code of conduct. France, meanwhile, has set a statutory quota of thirty per cent women by 2027 and forty per cent by 2030 (Le Monde, 2021), and has already seen some considerable progress.

For targets, whether voluntary or imposed by a statutory quota, to be effective, it's necessary to address the dissonance felt by many senior decision-makers, who are caught in the dilemma of wanting to support women but ultimately, for various reasons, not doing so. To reduce their feelings of dissonance, they unconsciously lean into biases and prejudices, and end up achieving the opposite of what they set out to. Specialised coaching can help to make them aware of the dilemma and, ideally, re-solve it – and so open the door for them to support qualified women.

Creating female role models at companies

Visibility of female role models in management is one very important factor to per-suade male CEOs who are not yet advocates of gender diversity, and to create accept-ance of more diverse leadership at all levels of a company. These role models are our alpha women: women who have already successfully made it into senior executive po-sitions at companies. Studies have shown that female role models pave the way for other women to follow in their footsteps. This is especially true in STEM fields (Herr-mann et al., 2016). The alpha men believe that greater visibility for successful women could persuade more sceptics of the principle and benefits of diversity. CEOs based in China described the effect of women in senior roles being 'normalised'. The large num-ber of women in top management has led to far wider acceptance than has so far been achieved in countries such as the USA, Germany and even France. In environments where the proportion of women in senior leadership positions is still low, alpha women are still rare exceptions. One example is Japan, where women remain uncom-mon even in middle management.

> Japanese CEO: I think many of those male executives never had a chance to work for female execu-tives themselves. If they were to have that experience, like I have myself, I think the world would be totally different. They might then realise that they're too biased about the role of gender in business settings. Once they have real experience working for a female boss, they may understand. I think they'd easily see there's no difference at all working for a male boss or a female one. Then that per-son could advocate for more women being promoted.

A lack of women in management or the existence of thinly veiled discrimination sends the message that women 'don't belong' in certain positions, industries or fields of study, which in turn diminishes women's interest in them. Enduring stereotypes about some degree subjects and professions also create barriers that discourage women from pur-suing certain careers (Steffens and Roth, 2016).

Role models are important motivators, who show women the goals they can aim for and how to achieve them (Herrmann et al., 2016). Effective role models must be seen as competent and must belong to the same gender or ethnic group (Lockwood and Kunda, 2006). Marx and Ko (2012) describe how direct contact with a role model is not necessary; what matters is awareness of the role model's achievements.

However, if a role model's achievements appear unattainable, this can lead to neg-ative social comparison (Collins, 2013). Lockwood and Kunda (1999) found that role models were effective when 'neutral-primed' participants were asked to think about their current professional self. Role model interventions reduce concerns about wom-en's representation in fields typically associated with men and help to combat stereo-types. Encountering a female role model increases career motivation and ambitions, fosters stronger identification with senior management roles, enhances women's performance and reduces internalised stereotypes that hold women back. These factors apply to female role models in management. Male role models tend to reduce women's interest and sense of belonging. Studies on identity-based motivation have shown that perceptions of a strong connection with one's own future self can bolster motivation. For instance, role models can show the benefits of perseverance in difficult times (Oyserman et al., 2006).

> *French CEO in Asia: If you take all the KPIs, we have what we call policy deployment with six strategy pillars. Four of them are managed by women. My successor, because we already know who my successor will be, is a woman. That's quite unique and not only because of me, it was already the case with my predecessor. For some reason, he had to reshape his organisation, and he found that the best candidates available at that time were women, and he selected them. It also looks like they are more loyal to the company, they stay a bit longer than men, so after a while you now have more and more women. They are performing – I won't say better than men, it doesn't mean anything to say better – but as well as men. We have more loyalty, probably more patience, less job hunting and maybe more dedication to the company. The most difficult thing is to fill in the pipe at the beginning with a sufficient number of young executives. Then you let them take more responsibility at a high level in the company. One day, twenty years later, they tend to have access to the top management roles. If you have nothing in the pipe, it's difficult. You can hire from outside, but then there's the company culture. Here we have a mix of women who joined the company five, six, seven years ago, and women who started here fifteen, twenty years ago. We have a mix of that.*

> *Australian CEO: I grew up with a very strong female presence around me, and it's ingrained in me that women are powerful, they're capable, they're competent and they can be senior to you because they're all older than me. You go to them for advice and you trust them. I always had that example around me growing up and I think it definitely influenced me. It feels just normal to me, but I've never seen anything different. I've never seen women around me who are incapable or incompetent or can't be somebody who I look up to and respect. I think that if growing up you're surrounded by women who are people you respect, it influences you.*

Much research on female leadership is based on the assumption of sisterhood and solidarity between women (Mavin, 2006). Women, it is assumed, will see other women as their natural allies. But that isn't always the case. Women who defy these expectations are often condemned for failing to support other women. They're seen as the 'wicked stepmother' rather than the 'good fairy'. For instance, the international press labelled Margaret Thatcher, Britain's first female prime minister, a 'queen bee' because she didn't further the careers of other women in her cabinet. The queen bee label is applied to women who seek to distance themselves from other women in organisations where the majority of leadership roles are held by men. These women strive for individual success by adapting to the organisation's predominantly masculine culture (Kanter, 1977; Staines et al., 1974). Examples from the literature of women who exhibit such behaviour stretch back decades. In male-dominated organisations, rather than showing solidarity with their fellow women, some women take the side of the status quo. They turn on other women, ignore disparaging remarks about them and refuse them any loyalty or respect (Nieva and Gutek, 1981).

However, it's questionable how much credence the theory of a 'queen bee syndrome' should be given, as it's difficult to establish a causal link between women's behaviour and the low proportion of women in top management positions. A report by Deloitte (2017) shows that organisations with women CEOs have almost twice as many women on their boards as male-led organisations.

Many authors argue that the prevalence of women in top positions depends on how women themselves respond to the stereotypes – still socially accepted in many countries – according to which men are better suited to leadership roles. These stereotypes insinuate that typically female traits are incompatible with the qualities needed by leaders. If more women make it to the top levels of companies, this will help to combat stereotypes and transform management norms (Arvate et al., 2018). In other words, the more visible women become in positions of power, the less that exclusively masculine stereotypes of leadership will dominate in organisations, which in turn will weaken the cognitive structures underlying the global 'think manager, think male' phenomenon (Schein et al., 1996). Seeing female role models increases other women's self-efficacy, that is, their belief in their ability to perform certain tasks. Having a high number of women in management reduces negative stereotypes among men and women alike (Hoyt and Simon, 2011).

> *Dutch CEO: It will change a little bit if they have more female leaders and if you have role models who are also involved in making those decisions. I was reading about the company that dislodged the boat that got stuck in the Suez Canal. The top team was completely male. I read that one of them actually said, 'It's also our culture that we're non-sensory.' All these biases about women. What he should understand is that if he had a diverse team, the company would do a lot better and be a lot more innovative. What happened at his company is that they made some acquisitions and there was a cultural clash and it didn't work out. He's called the Bulldozer. There was an interview and he was complaining about some of the mergers that didn't work. If he'd adopted a more female leadership style, with more listening, more understanding of cultural patterns, more looking from a systematic or systemic perspective, imagine what the company's results would have been. And just think how much shareholder value has been lost by this macho leadership. It really helps if you want to get a ship out of the Suez Canal in a few days, but not if you want to grow your company, not if you want to buy a company, not if you want to work together with other companies. Then you'll hit a wall for sure.*

Alpha men want to act as sponsors for alpha women

Given that they are still a minority in management, and continue to face challenges and barriers because of their sex, sponsorship can be a very effective career development strategy for women, perhaps even an essential one (Rastetter and Cornils, 2012; Tharenou et al., 1994).

The alpha men interviewed for this study regard sponsorship as one of the most important ways to support qualified women. And they conversely see their own role as being to sponsor talented women who want to pursue an executive career.

The terms sponsorship and mentoring are often used interchangeably in management practice and theory, even though they refer to different approaches, albeit ones that can be used synergistically by experienced leaders. Sponsorship and mentoring help women to expand their network and build lasting, career-promoting relationships. They also provide opportunities to receive constructive feedback and learn from the experiences of senior executives.

The main difference between mentoring and sponsorship is that the former primarily concentrates on the experienced manager sharing their expertise and helping the mentee to develop their leadership skills and industry knowledge. Ragins (1997) emphasises the importance of mentoring for women: 'Mentoring relationships, while important for men, may be essential for women'. Sponsorship, by contrast, aims to raise women's visibility in important decision-making forums and help get them assigned to key projects. A sponsor makes sure that their protégé's name is included among the candidates considered for promotion and helps them to secure opportunities for advancement.

> *Spanish CEO: It's a little bit dangerous. Let me explain. I think that it's good we support women, but there's a kind of paternalistic attitude. 'It's OK, ladies, don't worry. The superhero is here and he's going to create the conditions for you to succeed.' The regard this shows to women is a little bit paternalistic. We're still in the same culture of, OK, they're like fragile animals that we need to protect, because without the protection of the superleader, without the protection of the superman, they won't survive. It's true at the same time that if you don't put in place the right mechanisms to avoid the kind of behaviours I've described, then the competition for a promotion won't be well balanced. We have to have both, that genuine attitude of protection but without any kind of paternalism.*

Sponsors introduce women to their networks. Mentors, by contrast, help women to build their own networks. That makes mentoring closer to coaching. Sponsors generally work in the same organisation, but that isn't necessarily the case for mentors. Definitions that encompass both mentoring and sponsorship describe two key factors: career development and psychosocial support. The former includes tasks such as coaching and protecting the mentee. A sponsor also helps boost their protégé's visibility by having them assigned to important and challenging projects. Psychosocial support, meanwhile, refers to factors such as encouragement, advice and feedback that help the mentee become more confident, competent and effective. The benefits of mentoring and sponsorship can be divided into those that can be measured objectively, such as promotions and salary, and subjective criteria, such as how satisfied they feel with their work and how committed they are to their career.

Previous research has tended to focus on the impact of mentoring on women's careers. From the alpha men's responses, it's clear they primarily see their role as that of a sponsor, supplemented by certain aspects of mentoring.

> *Australian CEO: We need more guys to open the door for women. Because, unfortunately, the people behind the door, who are keeping the door closed, are mostly guys. The ones who are in the room already, where we need more diversity, should open the door. It makes it easier. Clearly, that*

would have to be a man because if there are one hundred people in a room and eighty of them are men, then it's easier to find a guy to open a door than to focus on the women.

In sum, studies comparing the effects of mentors and sponsors on women's and men's careers show that women primarily benefit in terms of career progression, while psychological effects are less pronounced (Lyness and Thompson, 2000). Sponsors focus their attention less on psychological aspects of women's career development and more on providing strategic support and protection within their organisation's systems – often in a way that aligns with the sponsors' own objectives (Allen et al., 2004).

Table 6.2: Tasks of female leaders' sponsors

Before promotion:	1. *Clarify ambitions**
	2. *Boost self-confidence**
In the run-up to a promotion:	3. **Create opportunities for visibility**
	4. **Open up networks**
After promotion:	5. **Assign important projects**
	6. **Provide protection in critical situations**

* Specialised coaching can also help with this

The alpha men are ambivalent about formal mentoring programmes, and want to free women from the victim role that they are often unintentionally assigned by company programmes. They view their own role as sponsors as essential, and believe men in senior leadership positions need to open doors for qualified women with clear career ambitions. Some of the alpha men also see a psychological aspect to their role as sponsor, in which they help women to focus more clearly on their careers and the goals they want to achieve. Through their sponsorship, they provide encouragement and positive reinforcement to talented women who are still hesitant to take the next step in their career. They see it as their task to help women who lack confidence to clarify their ambitions. Others believe that women should do this 'homework' themselves or with the support of a coach. They see their job as primarily being to open doors that would otherwise be closed for talented women who have what it takes to succeed at the top.

Men who decide to act as a sponsor for a woman will, again, need to resolve a certain dissonance: although they want to be supportive of women, some of the interviewees were mindful that if a woman they are sponsoring fails, it could have consequences for their own careers. Women in top management are still the exception in most fields and are subject to a lot of scrutiny. In very traditional environments, men may have to deal with critical reactions from other men – and some women – who are prejudiced against women in senior management. Men who sponsor women also have to tread a 'fine line' due to the risk of being victims of malicious rumours about their intentions.

More positively, successful sponsorship can be a personal success for the CEO, as many companies around the world have targets for the proportion of women in management. But in order to make a success of sponsorship, men will need to address these tensions and the often justified feelings of dissonance they elicit.

French CEO: She was a strategy director working for me, the CEO, and she had no experience in an MD role. People told me, 'But you're an exception,' and I said, 'I was an exception and she's a second one.' What's interesting is that at some point I realised that I needed to defend her very strongly before she joined. Otherwise, she'd be killed and I'd be killed, because if she wasn't my strong choice she would fail and I would fail as a result. When I made my speech to introduce her in the Parisian region, I told the team, 'Guys, this is my choice. You will judge me on this choice. If it's the wrong choice, then I'm not the right leader for the company.' I remember feeling, 'Wow, I hope she'll succeed.' I remember being shown a bundle of pictures of leaders. One was Elizabeth I of England. There are many pictures of her, some from her early reign and some from her late reign. One is her final painting with a sieve, which was used to separate seeds from chaff. She was painted with this sieve and with many men behind her. The presenter's point was, 'What do you understand from this painting?' We all answered, 'Nothing,' and he said, 'The sieve and the men behind, you'll judge me on how I chose the right leaders. This sieve is the example that if I choose well I will be a good manager. If I choose the right person.' I remember this painting, which I can send to you if you want.

Australian CEO: If you have male leaders and they're not supporting female team members, then they're going to be disadvantaged. If you have male leaders who gravitate towards working with men, it'll create a bias. It's exactly the same as if I had a female leader and she gravitated towards women, that would be a challenge for men. There is one element that I have seen data on, and that from conversations with women I know is an opportunity, which is that men will tend to put their name forward for something if they believe they could do it in the future and women will be more reserved about applying for something that they haven't done before or that they feel they may only be fifty per cent ready for. If I talk to a peer of mine who is a woman, she'll be like, 'Well, I'm not sure that I'm ready for that.' I'm like, 'What? You and I have done the same work in the same job and you're as capable, if not more capable than me. Why wouldn't you go for it?' That's one of the roles of male leaders: we provide that confidence and we talk about the possible risk with qualified women.

The men also recognise that women can play an important role as sponsors for other women. Successful women themselves can share their experiences of the obstacles faced by women in management and strategies for dealing with them. Previous attempts to encourage more female sponsors to come forward have often failed due to the lack of available women in senior positions, so the interviewees recommended that male executives get the ball rolling on sponsorship. One way to do this is by launching special programmes at their companies and raising awareness of the main challenges faced by qualified women. The men see their role as being to champion the benefits of sponsorship and encourage other senior male colleagues to sponsor talented women.

American CEO: Hopefully, someday women will need the support of women leaders in order to get to those positions, but the reality now is that C-suite and above is still male-dominated, so creating that support and connection with male leaders is really important. I've tried to create sponsor relation-

ships between my women in C-suite positions and up-and-coming women regardless of function, so that they had some role models. Female sponsorship is important to get the inside scoop on how to navigate through this corporate culture and rise up, but at the end of the day, if eighty per cent of the decision-makers on someone's promotion are men, you need to also create that support among influential male colleagues.

Establishing a diverse recruitment and selection strategy

Executives with responsibility for hiring decisions are, like everyone else, not immune to gender stereotypes and bias (Bonet et al., 2020). So organisations need to implement processes that prevent women's potential being misjudged and the wrong decisions being made about who to hire or promote to management positions. That includes establishing a culture that signals even outside the company that gender diversity is one of the company's core values. The strategies recommended to achieve this goal can be either global or local in scope. Romero (2015) recommends that organisations adopt a growth mindset rather than a fixed, unchangeable one. Organisations with a growth mindset place lifelong learning at the heart of their value hierarchy and help facilitate employees' continued development. Such organisations can be contrasted with ones that primarily look for 'ready-made' candidates who already have fully fledged management skills. Lifelong learning makes companies more agile and flexible, which is crucial to remaining successful in changing environments. Research shows that women place more trust in companies that present themselves as learning organisations and show a commitment to the associated values and principles.

In this context, it's important to assess managers not just in terms of whether they hit their targets, but also to consider other parameters such as the ability to change or to take calculated risks. The findings of Romero (2015) suggest that companies which primarily assess executives based on the brilliance of their previous accomplishments will have fewer women in leadership positions. Companies that want to recruit a diverse leadership team will have more success if they target candidates who are eager to learn. Such candidates are more willing to take risks, more resilient in the face of setbacks and better able to learn from mistakes – all traits that are necessary for innovation.

HR experts must also ensure their organisation has gender-inclusive selection processes. Knight (2017) describes seven practical steps that companies can take to reduce bias in their hiring processes and build a gender-inclusive culture. Regnet (2017) also provides a good overview of effective ways to prevent selection decisions from being influenced by stereotypes.

German executive: If you're a man with that kind of executive responsibility, what can you do yourself? To give one example, I very deliberately said to my headhunter, 'I want a woman as a direct report. I won't look any CVs of men.' What individual contribution can a leader make to supporting diversity? You might ask, 'Mr Director, if you're in favour of hiring or promoting more women, what exactly are you doing to make sure it happens? And what are you doing to make sure it isn't just lip service?' I've occasionally set an example, by trying to do something in our practical day-to-day business.

Dutch CEO in Asia: If that situation had occurred, then I would have known it upfront, and I would probably have stepped away from it for two reasons. I really am a strong advocate for diversity. I would say, 'If there's a woman candidate and there's me, please, by all means, go for the woman.' Because, in my view, it would clearly be easier to move on from this situation than it would be for her, because she will always have to explain, 'Why didn't you get that fantastic job?' That would always be the first question at her next job interview, but not for me. And whatever answer she gave – if she said, 'Well, I didn't like the opportunity,' then it'd be, 'Oh, she was full of crap.' If I said it, people would say, 'Yes, I get that attitude.' If she said it, she'd have to sell herself again. I don't like to be measured like that. If that's where the organisation is at, and that's the yardstick they measure people against, I think that's the wrong starting point. You shouldn't put me next to a woman in a position where both of us are competing for a job.

Dealing with the 'paradox of meritocracy'

Nowadays, companies are adopting various strategies to achieve the goal of a diverse leadership culture.

One is the strategy recommended by the alpha men, whereby teams are assembled based on a principle of broad diversity that encompasses not just gender but also age, ethnicity, nationality, sexual orientation and other factors. A common theme throughout the interviews was that the alpha men want women to be subject to the same standards as men in their companies: women should be given the same opportunities for advancement, provided they have demonstrated the same level of performance.

Most company boards now believe that in order to secure long-term success and remain competitive, they need to recruit and retain top talents. This human resources strategy is pursued both locally and internationally, with many companies adopting a merit-based approach in which they seek out, reward and promote the best employees.

This raises the question of how women fare under a purely merit-based HR development strategy. A study of 16,000 leaders using 360-degree feedback instruments (Sherwin, 2014) found that women scored significantly higher than men on 'leadership effectiveness', while men scored higher on 'technical or professional expertise'. A study of leaders from 149 countries (Ibarra and Obodaru, 2009) likewise found that female leaders were rated extremely favourably. These results suggest that women benefit from being assessed over a longer period. But despite the positive ratings of their performance, women still rise through the ranks more slowly and significantly less often (Wippermann, 2010). One reason is that women's career ambitions decline significantly faster than those of men. Findings from the USA (Gadiesh and Coffman, 2015) show that after just a few years of work, women's career ambitions more than halve, while men remain just as career-focused as before. A merit-based HR development strategy does not appear to protect against demographic bias. Research has found that certain gender-based prejudices (as well as prejudices about other minorities) persist in strongly merit-based company cultures. The 'paradox of meritocracy' (Castilla and Benard, 2010) is that formal processes that evaluate and reward employees based purely on merit can actually increase women's inequality. This phenomenon can be counteracted by mechanisms that make senior executives directly accountable and ensure open, transparent processes at all levels.

> French CEO: They assume the same responsibility and the same risk. Doesn't matter to me if they're male or female. But what I hate is when targets are discussed along the lines of, 'That works, but not for me.'

> French CEO: No, it's the cultural, political, social environment in Europe now. The trend is the victimisation of minorities, whichever minority you want to talk about. You just focus your discussion on discrimination, on victimisation. You don't do anything, you just talk about it. I think in China there are now so many women who have access to top management positions that they've stopped discussing it. Maybe also because of the Cultural Revolution in China and the Communist Party and so on. I don't know. It's probably true even in China that men still have a dominant position compared to women. But you don't spend all day talking about that, you just get on with things. So you don't discuss it, you give women the job, but if they don't perform well you fire them the same way you would fire a man. They don't have protection. They don't have special treatment.

Table 6.3: Steps to make a company both meritocratic and gender-inclusive

- Increase organisational transparency and accountability
- Introduce formalised processes for awarding merit-based pay rises
- Implement gender-inclusive performance evaluation
- Establish committees with the power to amend decisions by senior management
- Appoint designated officers to oversee these processes

Adapted from Castilla and Ranganathan (2020)

Raising awareness of bias against female managers

Bias, or unconscious prejudice, can impair people's ability to evaluate candidates in recruitment and promotion processes, causing decisions to favour certain groups at the expense of others. As a result of bias, women are often not considered for promotions to senior management roles, or rejected in favour of male candidates. Stereotypes and prejudices can affect the whole chain of recruitment decisions, from the job advert to the selection and hiring process to the salary negotiations. They can also affect HR development, especially when it comes to senior management positions. This explains, among other things, the discrepancy in the proportion of women in middle and top management. Specialised training can help make people aware of their unconscious bias, so that they can avoid it in future. Studies (e.g. Regnet, 2017) have shown the positive effects of implementing a gender-inclusive strategy for all selection and hiring processes.

Younger generations want new career models

Most companies do not yet have a strategy for addressing the changing attitudes and expectations of the younger generations. Nowadays, talented young men are often committed to supporting their partner's career as well as their own, while young women are no longer content to follow their partner but want to pursue their own professional ambitions. So young couples look for employers who will allow both partners to have successful careers and combine work with family life. The top managers interviewed for this study have observed these trends, and believe that over the course of time they will automatically work in women's favour.

At the moment, international companies are still focused on cultivating future leaders who will follow traditional career paths, which require them to relocate around the globe and progress through different roles and departments (Petriglieri and Kinias, 2020). But they are faced with the challenge that younger people, especially women, will quit if they are confronted by demands for flexibility and mobility. Traditional international career models impose rigid requirements in terms of working hours, attendance culture and multiple relocations. Women can only meet these requirements if their families are prepared to adapt to their careers. International companies can remove barriers to women's and younger people's advancement by allowing new kinds of career models. Features of these new models include job rotations, job sharing, working from home and a different approach to career breaks or lateral phases, which are especially common among mothers in middle management but in traditional models make further progression almost impossible. With the new models, companies can support careers by trusting their employees and giving them a high degree of flexibility and independence, including greater freedom to choose where and when they work. Many executives at global companies, where it's often necessary to lead teams virtually, see this flexibility as an advantage. It's also helpful for dual-career couples. Companies need to rethink the ways they expect their employees to work and the kinds of tasks they expect them to complete. They also need to look at how they can enable more diverse approaches. A focus on employees' autonomy makes monitoring largely unnecessary and increases mutual trust. Instead of targets handed down from above, managers and employees work together to set goals.

Another reason to introduce new career models is to address the psychological needs of highly motivated women. For most women in management, variety and positive challenges in their work are key aspects that can either motivate them or lead to drop-out. New career models can accommodate this fact by linking the acceptance of challenging projects to progression within the organisation.

Research on female top managers from five countries who participated in the Global Women Career Lab found that women's careers follow a variety of paths and patterns (Al-Sadik-Lowinski, 2020). The women's careers were analysed using an international typology that categorises female executive careers into five different types (Al-Sadik-Lowinski, 2021). Only one of these career types, the 'bounded career', is a traditional vertical career where a woman rises up the ranks at a single company. This career type applies to just seven per cent of top female managers in the Global Women Career Lab; the remaining ninety-three per cent built their careers by switching between companies. Most switched locally (forty-four per cent), others followed international career paths with multiple changes of employer (twenty-eight per cent). The far higher proportion of women who pursue local careers highlights the dilemma that expat careers pose for women; alongside the benefits that they can offer, such as being able to work in new cultural environments, they also require the women's partners and children to up sticks too, often taking no account of their needs. That also applies to men. But right from the selection process, women are often excluded due to gender bias, or else exclude themselves because even today international careers still demand extremely high flexibility and mobility from their families. Many women fear they will not be promoted back to the head office and worry about the negative long-term impact on their partner and children from having to constantly adjust to different countries, and so opt for local careers instead.

International companies can use the possibilities opened up by new career models to attract and retain top talents, in particular women and young people, and create a gender-inclusive corporate culture.

Fathers can serve a role model function in companies

There are still too few positive examples of fathers in leadership positions who serve a role model function for all parents in their company. This is due in part to the possibility that it could have drawbacks for their careers. Another reason may be that most high-flying men (and the same is true for high-flying women) have a partner by their side who supports them by taking care of everyday chores and parenting. This traditional division of roles makes it easier for male executives than female ones to devote a lot of time to their work while also being a parent. Evening meetings, for instance, remain common at most companies.

Male leaders who actively play a role in their family send a message to their whole organisation and help to promote the compatibility of career and parenthood (Gaida, 2022).

The long excerpt below from an interview with one of the alpha men highlights the challenges for fathers in leadership roles. It also shows the enormous impact that male role models in companies can have.

French CEO: When I divorced, I felt like I became a man. From a professional point of view, let me explain why. I had a position that many people wanted. My wife and I decided to divorce during that period, which was very destabilising for me. We were living together with our family in Asia. She essentially went back to France for her job. I encouraged her to do so. For many months, I was travelling back and forth from Europe to Asia, which was quite tough for me, because I wanted to be with my kids. My father died when I was eleven. I think it's a consequence of that that I'm extremely close to my kids. I know what it means not to have a father. When she was back in France, with the kids, I was travelling back and forth. Then I needed to make a decision: would I take another role? I had a meeting with my current boss. He proposed a job to me and I said, 'It's a dream job. I'll tell you my only condition. I want this job because I now want to work in a single country with no jet flights. I want to be no more than three hours from home when I travel.' In Asia, I had three passports in two-and-a-half years. The largest version, with fifty-two pages. I told my boss, 'That's why I want this job. The thing is, I'm getting divorced.' I know he's quite traditional. I said, 'I have my kids one week out of two, which is appealing for me. I won't ever miss taking them to school in the morning and I'll be back home by seven in the evening max.' He looked at me and he said, 'Well, you can't have the job and do that.' No, he didn't say that. That's not honest. He said, 'Do you think you can do the job and do that?' I said, 'Yes, I think I can. I think it can have great value by setting an example.' We attached great value to setting an example. The boss would be there when the branch opened, and it opened very early. I had to set an example to the staff as well. The good guys would be there very early and go back very late. When I was in north Asia in 2013, I told the team on my first day, 'Guys, I'm going to leave at ten to six in the evening because I want to see my kids.' It made a huge impact in the company. If it was possible for me, of course everyone would do it. People had more time with their family. Because I was asking a lot from them, they had time with their family, but they were contributing a lot. He told me, 'Right, I understand about the evening, but in the morning, can't you get a nanny to take your kids to school?' I said, 'Of course I can't. If I get a nanny to take the kids to school, I won't see them.' He said, 'OK.' I told him, 'When you say OK, it's not a full OK. For example, you're doing executive committee at seven thirty or eight in the morning. I can't do that. I can only do from nine a.m.' At this point, he said, 'OK. For one year, we'll start executive committee at nine a.m.' In our business, nine a.m. is the middle of the day. Our customers start work at six a.m. It's a bit personal, but I had the kids one week out of two. The other week, I was gone from Monday morning to Friday evening, visiting branches from six a.m. until late evening, when I had dinner with people who wanted to have dinner because I was introducing myself. My message was, 'This is what I'm doing because I'm getting divorced and I want to see my kids.' The first time, I was a bit embarrassed. I saw relief in many people who had kids, divorced or not. They told me, 'I feel bad when I have to leave my kids with a nanny and go to the office very early.' I saw the value of setting an example.

The head of the Parisian region decided to resign because he wanted my job, so he left. This guy was doing executive committee for the Parisian region not at eight, but at seven in the morning. To get there for seven in the morning, you needed to leave home at six. Because he left, I had no replacement. I did my job there for six months, and my first decision was, 'Guys, exec now starts at nine a.m. You think it's for my personal convenience, but I can tell you you'll never have a young mum at this exec if it starts at seven.' Today, the very successful MD of this Parisian region – which is a big region, with forty million of operating income – is a woman with two kids, including a two-year-old. I was able to recruit this very talented person, who would never otherwise have come to us, by saying, 'Well, just look at me. I'm doing it one week out of two. I don't know what your personal organisation will mean, but you can do it.' It's very helpful for me to be able to recruit people not only with regard to gender diversity but also geographic mobility. I recruit a lot of people for national jobs who've said, 'I can't live in Paris,' and I said, 'I don't care, you have kids, you can have the job.' I'm always sharing my experience. I say, 'When I have the kids, I don't shower, and as you can see, I'm in the car, I have the kids this week. I took my kids to school at eight thirty. I left with the car at eight thirty-five and I drove three hours to visit branches in Burgundy. Now, I'm in Burgundy, and that's it.' I made a joke. When you asked what it means to me, because the mentality is still like that I made a bad joke, saying, 'I'm like a mum.' I shouldn't say I'm like a mum, I should say, 'This is valid for all mums and dads, and we have a huge advantage for recruiting people.' They can feel relaxed because they don't have to choose between family and job. Of course, today it applies a bit more to mums, because society is like that, but I'm not sure it's a question of gender diversity. It's a question which applies to everyone.

A company that wants to be fit for the future will need to develop a culture that allows people of all genders to combine career and family. In times of global shortages of skilled workers and competition over top talents, introducing working hours and career models to suit all parents gives companies a competitive advantage. In many countries and international corporations, these parent-friendly measures are already well established. In others, they're still a distant prospect.

Creating a meeting culture where all voices are heard

As we saw in the previous chapters, the alpha men claim that women often don't speak up in male-dominated meetings, especially in traditional environments that were men-only spaces until recently and where women are still in the minority. However, if women deviate from the expected behaviour and speak up frequently and confidently in meetings, they are punished for it in performance reviews. A group of INSEAD researchers (Petriglieri and Kinias, 2020) found that women often get no recognition if they point out problems or propose solutions. They are also more likely to be interrupted in meetings. At the same time, meetings are a forum where participants can position themselves for senior management roles by raising their profile and making a good impression. Especially in virtual meetings, which are becoming increasingly common at global companies, it's important to regularly listen to all voices on a topic or project, rather than some employees staying silent. Certain easily implemented mechanisms can help ensure everyone's voices, perspectives and proposals are heard.

> British CEO: Do you know what I do? I write down all the names and tick off the people who've already said something. And I look at the clock. Then I ask the people who haven't spoken yet to share their views. That works pretty well with the women, and also with Asians who are too polite to speak up.

First and foremost, this requires the chair of the meeting to be aware of the problem and interested in fixing it, so that the meeting's full potential can be harnessed. Measures such as having set speaking times, offering encouragement and inviting people to contribute can help to establish a gender-inclusive meeting culture. They can also help to overcome cultural differences in self-presentation at meetings with international participants, and ensure it isn't just the more extroverted individuals whose voices get heard. Alongside scheduling meetings at times suitable for parents, improving a company's meeting culture is key to establishing a gender-inclusive culture in general.

How companies can lead the way on gender diversity

Company culture has a crucial part to play in getting more women into top executive roles. As its own little microcosm, a company can do a lot to support ambitious women and build diverse leadership teams even in less favourable sociocultural conditions. Creating a diverse, gender-inclusive company culture is an important step, so that companies can then implement specific measures to recruit and develop women over the longer term. One core element of an inclusive culture is a guiding vision that gives women and other groups a firm place at the heart of the company. It's important to raise awareness among all employees of existing bias and stereotypes and gradually eliminate them. An inclusive corporate culture will always trickle down from the CEO, but everyone in the company needs to be involved. It's vital that everyone is aware of the benefits of diverse management teams and is committed to harnessing those benefits for their organisation. Only then can diversity be made a lasting reality.

The international alpha men who participated in the research for this book all support the principle that qualified women should be given the same opportunities as their male colleagues. The best way to win over unpersuaded male executives is to explain how promoting more women will improve the company's performance, which in turn will have personal benefits for those executives. Not all of the alpha men's male colleagues have been persuaded of the benefits of mixed leadership teams or made sufficiently aware of how promoting capable women could further their own goals. The alpha men believe hard facts about long-term profits that diverse leadership teams will generate for companies are the most effective argument. They also favour broadening the focus and talking about the benefits of diversity in general. In their view, striving for equal opportunities for all groups in a company is the right way to tackle the challenges of gender diversity. This expanded scope places less emphasis on the specific issues faced by women and instead considers wider problems. According to the men, solving these wider problems would automatically alleviate the problem of gender representation in management. The men take a positive view of voluntary targets, and also support statutory quotas on a temporary basis as a way to accelerate the pace of change. But they stress the need to combine targets and quotas with clear quality and performance criteria so that they don't become ends in themselves that negatively impact on diversity overall. When asked about specific measures, the alpha men's answers focused on two main areas. Firstly, creating female role models; secondly, men in positions of power acting as sponsors of talented women. The men agree that having more successful female role models will encourage other women in those companies to follow in their footsteps. The more visible success stories there are in a given company or sector, the easier it will be for women to imagine themselves in powerful positions. In Japan, more men need to experience having women as bosses so that they can come to appreciate the qualities and benefits of female leadership. In China and some other Asian countries, meanwhile, the alpha men believe there are already enough female executives. It is striking that the higher the proportion of women in senior management in a country, the more restrained the interviewees were about making specific proposals. In those countries, the men believe it's down to women themselves whether they rise up the ranks or not, as they have plenty of positive examples of what is possible.

Especially in STEM industries, there are often not enough women in the 'talent pipeline'. The alpha men identified this as an area where there are opportunities to recruit and promote more women. The alpha men believe that sponsoring talented women is probably the most efficient approach. They imagine themselves steering the process and exerting their influence. They want to help women who meet their standards of good leadership (as discussed above) to secure promotions by adeptly positioning them on key committees. In some companies this still brings personal risks with it, but the men are willing to take a calculated risk if they believe in their protégés' loyalty and leadership qualities.

Men recommend building bridges so as to make diverse leadership more than a buzzword

A growing number of company boards are opting to create an inclusive environment that allows them to harness their employees' diverse strengths. They believe this will make their company more competitive and secure its long-term future. These efforts include firmly integrating women, who represent half the global population, into senior management.

For women in executive teams and on the board to become the norm, there needs to be a forward-looking vision of gender diversity at all levels of the company, backed up by persuasive arguments.

First of all, male and female executives must themselves be convinced of the benefits of mixed-gender leadership teams for the company, and must address the dissonance that can result from personal and societal stereotypes about men's and women's roles, including in management. Furthermore, they need to understand that a desire for identity exists on both sides and that this influences attitudes and behaviour in management. Only when both men and women find a way to work together as partners, harmonise their strengths and tolerate each other's weaknesses will diverse leadership be possible – to everyone's benefit. Specialist coaching for top executives may be helpful in getting to that point.

> German head of region: I think that if women were really women for once and men were more considerate, things would be better. We're getting there, but far too slowly. To reach that goal, women need to stay women and not become copies of us in leadership positions.

Researchers have linked myriad benefits to diverse leadership teams. To recap: mixed-gender teams are more effective and innovative than homogeneous ones and can develop better solutions to future challenges, as they combine numerous different perspectives. They also increase acceptance among customers and suppliers, who feel equally represented, and help companies to attract top talents, as the next generation of leaders have different ideas about equality than those that currently persist in many international companies around the world.

> Dutch CDO: I think the biggest trouble, really, is on both the male and the female side. The two apparently don't meet in the middle, because when men think about diversity, it means they're getting more women into their corner, and the women on the other side of the spectrum maybe think, 'I need more opportunities on my side.' Both of them, willing or unwilling, consciously or subconsciously, are maintaining the divide, and they're not asking, 'How do we bridge it? How do we make a bridge

from you to me?' Maybe we also need a meeting point in the middle of that bridge. No one seems to think or talk about that meeting point or the idea of, 'If we built this bridge, where do we then meet? Do we meet on your side or do we meet on my side?' That seems to be the attitude. Let's build a bridge and then agree that you meet on my side. 'I'm in the boardroom but you're not, so why don't you come here?' Not the other way around: 'Why don't I leave the boardroom and come to you?'

Numerous studies indicate that women are just as motivated to obtain leadership positions as men. However, this motivation declines over time in companies with cultures that don't view women as key to achieving good results and so don't develop strategies to retain them. Although women's performance is just as strong as men's, and sometimes stronger, few women make it to the upper echelons of companies. For CEO roles, that's true worldwide. The number of women who make it to board level primarily by dint of their own efforts remains low. Women often feel inhibited from expressing their ambitions, particularly if overprotective superiors try to take decisions out of their hands. Discrimination has become more subtle than it was in the past, when it was still accepted by most people as normal. Although women are highly adaptable, many qualified women around the world opt to switch companies rather than adapting to conditions in their current workplace, and at a certain point go their own way and start their own company (Reynolds et al., 2010). Executive teams that want to productively combine men's and women's potential need to understand these factors and create a culture that is not based solely on masculine norms but also incorporates feminine strengths and rejects prejudice against women. It is important that men in general are not denounced as villains or obstacles to progress, and that women stop seeing themselves only as victims.

Some countries are closer to the goal of equality in senior management, others are still a long way off. Companies in all countries, however, need to have a vision of a diverse, gender-inclusive culture where women have equal opportunities to rise to the top. Every company should develop its own vision, using its own words and making sure to involve all employees, that sets out a clear path to this future of diverse leadership and highlights the benefits it will bring. This vision should be integrated within a broader overall diversity and inclusion strategy, and accompanied by suitable measures to make diverse leadership a reality at the company.

In this book, readers have had the opportunity to hear what male business leaders have to say about gender diversity in senior management. It's time to unite their perspective with that of alpha women, so that together they can win over the sceptics and foot-draggers of both genders and achieve positive outcomes. For a new, diverse leadership culture to be established, more alpha men will need to open doors for women – and more ambitious women will need to step up and work with their male colleagues to create a leadership style that combines the best of both worlds.

7 The global research project behind this book

The qualitative study with selected male top managers that was carried out for this book feeds into the research by the Global Women Career Lab, which has been investigating the career paths and patterns of women in top management from around the world since 2014. The Global Women Career Lab offers company leadership teams consultancy services on their international diversity strategies and specialised executive coaching for women in management.

For this study, qualitative, semi-structured, in-depth interviews were conducted with twenty-eight male CEOS, directors and executives from eleven countries: the USA, France, the UK, China, the Netherlands, Russia, Spain, Japan, Ireland, Australia and Germany. The men have also held positions in other countries over the course of their careers. The study participants were recruited based on a theoretical sampling method, with selection criteria including hierarchical level, nationality and having an international career. At the time of the study, the men were working in a variety of industries, including both male-dominated ones, such as manufacturing and IT, and ones with more women, such as fashion and pharma. On average, the study participants were forty-five to sixty years old. In terms of ethnicity, most were white or of Asian origin. The majority of participants are fathers of daughters. Apart from two divorcees, at the time of the interviews all participants were married. The married participants are supported by their wives, who have either adapted their own careers to those of their husbands or do not work.

By agreeing to participate in the confidential interviews, the top managers signalled an interest in the topic of diversity and mixed leadership. Men who are critical of women in senior management are thus not represented in the study.

The average duration of the interviews was one-and-a-half to two hours. The interviews were conducted by the author herself in English, German or French, following a structured script. Depending on the course of the conversation, certain issues were explored in greater depth or new topics not included in the script were discussed. The transcripts were analysed using the method of structured content analysis.

The study with the male top managers was supplemented by shorter, qualitative interviews with female top managers. For these interviews, a questionnaire was developed that built on the findings from the first part of the study. The women were also selected using a sampling method that ensured they held board or C-level positions. The book also includes quotations from an earlier study with 110 female top managers (Al-Sadik-Lowinski, 2020).

https://doi.org/10.1515/9783111172651-007

The roadmap to getting more women into boardrooms: the FemCareer-Model

The analysis in this book makes use of the FemCareer-Model (figure 7.1), which offers a structured approach to the determinants of women's managerial careers (Al-Sadik-Lowinski, 2018). There are many such determinants, which can affect women's career success and career trajectories in a variety of ways.

The model helped to structure the qualitative interviews and their analysis, and illustrates the perspective adopted in the book on this complex topic. Women's careers in management are shaped by an interplay of contextual factors, such as social views of women's roles and the opportunities available to women in the labour market, as well as each individual woman's own goals and ambitions. The challenge for researchers is to adequately grasp the complexity of women's careers and take account of these various determinants.

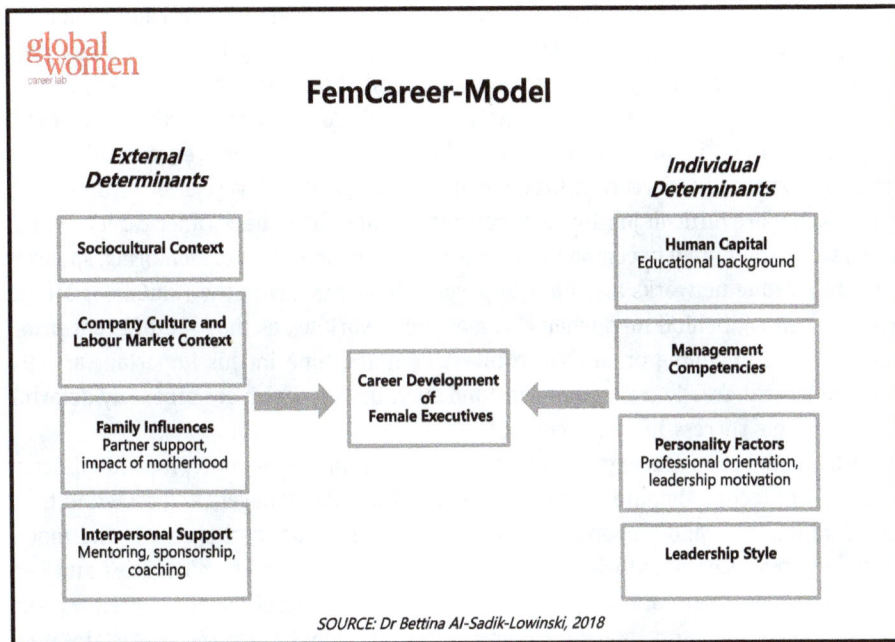

global women career lab

FemCareer-Model

External Determinants

- Sociocultural Context
- Company Culture and Labour Market Context
- Family Influences
  Partner support, impact of motherhood
- Interpersonal Support
  Mentoring, sponsorship, coaching

Career Development of Female Executives

Individual Determinants

- Human Capital
  Educational background
- Management Competencies
- Personality Factors
  Professional orientation, leadership motivation
- Leadership Style

SOURCE: Dr Bettina Al-Sadik-Lowinski, 2018

Figure 7.1: The FemCareer-Model (Al-Sadik-Lowinski, 2018)

At the centre of the model is the career development of female executives. The model provides a framework for analysing women's career paths and patterns, as well as their attitudes to and motivations for their careers. Women's career decisions differ from men's due to their early socialisation experiences and the structural opportunities available to them, which need to be analysed in their cultural context. Although women's career development does not differ fundamentally from that of men, it is demonstrably more complex due to a socialisation process that in many parts of the world emphasises the dichotomy of career and family. As a result, women's career paths are more varied and diverse than men's.

The model distinguishes between external and individual determinants of women's careers; the latter are ones attributable to the women themselves. The first category of external determinants comprises the society and culture in a given country and the specific conditions for women there. Sociocultural influences vary from place to place, resulting in differences in the proportion of women in top management in different countries. These influences include women's socialisation experiences and the political and social conditions for women's careers. Women will thus, depending on which country they come from, internalise different ideas and assumptions about careers, the goals they can hope to achieve and the characteristics of female leadership. Cultural stereotypes are often cited as a reason why women are still underrepresented in senior management. Conversely, sociocultural contexts with fewer stereotypes can positively open things up and create opportunities for women. Another external determinant of women's career opportunities is the labour market in their country and the culture at their company. One factor that affects female managers' careers more than men's is family, including family organisation and choice of partner. The expression 'motherhood penalty' refers to the negative correlation between motherhood and a successful career in management. In traditional corporate cultures, executives can only have successful careers if they put their job first and invest a lot of time in it, which is a more difficult juggling act for mothers than for fathers. Older career models place work and family in competition for a share of women's time. Mentoring, sponsorship and strong networks are other important determinants in the FemCareer-Model. Women still lag behind men when it comes to networking, as they set different priorities and are unwilling or unable to invest as much time in this important activity. Women benefit greatly from mentoring and sponsorship, which are other key determinants of their success in management.

The model contrasts external determinants with individual ones. Individual determinants are factors that are specific to individual female managers and rooted in their personal qualities and personality traits. The determinants on this side of the model include human capital (educational background), management competencies and personality factors. There are certain abilities that any successful manager, of either gender, will need to possess; but since men and women may be stronger in certain areas than others, it makes sense for organisations to try and harmonise male and female strengths. Another determinant in the model is women's leadership style. Particular roles demand a particular leadership style, so it may seem logical that men and women who hold the same role at a company should exhibit the same leadership style. But unlike men, women are caught between conflicting role expectations – the expectation of a typically feminine way of acting on the one hand and the expectation of complying with masculine leadership norms on the other. Women who adopt a male leadership style tend to be judged negatively. So leadership style is not a gender-neutral phenomenon and women need to do more work on this aspect than men if they wish to progress at their organisations.

Both the external and individual determinants in the model can affect women's prospects of securing a leadership role, though the degree of influence will vary depending on context. In this book, the determinants described by the model have been augmented by the experiences and suggestions of the male study participants, who shared their observations on women from a male perspective.

Acknowledgements

I'd like to thank all the men and women from across the world who participated in the research for this book for the time and trust they gave me. Special thanks go to the team at de Gruyter, my translator Andrew Godfrey-Collins and my friend Ian Lawrance, a big fan of gender diversity, who once again supported me by editing the English version of the book.

In memory of Gundula Fichtler, without whom this book would never have been written.

https://doi.org/10.1515/9783111172651-008

Bibliography

Adams, R. B., and Ferreira, D. (2008), 'Women in the Boardroom and Their Impact on Governance and Performance', *Journal of Financial Economics* 94(2): 291–309.

Adams, R. B., and Kirchmaier, T. (2011), 'Women in the Boardroom: A Global Perspective?', paper given at the Conference on Board Diversity and Economic Performance, Copenhagen Business School, 29–30 September 2011.

Allen, T. D., Eby, L. T., Poteet, M. L., Lentz, E., and Lima, L. (2004), 'Career Benefits Associated with Mentoring for Protégés: A Meta-Analysis', *Journal of Applied Psychology* 89(1): 127–136.

Al-Sadik-Lowinski, B. (2018), *How Chinese Women Rise: What We Can Learn from Chinese Women with Successful Careers in Top Management*, Cuvillier.

Al-Sadik-Lowinski, B. (2020), *Women in Top Management*, De Gruyter.

Al-Sadik-Lowinski, B. (2021), *Typology of Career Paths of International Top Women Managers – Global Orientation Pattern for Qualified Women in Management · Typologie der Karrierewege von internationalen Topmanagerinnen – Orientierungsmuster für qualifizierte Frauen im Management*, Cuvillier.

Amaram, D. I. (2007), 'Cultural Diversity: Implications for Workplace Management', *Journal of Diversity Management* 2(4): 1–6.

Ankersen, W., and Berg, C. (2018), 'Germany Last Place: Corporations across the World Get More Women into Top Management', <https://www.allbright-stiftung.de/s/Allbrightbericht_English.pdf>, last accessed 5 January 2023.

Ankersen, W., and Berg, C. (2020), 'Deutscher Sonderweg: Frauenanteil in DAX-Vorständen sinkt in der Krise', <https://static1.squarespace.com/static/5c7e8528f4755a0bedc3f8f1/t/5f7cb22f2f46821aa896e185/1602007640517/AllBrightBericht_Herbst+2020.pdf>, last accessed 5 January 2023.

Ankersen, W., and Berg, C. (2021), 'Aufbruch oder Alibi: Viele Börsenvorstände erstmals mit einer Frau', <https://www.allbright-stiftung.de/s/AllBright-Bericht-Herbst-2021_Aufbruch-oder-Alibi_.pdf>, last accessed 5 January 2023.

Ardichvili, A., and Gasparishvili, A. (2001), 'Human Resource Development in an Industry in Transition', *Human Resource Development International* 4(1): 47–63.

Arnett, J. (1992), 'Reckless Behavior in Adolescence: A Developmental Perspective', *Developmental Review* 12(4): 339–373.

Arvate, P. R., Galilea, G. W., and Todescat, I. (2018), 'The Queen Bee: A Myth? The Effect of Top-Level Female Leadership on Subordinate Females', *Leadership Quarterly* 29(5): 533–548.

Ashwin, S., and Yakubovich, V. (2005), 'Cherchez la Femme: Women as Supporting Actors in the Russian Labour Market', *European Sociological Review* 21(2): 149–164.

Assig, D., and Echter, D. (2012), *Ambition: wie große Karrieren gelingen*, Campus.

Astin, H. S. (1984), 'The Meaning of Work in Women's Lives: A Sociopsychological Model of Career Choice and Work Behavior', *Counseling Psychologist* 12(4): 117–126.

Athanasopoulou, A., Moss-Cowan, A., Smets, M., and Morris, T. (2018), 'Claiming the Corner Office: Female CEO Careers and Implications for Leadership Development', *Human Resource Management* 57(2): 617–639.

Babcock, L., Laschever, S., Gelfand, M., and Small, D. (2003), 'Nice Girls Don't Ask', *Harvard Business Review* 81(10): 14–14.

Baines, D. (2010), 'Gender Mainstreaming in a Development Project: Intersectionality in a Post-Colonial Un-Doing?', *Gender, Work & Organization* 17(2): 119–149.

Ballakrishnen, S., Fielding-Singh, P., and Magliozzi, D. (2019), 'Intentional Invisibility: Professional Women and the Navigation of Workplace Constraints', *Sociological Perspectives* 62(1): 23–41.

https://doi.org/10.1515/9783111172651-009

Barsh, J., Devillard, S., and Wang, J. (2012), 'Women Continue to Be Underrepresented at Senior-Management Levels in Asia, Europe, and North America. McKinsey Research Suggests Some Answers', <https://www.mckinsey.com.br/capabilities/people-and-organizational-performance/our-in sights/the-global-gender-agenda>, last accessed 5 January 2023.

Basow, S. A., and Rubenfeld, K. (2003), '"Troubles Talk": Effects of Gender and Gender-Typing', *Sex Roles* 48(3): 183–187.

Berger, L., Benschop, Y., and van den Brink, M. (2015), 'Practising Gender When Networking: The Case of University–Industry Innovation Projects', *Gender, Work & Organization* 22(6): 556–578.

Betz, N. E., and Fitzgerald, L. F. (1987), *The Career Psychology of Women*, Academic Press.

Bianchi, S. M., Milkie, M. A., Sayer, L. C., and Robinson, J. P. (2000), 'Is Anyone Doing the Housework? Trends in the Gender Division of Household Labor', *Social Forces* 79(1): 191–228.

Bierach, B. (2011), *Das dämliche Geschlecht: Warum es noch immer kaum Frauen im Management gibt*, John Wiley & Sons.

Boll-Palievskaya, D. (2009), *Russische Frauen: Innen und Außenansichten*, Books on Demand.

Bond, M. H., and Hwang, K. (1986), 'The Social Psychology of Chinese People', in M. H. Bond (ed.), *The Psychology of the Chinese People*, Oxford University Press, pp. 213–266.

Bonet, R., Cappelli, P., and Hamori, M. (2020), 'Gender Differences in Speed of Advancement: An Empirical Examination of Top Executives in the Fortune 100 Firms', *Strategic Management Journal* 41(4): 708–737.

Bosak, J., and Sczesny, S. (2008), 'Am I the Right Candidate? Self-Ascribed Fit of Women and Men to a Leadership Position', *Sex Roles* 58(9): 682–688.

Bourdieu, P. (1986), 'The Forms of Capital', in J. G. Richardson (ed.), *Handbook of Theory and Research for the Sociology of Education*, Greenwood, pp. 241–258.

Bourdieu, P. (2001), *Masculine Domination*, Stanford University Press.

Budig, M. J., Misra, J., and Boeckmann, I. (2012), 'The Motherhood Penalty in Cross National Perspective: The Importance of Work–Family Policies and Cultural Attitudes', *Social Politics: International Studies in Gender, State & Society* 19(2): 163–193.

Burke, R. J., and McKeen, W. (1990), 'Mentoring in Organizations: Implications for Women', *Journal of Business Ethics* 9: 317–332.

Carli, L. L. (1999), 'Gender, Interpersonal Power, and Social Influence', *Journal of Social Issues* 55(1): 81–99.

Castilla E. J., and Benard, S. (2010), 'The Paradox of Meritocracy in Organizations', *Administrative Science Quarterly* 55(4): 543–676.

Castilla, E. J., and Ranganathan, A. (2020), 'The Production of Merit: How Managers Understand and Apply Merit in the Workplace', *Organization Science* 31(4): 909–935.

Catalyst (2004), 'The Bottom Line: Connecting Corporate Performance and Gender Diversity', <https://www.catalyst.org/wp-content/uploads/2019/01/The_Bottom_Line_Connecting_Corporate_Performance_and_Gender_Diversity.pdf>, last accessed 5 January 2023.

Cejka, M. A., and Eagly, A. H. (1999), 'Gender-Stereotypic Images of Occupations Correspond to the Sex Segregation of Employment', *Personality and Social Psychology Bulletin* 25(4): 413–423.

Celik, G. (2020), 'Does China's Tech Ecosystem Present a Level Playing Field for All?', <https://kr-asia.com/does-chinas-tech-ecosystem-present-a-level-playing-field-for-all>, last accessed 5 January 2023.

Chirikova, A. E., and Krichevskaia, O. N. (2002), 'The Woman Manager', *Sociological Research* 41(1): 38–54.

Coler, R. (2007), *El reino de las mujeres: el último matriarcado*, Temas de Hoy.

Collins, K. M. (2013), *Ability Profiling and School Failure: One Child's Struggle to Be Seen As Competent*, Routledge.

Cornils, D., and Rastetter, D. (2012), '"... und schon gar nicht Tränen einsetzen": Gender, Emotionsarbeit und Mikropolitik im Management', in G. Krell, D. Rastetter and K. Reichel (eds), *Geschlecht macht Karriere in Organisationen: Analysen zur Chancengleichheit in Fach- und Führungspositionen*, Edition Sigma, pp. 157–178.

Correll, S., and Mackenzie, L. (2016), 'To Succeed in Tech, Women Need More Visibility', <https://hbr.org/2016/09/to-succeed-in-tech-women-need-more-visibility>, last accessed 5 January 2023.

Costa, P. T., and McCrae, R. (1992), NEO Five Factor Inventory (NEO-FFI).

Cox, T. (1994), *Cultural Diversity in Organizations: Theory, Research and Practice*, Berrett-Koehler Publishers.

Davies, M. (2015), *Women on Boards Davies Review: Five Year Summary October 2015*, KPMG and Cranfield University.

Deloitte (2017), 'Progress at a Snail's Pace: Women in the Boardroom: A Global Perspective', <https://www2.deloitte.com/content/dam/Deloitte/global/Documents/gx-women-in-the-boardroom-seventh-edition.pdf>, last accessed 5 January 2023.

Doppler, D. (2007), 'Männerbund Management: Geschlechtsspezifische Ungleichheit im Spiegel soziobiologischer, psychologischer, soziologischer und ethnologischer Konzepte', *German Journal of Human Resource Management* 21(4): 482–486.

Eagly, A. H., and Carli, L. (2007), *Through the Labyrinth – The Truth about How Women Become Leaders*, Harvard Business School Press.

Eagly, A. H., and Wood, W. (2012), 'Social Role Theory: A Biosocial Analysis of Sex Differences and Similarities', in P. A. M. Van Lange, A. W. Kruglanski and E. T. Higgins (eds), *The Handbook of Theories of Social Psychology*, Sage Publications, vol. 2, pp. 458–476.

Eklund, K. E., Barry, E. S., and Grunberg, N. E. (2017), 'Gender and Leadership', in A. Alvinius (ed.), *Gender Differences in Different Contexts*, InTech, 129–150.

Fernandez, R. M., and Fernandez-Mateo, I. (2006), 'Networks, Race, and Hiring', *American Sociological Review*, 71(1): 42–71.

Fietze, S., Holst, E., and Tobsch, V. (2011), 'Germany's Next Top Manager: Does Personality Explain the Gender Career Gap?', *Management Revue* 22(3): 240–273.

Fitzgerald, L. F., and Weitzman, L. M. (1992), 'Women's Career Development: Theory and Practice from a Feminist Perspective', in Z. Leibowitz and D. Lea (eds), *Adult Career Development: Concepts, Issues and Practices*, National Career Development Association, 125–157.

Flynn, J., Heath, K., and Holt, M. D. (2011), 'Four Ways Women Stunt Their Careers Unintentionally', <https://hbr.org/2011/10/four-ways-women-stunt-their-careers>, last accessed 5 January 2023.

Fondas, N. (1996), 'Feminization at Work: Career Implications', in M. Arthur and D. Rousseau (eds), *The Boundaryless Career*, Oxford University Press, 282–293.

Gadiesh, O., and Coffman, J. (2015), 'Companies Drain Women's Ambition after Only 2 Years', <https://hbr.org/2015/05/companies-drain-womens-ambition-after-only-2-years>, last accessed 5 January 2023.

Gaida, R. (2022), *Working Dad: Vereinbarkeit von aktiver Vaterrolle und Karriere leben*, Campus.

Gamson, W. A. (1968), 'Stable Unrepresentation in American Society', *American Behavioral Scientist* 12(2): 15–21.

Geisler, K. (2009), 'Karriere – ein Zusammenspiel aus Individualität und organisationaler Struktur: Eine Studie über die Beziehung zwischen Karriereorientierungen und organisationalen Sozialisationserfahrungen', thesis, LMU Munich.

Gill, R., and Orgad, S. (2015), 'The Confidence Cult(ure)', *Australian Feminist Studies* 30(86): 324–344.

Gorbachev, M. (1987), *Perestroika: New Thinking for Our Country and the World*, Collins Publishing.

Goskomstat (2006), assorted reports: <http://www.gks.ru/free_doc/2006/b06_13/04-01.htm>; <www.gks.ru/free_doc/2007/b07_11/05-01.htm>; <www.gks.ru/bgd/free/b07_00/IssWWW.exe/Stg/d06/80.htm>; <www.gks.ru/bgd/free/b07_00/IssWWW.exe/Stg/d100/8-0.htm>, last accessed 27 October 2019.

Granrose, C. S. (ed.) (2005), *Employment of Women in Chinese Cultures: Half the Sky*, Edward Elgar.

Granrose, C. S. (2007), 'Gender Difference in Career Perception in the People's Republic of China', *Career Development International* 12: 9–27.

Grant Thornton (2014), 'Women in Business: From Classroom to Boardroom', <https://www.grantthornton.global/en/insights/articles/Women-in-business-classroom-to-boardroom/>, last accessed 5 January 2023.

Grant Thornton (2017), 'Women in Business: New Perspectives on Risk and Reward', <https://www.grant thornton.com.au/insights/reports/women-in-business-new-perspectives-on-risk-and-reward/>, last accessed 5 January 2023.

Grant Thornton (2021), 'Women in Business 2021: A Window of Opportunity', <https://www.grantthornton ni.com/insights/publications/women-in-business-2021-a-window-of-opportunity/>, last accessed 5 January 2023.

Gray, J. (1993), *Men Are from Mars, Women Are from Venus*, HarperCollins.

Greguletz, E., Diehl, M. R., and Kreutzer, K. (2019), 'Why Women Build Less Effective Networks than Men: The Role of Structural Exclusion and Personal Hesitation', *Human Relations* 72(7): 1234–1261.

Griffin, C. (2000), 'Girls Just Wanna Have Funds', *Entrepreneur* 28(3): 38.

Guillén, L., Mayo, M., and Karelaia, N. (2018), 'Appearing Self-Confident and Getting Credit for It: Why It May Be Easier for Men than Women to Gain Influence at Work', *Human Resource Management* 57(4): 839–854.

Gvozdeva, E. S., and Gerchikov, V. L. (2002), 'Sketches for a Portrait of Women Managers', *Sociological Research* 41(1): 55–68.

Hakim, C. (2010), 'Erotic Capital', *European Sociological Review* 26(5): 499–518.

Hakim, C. (2011), *Erotic Capital*, Basic Books.

Hall, D. T., and Hall, F. S. (1976), 'What's New in Career Management', *Organizational Dynamics* 5(1): 17–33.

Hays (2016), 'Only One in 10 British Women Aspire to Reach the Top', <https://www.haysplc.com/media/ press-releases/2016/pr-2016-03-08>, last accessed 5 January 2023.

Heinemann, I. (2011), '"Concepts of Motherhood": Öffentliche Debatten, Expertendiskurse und die Veränderung von Familienwerten in den USA (1890–1970)', *Zeithistorische Forschungen – Studies in Contemporary History* 8(1): 60–87.

Henn, M. (2012), *Die Kunst des Aufstieges: Was Frauen in Führungspositionen kennzeichnet*, Campus.

Herrmann, S. D., Adelman, R. M., Bodford, J. E., Graudejus, O., Okun, M. A., and Kwan, V. S. (2016), 'The Effects of a Female Role Model on Academic Performance and Persistence of Women in STEM Courses', *Basic and Applied Social Psychology* 38(5): 258–268.

Hervé, F. (1995), 'Französische Frauen: Die Entwicklung des Feminismus in Frankreich', *Via Regia – Blätter für internationale kulturelle Kommunikation* 24.

Hinchliffe, E. (2021), 'The Female CEOs on This Year's Fortune 500 Just Broke Three All Time Records', *Fortune*, 2 June 2021, <https://fortune.com/2021/06/02/female-ceos-fortune-500-2021-women-ceo-list-roz-brewer-walgreens-karen-lynch-cvs-thasunda-brown-duckett-tiaa/>, last accessed 5 January 2023.

Hogan, R., Perrucci, C. C., and Behringer, A. (2005), 'Enduring Inequality: Gender and Employment Income in Late Career', *Sociological Spectrum* 25: 53–77.

Hollstein, W. (2004), *Geschlechterdemokratie*, VS Verlag für Sozialwissenschaften.

Hollstein, W. (2011), 'Frauenquote – Auf Kosten der Männer', *Financial Times Deutschland*, 20 February 2011, <https://web.archive.org/web/20110221101049/http://www.ftd.de/politik/deutschland/:gleichber echtigung-frauenquote-auf-kosten-der-maenner/60014280.html>, last accessed 5 January 2023.

Holst, E., Busch-Heizmann, A., and Wieber, A. (2015), *Führungskräfte-Monitor 2015: Update 2001–2013*, vol. 100, DIW Berlin.

Hossiep, R., and Paschen, M. (2003), Business-Focused Inventory of Personality (BIP).

Hoyt, C. L., and Simon, S. (2011), 'Female Leaders: Injurious or Inspiring Role Models for Women?', *Psychology of Women Quarterly* 35(1): 143–157.

Ibarra, H., Ely, R., and Kolb, D. (2013), 'Women Rising: The Unseen Barriers', *Harvard Business Review* 91(9): 60–66.

Ibarra, H., and Obodaru, O. (2009), 'Women and the Vision Thing', <https://hbr.org/2009/01/women-and-the-vision-thing>, last accessed 5 January 2023.

Ifak (2018), 'Umfrage: Kontaktbörse Arbeitsplatz', <https://www.ifak.com/neuigkeiten/umfrage-kontakt boerse-arbeitsplatz>, last accessed 5 January 2023.

Iwao, S. (1998), *Japanese Woman*, Simon & Schuster.

Jeffries, J. W. (2018), *Wartime America: The World War II Home Front*, Rowman & Littlefield.

Johnson, A. C. (2021), 'Abenomics' Effect on Gender Inequality in Japanese Society and the Workplace', thesis, Georgia Southern University.

Jüngling, C., and Rastetter, D. (2009), 'Machtpolitik oder Männerbund? Widerstände in Organisationen gegenüber Frauen in Führungspositionen', in M. W. Fröse and A. Szebel-Habig (eds), *Mixed Leadership: Mit Frauen in die Führung*, Haupt, pp. 131–146.

Kanter, R. M. (1977), *Men and Women of the Corporation*, Basic Books.

Karl, A. L., Schwidder, S., Weingarten, J., and Weckes, M. (2020), 'Ambition oder Symbolpolitik: Europäische Geschlechterquoten für Führungspositionen im Vergleich', Mitbestimmungsreport no. 59, Hans-Böckler-Stiftung, Institut für Mitbestimmung und Unternehmensführung (IMU), Düsseldorf.

Kay, K., and Shipman, C. (2014), *The Confidence Code*, Harper Business.

Kierski, W., and Blazina, C. (2010), 'The Male Fear of the Feminine and Its Effects on Counseling and Psychotherapy', *Journal of Men's Studies* 17(2): 155–172.

Kim, E. J., and Parish, S. L. (2020), 'Family-Supportive Workplace Policies and South Korean Mothers' Perceived Work–Family Conflict: Accessibility Matters', *Asian Population Studies* 16(2): 167–182.

King, M. M., Bergstrom, C. T., Correll, S. J., Jacquet, J., and West, J. D. (2017), 'Men Set Their Own Cites High: Gender and Self-Citation across Fields and over Time', *Socius* 3.

Kipnis, D., and Lane, W. P. (1962), 'Self-Confidence and Leadership', *Journal of Applied Psychology* 46(4): 291–295.

Kirchmeyer, C. (1998), 'Determinants of Managerial Career Success: Evidence and Explanation of Male–Female Differences', *Journal of Management* 24: 673–692.

Kite, M. E. (2001), 'Changing Times, Changing Gender Roles: Who Do We Want Women and Men to Be?', in R. K. Unger (ed.), *Handbook of the Psychology of Women and Gender*, John Wiley & Sons.

Knight, R. (2017), '7 Practical Ways to Reduce Bias in Your Hiring Process', <https://hbr.org/2017/06/7-practical-ways-to-reduce-bias-in-your-hiring-process>, last accessed 5 January 2023.

Kray, L. J., Howland, L., Russell, A. G., and Jackman, L. M. (2017), 'The Effects of Implicit Gender Role Theories on Gender System Justification: Fixed Beliefs Strengthen Masculinity to Preserve the Status Quo', *Journal of Personality and Social Psychology* 112(1): 98–115.

Krishnan, G. V., and Parsons, L. M. (2008), 'Getting to the Bottom Line: An Exploration of Gender and Earnings Quality', *Journal of Business Ethics* 78(1): 65–76.

Kröll, J., Szlusnus, T., Hüttermann, H., and Boerner, S. (2014), 'Sind gemischt-geschlechtliche Führungsteams erfolgreicher? Der Zusammenhang zwischen Mixed Leadership und Unternehmenserfolg', *Betriebswirtschaftliche Forschung und Praxis* 66(6): 602–625.

Krone-Schmalz, G. (1992), *In Wahrheit sind wir stärker: Frauenalltag in der Sowjetunion*, Fischer.

Laible, M. C. (2013), 'Gender Diversity in Top Management and Firm Performance: An Analysis with the IAB-Establishment Panel', paper given at the Comparative Analysis of Enterprise Data Conference, Atlanta, 18–20 September 2013.

Lalanne, M., and Seabright, P. (2022), 'The Old Boy Network: Are the Professional Networks of Female Executives Less Effective than Men's for Advancing Their Careers?', *Journal of Institutional Economics* 18(5): 725–744.

Leaper, C., and Ayres, M. M. (2007), 'A Meta-Analytic Review of Gender Variations in Adults' Language Use: Talkativeness, Affiliative Speech, and Assertive Speech', *Personality and Social Psychology Review* 11(4): 328–363.

Le Monde (2021), 'Parité femmes-hommes: le Sénat vote pour l'établissement de quotas aux postes de direction des grandes entreprises', *Le Monde*, 28 October 2021, <https://www.lemonde.fr/politique/article/2021/10/28/parite-homme-femme-le-senat-vote-pour-l-etablissement-de-quotas-aux-postes-de-direction-des-grandes-entreprises_6100145_823448.html>, last accessed 5 January 2023.

Leung, A. S. M. (2002), 'Gender and Career Experience in Mainland Chinese State-Owned Enterprises', *Personnel Review* 31: 602–619.

Lewis, L. (2015), 'Japan: Women in the Workforce', *Financial Times*, <https://www.ft.com/content/60729d68–20bb-11e5-aa5a-398b2169cf79>, last accessed 5 January 2023.

Li, C. (2000), 'Confucianism and Feminist Concerns: Overcoming the Confucian "Gender Complex"', *Journal of Chinese Philosophy* 27: 187–199.

Lockwood, P., and Kunda, Z. (1999), 'Increasing the Salience of One's Best Selves Can Undermine Inspiration by Outstanding Role Models', *Journal of Personality and Social Psychology* 76(2), 214–228.

Lyness, K. S., and Thompson, D. E. (2000), 'Climbing the Corporate Ladder: Do Female and Male Executives Follow the Same Route?', *Journal of Applied Psychology* 85: 86–101.

Marion, H. (1880), 'Le nouveau programme de philosophie', *Revue Philosophique de la France et de l'Étranger* 10: 414–427.

Marx, D. M., and Ko, S. J. (2012), 'Superstars "Like" Me: The Effect of Role Model Similarity on Performance under Threat', *European Journal of Social Psychology* 42(7): 807–812.

Mathe, K., Michie, S., and Nelson, D. L. (2011), 'Women in Management in the USA', in M. J. Davidson and R. J. Burke (eds), *Women in Management Worldwide*, Gower, pp. 223–240.

Mavin, S. (2006), 'Venus Envy: Problematizing Solidarity Behaviour and Queen Bees', *Women in Management Review* 21(4): 264–276.

Maxfield, S., Shapiro, M., Gupta, V., and Hass, S. (2010), 'Gender and Risk: Women, Risk Taking and Risk Aversion', *Gender in Management* 25(7): 586–604.

McClain, L. C. (2018), 'Male Chauvinism Is under Attack from All Sides at Present: Roberts v. United States Jaycees, Sex Discrimination, and the First Amendment', *Fordham Law Review* 87: 2385–2416.

McDonald, S. (2011), 'What's in the "Old Boys" Network? Accessing Social Capital in Gendered and Racialized Networks', *Social Networks* 33(4): 317–330.

McGrath, J. E. (1964), 'A Social Psychological Approach to the Study of Negotiation'. government research report, University of Illinois.

McKinsey (2012), 'Women Matter: Making the Breakthrough', <https://www.mckinsey.com/capabilities/people-and-organizational-performance/our-insights/making-the-breakthrough>, last accessed 5 January 2023.

McKinsey, (2020), 'Women in the Workplace 2020', <https://wiw-report.s3.amazonaws.com/Women_in_the_Workplace_2020.pdf>, last accessed 5 January 2023.

Merriam-Webster (2022), 'Ambition', <https://www.merriam-webster.com/dictionary/ambition>, last accessed 5 January 2023.

Metcalfe, B., and Afanassieva, M. (2005), 'The Woman Question? Gender and Management in the Russian Federation', *Women in Management* 20: 429–445.

Metcalfe, B., and Linstead, A. (2003), 'Gendering Teamwork: Rewriting the Feminine', *Gender Work and Organization* 19(1): 94–119.

Meuser, M. (2008), 'Ernste Spiele: Zur Konstruktion von Männlichkeit im Wettbewerb der Männer', in N. Baur and J. Luedtke (eds), *Die soziale Konstruktion von Männlichkeit: Hegemoniale und marginalisierte Männlichkeiten in Deutschland*, Opladen, pp. 33–44.

Miller, C. C. (2017), 'Unintended Consequences of Sexual Harassment Scandals', *New York Times*, 9 October 2017, <https://www.nytimes.com/2017/10/09/upshot/as-sexual-harassment-scandals-spook-men-it-can-backfire-for-women.html>, last accessed 5 January 2013.

Miner, J. B. (1978), 'Twenty Years of Research on Role-Motivation Theory of Managerial Effectiveness', *Personnel Psychology* 31(4): 739–760.

Mischke, R. (2011), 'Sex-Appeal hilft auf dem Weg zum beruflichen Erfolg', *Welt*, 24 October 2011, <https://www.welt.de/partnerschaft/article13676658/Sex-Appeal-hilft-auf-dem-Weg-zu-beruflichem-Erfolg.html>, last accessed 5 January 2013.

Mulac, A., Bradac, J. J., and Gibbons, P. (2001), 'Empirical Support for the Gender-as-Culture Hypothesis: An Intercultural Analysis of Male/Female Language Differences', *Human Communication Research* 27(1): 121–152.

Neubauer, W., and Rosemann, B. (2006), *Führung, Macht und Vertrauen in Organisationen*, Kohlhammer.

Nieva, V. F., and Gutek, B. A. (1981), *Women and Work: A Psychological Perspective*, Greenwood.

Noland, M., Moran, T., and Kotschwar, B. (2016), 'Is Gender Diversity Profitable? Evidence from a Global Survey', Peterson Institute for International Economics Working Paper no. 16–3, <https://papers.ssrn.com/sol3/papers.cfm?abstract_id=2729348>, last accessed 5 January 2023.

Oakley, J. G. (2000), 'Gender-Based Barriers to Senior Management Positions: Understanding the Scarcity of Female CEOs', *Journal of Business Ethics* 27(4): 321–334.

O'Neill, D. A., and Hopkins, M. M. (2013), 'Patterns and Paradoxes in Women's Careers', in W. Patton (ed.), *Conceptualising Women's Working Lives: Moving the Boundaries of Discourse:* Sense Publishers, pp. 63–79.

Ortmann, G., and Sydow, J. (2003), 'Grenzmanagement in Unternehmungsnetzwerken: Theoretische Zugänge', in J. Zentes, B. Swoboda and D. Morschett (eds), *Kooperationen, Allianzen und Netzwerke*, Gabler, pp. 895–920

Oyserman, D., Bybee, D., and Terry, K. (2006), 'Possible Selves and Academic Outcomes: How and When Possible Selves Impel Action', *Journal of Personality and Social Psychology* 91(1): 188–204.

Palmer, C. (2000), 'A Job, Old Boy? The School Ties That Still Bind', *The Guardian*, 11 June 2000, <https://www.theguardian.com/money/2000/jun/11/workandcareers.madeleinebunting2>, last accessed 5 January 2023.

Pande, R., and Ford, D. (2011), 'Gender Quotas and Female Leadership: A Review', background paper for the World Development Report on Gender.

Paustian-Underdahl, S. C., Walker, L. S., and Woehr, D. J. (2014), 'Gender and Perceptions of Leadership Effectiveness: A Meta-Analysis of Contextual Moderators', *Journal of Applied Psychology* 99(6): 1129–1145.

Penz, O., and Sauer, B. (2016), *Affektives Kapital: Die Ökonomisierung der Gefühle im Arbeitsleben*, Campus.

Petriglieri, G., and Kinias, Z. (2020), INSEAD Gender Diversity Programme, held online March to May 2020.

Pleck, J. H. (1975), 'Masculinity – Femininity', *Sex Roles* 1(2): 161–178.

Pohl, W., and Theiss, L. (2009), *Die schmutzige Emanzipation: wie Frauen über Männer an die Macht kommen*, Edition A.

Powell, G. N. (2011), *Women and Men in Management*, SAGE.

PWC (2013), 'Spotlight on Russia – Women Leaders in Russian Businesses', <https://pwc.blogs.com/gender_agenda/2013/08/spotlight-on-russia-women-leaders-in-russian-business.html>, last accessed 11 March 2022.

Ragins, B. R. (1997), 'Diversified Mentoring Relationships in Organizations: A Power Perspective', *Academy of Management Review* 22: 482–521.

Rastetter, D., and Cornils, D. (2012), 'Networking: Aufstiegsförderliche Strategien für Frauen in Führungspositionen', *Gruppendynamik und Organisationsberatung* 43(1): 43–60.

Regnet, E. (2017), *Frauen ins Management – Chancen, Stolpersteine und Erfolgsfaktoren*, Hogrefe.

Reiners, F. (2008), *Networking in Organisationen*, Hampp.

Reinwald, M., Hüttermann, H., Kröll, J., and Boerner, S. (2015), 'Gender diversity in Führungsteams und Unternehmensperformanz: Eine Metaanalyse', *Schmalenbachs Zeitschrift Für Betriebswirtschaftliche Forschung* 67(3): 262–296.

Reischauer, E. O. (2020), *Japan: The Story of a Nation*, Knopf.

Ren, X. (2010), 'A Critical Examination of Women's Work–Family Conflict and Career Aspirations in the Chinese Airline Industry', thesis, Cardiff University.

Reynolds, K. J., Eggins, R. A., and Haslam, S. A. (2010), 'Uncovering Diverse Identities in Organisations: AIRing versus Auditing Approaches to Diversity Management', *Asia Pacific Journal of Human Resources* 48(1): 45 – 57.

Richardson, M. S. (1974), 'The Dimensions of Career and Work Orientation in College Women', *Journal of Vocational Behavior* 5(1): 161 – 172.

Romero, C. (2015), 'What We Know about Growth Mindset from Scientific Research', <http://studentexper iencenetwork.org/wp-content/uploads/2015/09/What-We-Know-About-Growth-Mindset.pdf>, last accessed 5 January 2023.

Rothbard, N. P. (2001), 'Enriching or Depleting? The Dynamics of Engagement in Work and Family Roles', *Administrative Science Quarterly* 46: 655 – 684.

Rzhanitsyna, L. (2000), 'Working Women in Russia at the End of the 1990s', *Problems of Economic Transition* 43(7): 68 – 86.

Sander, G., and Keller, N. J. (2021), 'McKinsey Gender Parity Report', in E. S. Ng, C. L. Stamper, A. Klarsfeld and Y. J. Han (eds), *Handbook on Diversity and Inclusion Indices*, Edward Elgar, pp. 164 – 175.

Schein, V. E., Mueller, R., Lituchy, T., and Liu, J. (1996), 'Think Manager – Think Male: A Global Phenomenon?', *Journal of Organizational Behavior* 17: 33 – 41.

Schmitt, D. P., Jonason, P. K., Byerley, G. J., Flores, S. D., Illbeck, B. E., O'Leary, K. N., and Qudrat, A. (2012), 'A Reexamination of Sex Differences in Sexuality: New Studies Reveal Old Truths', *Current Directions in Psychological Science* 21(2): 135 – 139.

Sherwin, B. (2014), 'Why Women Are More Effective Leaders than Men', <https://www.businessinsider.com/study-women-are-better-leaders-2014-1?r=US&IR=T>, last accessed 5 January 2023.

Shrauger, J. S., and Schohn, M. (1995), 'Self-Confidence in College Students: Conceptualization, Measurement, and Behavioral Implications', *Assessment* 2(3): 255 – 278.

Soklaridis, S., Zahn, C., Kuper, A., Gillis, D., Taylor, V. H., and Whitehead, C. (2018), 'Men's Fear of Mentoring in the #MeToo Era – What's at Stake for Academic Medicine', *New England Journal of Medicine* 379(23): 2270 – 2274.

Sparwelt (2017), 'Mit dem Job im Bett: Jeder Dritte hatte schon eine Beziehung am Arbeitsplatz', <https://www.presseportal.de/pm/75733/3666228>, last accessed 5 January 2023.

Sperling, V. (1999), *Organising Women in Contemporary Russia: Engendering Transition*, Cambridge University Press.

Spiegel (2013), 'Jeder zehnte unter 30-jährige würde sich hochschlafen', *Spiegel*, 25 July 2013, <https://www.spiegel.de/karriere/sex-mit-dem-chef-jeder-zehnte-wuerde-sich-hochschlafen-a-913031.html>, last accessed 5 January 2023.

Staines, G., Tavris, C., and Jayaratne, T. E. (1974), 'The Queen Bee Syndrome', *Psychology Today* 7(8): 55 – 60.

Steffens, M. C., and Roth, J. (2016), 'Diversity Kompetenz in Bezug auf Gender: Sozialpsychologisches Wissen über Geschlechterstereotype und Geschlechterrollen', in P. Genkova and T. Ringeisen (eds), *Handbuch Diversity Kompetenz*, Springer, vol. 2, pp. 273 – 283.

Strunk, G. (2009), 'Eine Frau muss ein Mann sein, um Karriere zu machen', in J. Dalhoff and J. Girlich (eds), *Frauen für die Stärkung von Wissenschaft und Forschung*, GESIS and CEWS, 38 – 45.

Sturges, J. (1999), 'What It Means to Succeed: Personal Conceptions of Career Success Held by Male and Female Managers at Different Ages', *British Journal of Management* 10: 239 – 252.

Swope, A. J. (2012), 'Under the Influence: An Examination of Men's Fears of Women Leaders', *Journal of Psychological Issues in Organizational Culture* 3(2): 6 – 16.

Tannen, D. (ed.) (1993), *Gender and Conversational Interaction*, Oxford University Press.

Tharenou, P., Latimer, S., and Conroy, D. (1994), 'How Do You Make It to the Top? An Examination of Influences on Women's and Men's Managerial Advancement', *Academy of Management Journal* 37: 899 – 931.

Thompson, C. A., Beauvais, L. L., and Lyness, K. S. (1999), 'When Work–Family Benefits Are Not Enough: The Influence of Work–Family Culture on Benefit Utilization, Organizational Attachment, and Work–Family Conflict', *Journal of Vocational Behavior* 54(3): 392 – 415.

Thorne, B., and Henley, N. (eds) (1975), *Language and Sex: Difference and Dominance*, Newbury House.

Türk, K. (1995), 'Zur Kritik der politischen Ökonomie der Organisation', in K. Türk, *Die Organisation der Welt*, VS Verlag für Sozialwissenschaften, pp. 37 – 92.

Vassilopoulou, J., Takkenberg, H., and Miedtank, T. (2021), 'Gender Inclusive Recruitment & Selection Toolkit for HR Professionals', <https://equal4europe.eu/wp-content/uploads/2021/10/D3.2_Toolkit-for-HR-Professionals.pdf>, last accessed 5 January 2023.

Wagner, W., and Brandstätter, H. (1994), 'Doppelte Erwerbsarbeit in Familien und innerfamiliäre Arbeitsteilung', *Österreichische Zeitschrift für Soziologie* 19: 76 – 90.

Warnecke, T., and Blanchard, A. (2010), 'Women in China, between Confucius and the Market', Rollins College Faculty Publications 225, <https://scholarship.rollins.edu/as_facpub/225/>, last accessed 5 January 2023.

Weber, M. (1978), *Economy and Society*, vol. 1, University of California Press.

Williams, S. J., and Bendelow, G. (1997), *Emotions in Social Life: Critical Themes and Contemporary Issues*, Routledge.

Wilson, M., and Daly, M. (1985), 'Competitiveness, Risk Taking, and Violence: The Young Male Syndrome', *Ethology and Sociobiology* 6(1): 59 – 73.

Wippermann, C. (2010), 'Frauen in Führungspositionen: Barrieren und Brücken', <https://www.bmfsfj.de/bmfsfj/service/publikationen/frauen-in-fuehrungspositionen-95850>, last accessed 5 January 2023.

WirtschaftsWoche (2008), 'Sex am Arbeitsplatz', *WirtschaftsWoche*, 9 June 2008, <https://www.wiwo.de/erfolg/trends/tatsachen-sex-am-arbeitsplatz/5433392.html>, last accessed 5 January 2023.

Wittenberg-Cox, A. (2010), *How Women Mean Business: A Step by Step Guide to Profiting from Gender Balanced Business*, John Wiley & Sons.

Women's Forum for the Economy & Society (2021), 'Unlocking Women's Leadership through STEM Skills Programmes', <https://www.womens-forum.com/2021/03/16/women4stem-report-2020/>, last accessed 5 January 2023.

World Economic Forum (2017), 'The Global Gender Gap Report 2017', <https://www.weforum.org/reports/the-global-gender-gap-report-2017>, last accessed 5 January 2023.

Wottawa, H., Montel, C., Mette, C., Zimmer, B., and Hiltmann, M. (2011), 'Eligo-Studie. Berufliche Lebensziele und Leistungspotenziale junger Hochschulabsolventinnen und Hochschulabsolventen', *Wirtschaftspsychologie* 13(3): 85 – 111.

Xing (2017), 'Flirt und Affäre ja, feste Partnerschaft nein: XING-Studie zeigt, was deutsche Arbeitnehmer von der Liebe am Arbeitsplatz halten', <https://www.new-work.se/de/newsroom/pressemitteilungen/flirt-und-affaere-ja-feste-partnerschaft-nein-xing-studie-zeigt-was-deutsche-arbeitnehmer-von-der-liebe-am-arbeitsplatz-halten>, last accessed 5 January 2023.

Yang, K. S. (1986), 'Chinese Personality and Its Change', in M. H. Bond (ed.), *The Psychology of the Chinese People*, Oxford University Press, pp. 106 – 170.

Zahidi, S., and Ibarra, H. (2010), 'The Corporate Gender Gap Report 2010', <https://www.weforum.org/reports/corporate-gender-gap-2010>, last accessed 5 January 2023.

Ziegler, H. (2011), 'Soziale Arbeit und das gute Leben – Capabilities als sozialpädagogische Kategorie', in C. Sedmak, B. Babic, R. Bauer and C. Posch (eds), *Der Capability-Approach in sozialwissenschaftlichen Kontexten*, VS Verlag für Sozialwissenschaften, pp. 117 – 137.

Zweigenhaft, R. (2021), 'Diversity among Fortune 500 CEOs from 2000 to 2020: White Women, Hi-Tech South Asians, and Economically Privileged Multilingual Immigrants from around the World', <https://whorulesamerica.ucsc.edu/power/diversity_update_2020.html>, last accessed 5 January 2023.

About the author

Dr Bettina Al-Sadik-Lowinski is an ICF Master Certified Coach, management researcher and founder of the Global Women Career Lab initiative. She teaches at several universities, has spoken at numerous international conferences and, alongside her own coaching work, also certifies other executive coaches. Originally from Germany, she has lived and worked in Japan, France and China.

As an executive coach, she draws on her own extensive corporate experience to deliver high-impact outcomes for her clients, who come from all over the world. She has partnered with global companies spanning a range of different industries, as well as academic institutions and research organisations. Through her Global Women Career Lab initiative, she provides consulting services to international organisations and helps them to formulate their diversity strategies. She also supports women leaders with training and coaching.

In her previous publications, *How Chinese Women Rise* (Excellent Topic Prize 2019), *Women in Top Management* and *Typology of Career Paths of International Top Women Managers*, Al-Sadik-Lowinski explored how female managers from around the world can rise to the highest positions. Her analysis and conclusions have been widely discussed in the international press.

Alpha Males and Alpha Females is both a call for greater gender equality at senior level in global companies and a guide to how it can be achieved. It gives women who are interested in pursuing a management career an insight into men's views, as well as advice on their personal career development. It also suggests strategies that executives can adopt to strengthen diversity, build mixed leadership teams and help secure their companies' long-term success. Al-Sadik-Lowinski shows how talented men and women can harmonise their strengths and work together to build a brighter future.

https://doi.org/10.1515/9783111172651-010

www.ingramcontent.com/pod-product-compliance
Lightning Source LLC
Chambersburg PA
CBHW080646270326
41928CB00017B/3209